"Busse takes the mystery out of employment law in this superbly written, balanced approach to relationships 'gone wrong' in the workplace. This compassionate practical guide is a *must read* for employees and employers alike."

Jody Larimore, MS, SPHR, CPCC
Human Resources Director
Wells Fargo Bank
Northwest Region

"A *jewel.* At last an understandable explanation of discrimination laws. This book is invaluable for community advocates often called [on] by the defenseless, suffering from employment discrimination."

Ron Herndon, Founder of the Black United Front
Chairman of the Board
National Head Start Association

"Busse demonstrates a thorough knowledge of workplace legal issues in a clear, easy-to-read style. His text is peppered with examples that show how the law actually works. The basic training he provides will help new recruits and veterans alike to navigate the employment relationship successfully."

Charles H. Fleischer, Attorney at Law
Author of *HR for Small Business*

Other books in the *Rights* series:

Attorney Responsibilities & Client Rights
by Suzan Herskowitz Singer

Gay & Lesbian Rights
by Brette McWhorter Sember

Teen Rights (and Responsibilities), 2nd Ed.
by Traci Truly

Unmarried Parents' Rights, 2nd Ed.
by Jacqueline D. Stanley

Your Rights at Work

All You Need to Know about Workplace Law—and How to Use it to Protect Your Job

Richard C. Busse
Attorney at Law

SPHINX® PUBLISHING
AN IMPRINT OF SOURCEBOOKS, INC.®
NAPERVILLE, ILLINOIS
www.SphinxLegal.com

First Edition: 2005

Published by: **Sphinx® Publishing, An Imprint of Sourcebooks, Inc.®**

Naperville Office
P.O. Box 4410
Naperville, Illinois 60567-4410
630-961-3900
Fax: 630-961-2168
www.sourcebooks.com
www.SphinxLegal.com

This publication is designed to provide accurate and authoritative information in regard to the subject matter covered. It is sold with the understanding that the publisher is not engaged in rendering legal, accounting, or other professional service. If legal advice or other expert assistance is required, the services of a competent professional person should be sought.

From a Declaration of Principles Jointly Adopted by a Committee of the American Bar Association and a Committee of Publishers and Associations

This product is not a substitute for legal advice.
Disclaimer required by Texas statutes.

Library of Congress Cataloging-in-Publication Data
Busse, Richard C.
Your rights at work : all you need to know about workplace law—and how to use it to protect your job / by Richard C. Busse.-- 1st ed.
p. cm.
Includes bibliographical references and index.
ISBN 1-57248-505-1 (pbk. : alk. paper)
1. Labor laws and legislation--United States--Popular works. 2. Employee rights--United States--Popular works. I. Title.

KF3319.6.B88 2005
344.7301--dc22

2005012695

Printed and bound in the United States of America.

BG — 10 9 8 7 6 5 4 3 2 1

ACKNOWLEDGMENT

I would like to thank Michael Bowen, Dianne Wheeler, and Mary Oberst for the masterful contribution they made in editing this book at its different stages.

I would also like to thank my loving wife, Kathy, for her eternal support and patience. Also, my partner Scott H. Hunt for his encouragement and indulgence; my legal assistant, Shirley Rayner; and my legal secretary, Lori Errico.

CONTENTS

INTRODUCTION

If you needed an *employment lawyer* twenty-eight years ago, when I first began to practice in the civil rights field, you could not find one. At that time, there was no subject area known as *employment law*. Over the past quarter century, whole industries to assist employers in protecting themselves from liability have been developed. Employers spend millions of dollars on lawyers, consultants, and seminars. Employees, on the other hand, have little to go on to get their legal bearings. Too often they are left to act completely oblivious of their rights, or worse still, under a misimpression of what their rights are. This book is meant to help level the playing field.

However, this book is not meant as a substitute for legal advice. The law is dynamic, and by the time you read this book, either your state legislature or appellate courts may have changed it. Moreover, what is presented here is necessarily stated in generalities. There are many exceptions to these general rules. Though a case on the surface appears to be similar to yours, there may be a small detail in your case that changes the entire result. The law does not operate in a vacuum. It applies to specific fact situations. Therefore, do not fall into the trap of thinking that this is a do-it-yourself diagnostics kit. Rather, the goal is to inform you of your rights so that you can better recognize a situation that may involve a violation of those rights.

One additional caution—you may be too close to a situation to objectively analyze it. Often, a person who has been the victim of unfair treatment either does not know why or is mistaken as to the reason. Sometimes only a lawyer's review of one's employment history can reveal a likely motivating factor for a discharge. This is important to know because you may tend to report that you are sure the mistreatment is for one reason, thereby failing to report other important facts that may be the key to a case.

Law school does not teach what the law is as applied to a specific case. Rather it is intended to provide a firm grounding in legal principles and training in how to spot and properly analyze issues that pertain to a case. If, after reading this book, you are more aware of the laws that protect you, one of its purposes will be served.

Too often, terminated employees who arrive at a lawyer's office with an employment problem have already contributed to their own demise, or have failed to take precautionary measures that give their lawyers something to work with. Hopefully, this book will educate employees so that they will be able to identify situations as they arise in the workplace, in which their legal rights are implicated before acting.

Sometimes, case studies are presented in this book to illustrate a legal principle. They are taken from court cases, but the case studies and case study captions do not necessarily reflect actual events or the conduct of the persons or entities that are named in, or are the subject of the cited cases.

This book is written in three parts. Section I is intended to educate you on the basics of employment law. Section II is devoted to the more practical aspects of your life as an employee and potential litigant. Section III identifies twenty-five of the most commonly asked questions about employment law.

Throughout this book, you will see names and citations to cases. End notes for many of the chapters are located at the end of the book. Do not be intimidated by all of the numbers and letters you see. They are included to give you information about the source that stands behind any legal proposition that is asserted. In citing you to a case, you are not expected to go find it in a law library and read it. The citation itself will give you information about the strength of the citation and whether it will likely apply to you.

For example, in the following citation: *Meritor Savings Bank v. Vinson*, 477 U.S. 57 (1986), the "U.S." means the case was decided by the United States Supreme Court. This tells you the decision will probably apply to you. The numbers before "U.S." refer to the volume of that reporter series, and the numbers afterward refer to the page within that volume where the case begins. The "(1986)," tells you the year of the decision. A lot has happened since 1986, but this case is still *good law* (case law that has not been overturned and otherwise is still in full force and effect).

Beneath the Supreme Court is the federal circuit courts of appeal. These courts are divided geographically and numbered 1st through the 11th and the D.C. Circuit. You may see a citation like this: *Ross v. Douglas County*, 234 F.3d 391 (8th Cir. 2000). You should know from the information within parenthesis that this case was decided in 2000 in the 8th Circuit. The "F.3d" just refers to a different set of books—the Federal Reporter, third series. If a federal circuit court case decides a question of federal law in the circuit in which your state lies, that decision will be *binding* within the circuit. All circuit decisions outside your circuit are said to be *persuasive* authority within it, but must yield to a circuit court case on point within the circuit.

You may refer to the list below to find out which circuit your state sits in:

- 1st Circuit: Maine, Massachusetts, New Hampshire, Puerto Rico, Rhode Island
- 2nd Circuit: Connecticut, New York, Vermont
- 3rd Circuit: Delaware, New Jersey, Pennsylvania, the Virgin Islands
- 4th Circuit: Maryland, North Carolina, South Carolina, Virginia, West Virginia
- 5th Circuit: Louisiana, Mississippi, Texas
- 6th Circuit: Kentucky, Michigan, Ohio, Tennessee
- 7th Circuit: Illinois, Indiana, Wisconsin
- 8th Circuit: Arkansas, Iowa, Minnesota, Missouri, Nebraska, North Dakota, South Dakota
- 9th Circuit: Alaska, Arizona, California, Hawaii, Idaho, Montana, Nevada, Oregon, Washington, Guam

- 10th Circuit: Colorado, Kansas, New Mexico, Oklahoma, Utah, Wyoming
- 11th Circuit: Alabama, Florida, Georgia

All other federal citations are to the decisions of the district, or trial courts, which are usually found in the reporter called the Federal Supplement. For example, *Cross v. CCL Custom Mfg.*, Inc. 951 F. Supp 124 (WD Tenn 1997). This citation tells you the volume and page to find the case in the Western District of Tennessee.

The state reporter series are even easier to decipher. They are divided by region: Atlantic (A.), Southern (So.), South Eastern (S.E.), South Western (S.W.), North Eastern (N.E.), North Western (N.W.), and Pacific (P.). You do not have to memorize these because the protocol is that whenever a regional reporter is cited, the state in which the case was decided is indicated in parenthesis before the year of the decision. So, for example, *Lord v. Souder*, 748 A.2d 393 (Del 2000). This means it is a state court case out of Delaware, decided by its highest appellate court in 2000. The "2d" or "3d" that follows, is simply a reference to the series of that regional reporter.

I hope you find this book informative and helpful in your employment-related situations.

Richard C. Busse
Portland, Oregon

SECTION ONE:

Understanding Employment Law

–1–
OUR LEGAL SYSTEM

At the time of the Revolutionary War in this country, the rule of *at-will employment* prevailed. Simply stated, at-will employment means that the employee works *at the pleasure of the employer*. An employee can be terminated for any reason or for no reason at all.

Two hundred years later, the at-will employment rule still prevails in almost every state. The development of civil service or merit personnel systems in the public sector and the rise of the organized labor movement in this century have created exceptions for government employees and union workers who are protected by provisions that require *cause* for termination. Until recently, the unorganized private sector workplace remained largely unprotected.

About forty years ago, the civil rights movement resulted in additional protections for certain classes of workers. Title VII of the *Civil Rights Act of 1964* established a rule of *nondiscrimination* in employment for persons who fit certain *protected class* categories—race, color, national origin, religion, and sex. Since 1964, other state and federal laws have established additional protected class categories for persons on the basis of, for example, age and disability.

For the past twenty-five years, however, courts have reexamined the nature of the employer/employee relationship. This reexamination has resulted in the now commonly accepted view that the employee shall not leave his or her civil rights at the door when he or she reports for work. This book focuses on that recent progress.

THE LAW

Law is made both by legislative bodies and judges. Congress enacts federal legislation of general applicability called *statutes*. Our state legislatures enact *state statutes*. Those statutes are not the only source of substantive law. Not only do federal and state level judges interpret state and federal statutes, but they also mold and fashion law through decisions. These decisions make or are based on *common law* or *judge-made law* that predate those statutes in many cases. Our common law was largely inherited from the English common law. As society has developed, so has the law. This development has been particularly rapid in the employment law field during the last twenty-five years.

At some point, you may have read about an employee who was wrongfully discharged and was awarded millions of dollars. However, you should know that except for federal laws passed by Congress that apply throughout the United States, each state has its own set of laws. The protection afforded to workers by the statutes and common laws vary widely between the states. In more populated states, the courts have had more opportunities to confront and resolve new questions of employment law. In those states, the law has generally developed faster and farther to provide rights to employees. Even in most rural and southern states, however, the development in recent years has been dramatic.

Each state's judicial framework is different. Each state has a first level *trial court*. Appeals from the trial court go to an *appellate court*. Some states have two layers of appellate courts above the trial court to review its decisions and provide for uniform application and interpretation of the law.

Some employment cases are filed in *federal court*. The federal court has its own uniform national system. The trial court level is the district courts. Each state has at least one judicial district. An appeal from a district court goes to a circuit court of appeals. A petition to review a decision of a circuit court of appeals goes to the United States Supreme Court in Washington, D.C.

Categorizing a Case

Our laws are categorized in two broad terms—*criminal* or *civil*. Criminal law generally deals with cases in which the *state* is the *prosecuting party* and the issue is whether the other party—the *defendant*—should be convicted of a crime. A conviction may involve a fine or jail sentence.

Civil law, on the other hand, deals with resolving wrongs between two parties—a *plaintiff* and a *defendant*. In civil cases, the issue is whether the defendant has wronged the plaintiff (in this case, you) under some noncriminal law and is therefore liable to the plaintiff for *damages* or money. Sometimes, other relief is also available in the form of an *injunction* or court order that compels a party to refrain from certain acts.

Civil law *liability* may arise from what we call either contract or tort principles. A *contract* is a legally enforceable agreement between two parties. A *tort* (which in French simply means wrong) is a wrong committed by one person against another that does not involve a breach of an agreement, but is of a kind for which the courts will nonetheless allow the recovery of damages. For example, if a stranger punches you in the nose without your consent, that person commits the tort of *battery* against you. You had no contractual promise from that person that he or she would not do that. Yet the law of torts says some social obligations are so well understood that the law will impose liability without a contract if people do not conduct themselves according to those principles.

There are important differences in the law of contracts and torts. One important difference in most states relates to available *remedies*. In a simple contract case, the remedies available are usually limited to the economic loss (past and future) that results from an illegal termination. Tort remedies are broader. In a tort case, generally, one may also recover for *noneconomic* and, in some cases in states where they are allowed, *punitive damages*. Noneconomic damages typically relate to the emotional distress associated with a termination. In certain cases, recovery for injury to reputation is also allowed.

There are different *labels* for legal wrongs. These are called *causes of action* or *claims of relief*, such as intentional infliction of emotional distress, battery, and defamation. The labels are important because the law does not give a remedy for every wrong in society. Only the wrongs that fit within certain legally recognized pigeonholes may be remedied in court. Unless a case falls within one of those pigeonholes, a lawyer can do nothing about the situation, no matter how *wrong* it seems.

Legal Claims

If there is a problem, you will need to understand your rights by reference to the various types of *legal theories* or claims for relief that are available and recognized by the courts. How your lawyer, the employer's lawyer, the judge, and the jury may ultimately approach, evaluate, and decide a case depends on this variable.

We inherited our law from England to a large extent. Historically, a commoner who came to the king would be entitled to relief only if that person's case fell under one of several established categories of cases for which the king would issue a *writ*. For example, there was one form of writ for cases involving trespass on another's land and another for cases involving a personal assault. To obtain a writ, your case had to fall within one of those established categories.

Over the years, the number of the categories for which one could obtain a writ has slowly increased. With respect to each category, each one of the *elements* or required subparts of the claim must be proven. Therefore, if you meet with a lawyer, you will find that his or her questions will be designed to ascertain whether your case satisfies all of the necessary elements of a particular claim. Your case may involve facts that would satisfy the elements of several different claims for relief. Under our court system, you would then be entitled to pursue as many different claims as you have. In this sense, the lawyer uses those various categories of claims that are generally available in employee rights cases like *tools in a bag* to vindicate your rights.

STAGES OF LITIGATION

Litigating a case is a process. As a process, it goes through various stages in which different activities are conducted and different decisions must be made.

Prefiling

If you decide to pursue a case, find a lawyer to hear you out and evaluate whether you have a case or not. *Most people do not have a case*. In most instances, what the employer did was unfair, but not illegal. The purpose of this stage is to help determine if you have a case, whether to assert it, and under what conditions. This typically involves meeting with a lawyer to tell your story, perhaps more than once.

The lawyer may ask you to provide documents or to write your story down in narrative form to flesh out the details. You may be asked to provide names of witnesses for the lawyer to contact in order to help the lawyer decide whether you have a case. In some cases, the lawyer may write a letter to the employer, known as a *demand letter*, to provide the employer an opportunity to settle the case before it is publicly filed. It may be necessary to initiate administrative proceedings before a court filing is made to satisfy certain legal requirements.

Filing

If you and your lawyer decide you have a case and it is in your best interest to proceed, the actual court case is initiated by the filing of a *pleading* known as a *complaint*. This is the document that contains the allegations of your case, organized by legal claims so the defendant and his or her attorney, as well as the judge, can understand what you are suing for.

Discovery

Once the case is filed, modern rules of civil procedure allow great leeway for attorneys of both parties in *discovering* facts relevant to their positions. These discovery rules are designed to take much of the surprise out of litigation. This helps identify those cases that are truly trial worthy, and also stimulates settlement.

In federal and state court, the plaintiff may request that the defendant produce documents that may lead to the discovery of relevant evidence. In federal court, and some state courts, the plaintiff may also require the defendant to answer written questions—called *interrogatories*—concerning the reasons for the discharge and other relevant matters. The defendant has reciprocal rights. Once the parties complete this phase of discovery, then the process turns to taking *depositions* of the plaintiff and the defendant's employees. A deposition is a formal interrogation that all parties and attorneys may attend, where questions are asked of a witness before a court reporter, and answers are given under oath.

Trial

If a case is not settled or disposed of on pretrial motions, it will be tried. Some states process cases more quickly than others. In some states, a trial may be held in about a year. In states with a more crowded docket, you may have to wait years to get to court.

The trial of an employment case typically lasts a few days. The rare case will take weeks. This is where live testimony is presented in court to help you win your case. Most often your case is presented to a jury, depending on what the statutory procedure and case law allows.

Appeals

A victory at trial does not mean the case is over. Employers often *appeal* judgments that award amounts of money. Employees, too, appeal from adverse judgments. An appeal involves further delay, typically one to two more years, before a final resolution is achieved. In the meantime, during the pendency of an appeal, interest is earned on the amount of any trial court judgment.

The appellate court has the power to either affirm, modify, or reverse the trial court judgment. Most often, jury verdicts are left undisturbed. But the appellate court will not be shy to reverse a case and send it back for a new trial (or dismiss it altogether) if it finds that serious legal error has been made at the trial court level. Once all appellate opportunities have been had, the case is finally decided. However, even then, it may not truly be resolved.

Settlement

Most cases *settle*. Opportunities for settling your case arise throughout the entire process. These windows of opportunity occur most frequently:

- just before filing the case;
- just before or after depositions are taken; and,
- just before, during, and after trial.

Cases are often settled on appeal as well. Your lawyer will be attuned to exploiting those opportunities. Court rules at the federal level, and in some states, now require the parties to discuss settlement before trial. The judge assigned to the case will expect the parties to have fully explored settlement before trial. Settlement judges or professional mediators may assist in the settlement process. (For more on settling your case, see Chapter 21.)

–2–
DISCRIMINATION

Since the *1964 Civil Rights Act,* many discrimination laws have been enacted by both Congress and many of the state legislatures. In 1964, Congress passed the Civil Rights Act, *Title VII,* which prohibits discrimination in the now familiar categories of race, color, religion, sex, and national origin. Then, in 1967, Congress passed the *Age Discrimination in Employment Act* to prohibit age discrimination. That was followed in 1972 by the *Rehabilitation Act,* which prohibits discrimination against disabled persons. Those Acts were followed in the nineties with the passage of the *Americans with Disabilities Act of 1990* and the *Family and Medical Leave Act* three years later. Various state legislatures followed Congress' lead and adopted a wide variety of statutes prohibiting discrimination.

The following is a listing of the principal federal statutes that protect you from discrimination.

- *Title VII of the Civil Rights Act of 1964*—prohibits *discrimination* in terms, conditions, or privileges of employment with respect to race, color, national origin, sex, and religion.
- *Equal Pay Act*—prohibits employers from paying different wages in a single establishment to a male and female employee for *equal work* on jobs that require equal skill, effort, and responsibility, and that are performed under similar working conditions.
- *Civil Rights Acts of 1870*—passed in the post-Civil War Reconstruction era, it provides more extensive remedies than Title VII for *intentional discrimination based on race.*

- *Age Discrimination in Employment Act* (ADEA)—prohibits discrimination in employment on the basis of *age* against any person 40 years of age and over.
- *Rehabilitation Act*—prohibits discrimination against *disabled persons* by federal construction contractors and requires affirmative action by those contractors to employ and advance qualified disabled persons; prohibits discrimination in employment by employers who receive federal financial assistance for the programs or activities supported by that assistance.
- *Vietnam Era Veterans Readjustment Act*—prohibits discrimination in employment against *Vietnam Era Veterans* and disabled veterans; requires affirmative action by contractors holding substantial federal contracts.
- *Americans with Disabilities* (ADA)—prohibits discrimination against *disabled persons* who can perform the essential functions of the position with or without reasonable accommodation.
- *The Family and Medical Leave Act*—prohibits discrimination for taking *family leave*; requires reinstatement to the position held or equivalent.

The very breadth of these laws demonstrates that discrimination laws may serve everyone at one time or another.

Often, the charge is made that discrimination laws require that minorities and women receive *special treatment*. As a rule, however, those laws do not require affirmative action or special consideration. Actually, Title VII and the ADEA merely require *nondiscrimination*. In other words, that the person be treated like everyone else. That is true as well of the Americans with Disabilities Act, except it requires employers to *reasonably accommodate* disabilities.

An exception to that rule also applies to federal contractors, when an affirmative action requirement is included in a federal contract as the *quid pro quo* for receiving federal funds. In addition, judges have the power to impose affirmative action requirements on employers in certain cases after discrimination has been proven. That power is used sparingly and only when, in the court's judgment, the offending party will not change its ways without court supervision.

A closely related criticism is that persons with frivolous discrimination claims end up obtaining huge judgments. Usually, however, since discrimination can be hard to prove, meritless cases tend to be screened out. Lawyers, who typically take those cases on a contingent fee basis, do not knowingly accept a losing case out of self-interest.

Once they are brought into court, the ones that are successful usually deserve it. Discrimination cases carry onerous proof requirements. If a case is deficient in proof, a judge has the power to kick it out of court before it even gets to a jury. If a judge allows the case to go to a jury, then the standard rule applies—juries usually get it right. A plaintiff who wins a verdict in a discrimination case probably deserved the victory.

Does discrimination still exist? Unfortunately, yes. Racial and ethnic epithets are still made. Women are still facing pregnancy discrimination, sexual harassment, sexually segregated job classifications, and glass ceilings. Injured workers are still being terminated for filing workers' compensation claims. Disabled workers are still being fired because of actual or perceived physical or mental impairments. Older workers are still being cast out and replaced by younger, less qualified workers.

The number of occasions and variety of ways in which workers are being discriminated against has not diminished. Those laws are needed now as much as ever. The *Equal Employment Opportunity Commission* (EEOC) has reported that 81,293 recent charges were filed with it against private sector employers alone. Of that number, about 20% were either settled or found to have merit at the administrative level.

PROVING DISCRIMINATION

Courts have recognized that there is rarely any direct evidence of discrimination. Most discrimination occurs through disparate or different treatment. For example, if an African American has been terminated, but no racial epithets were used, where would you look for any proof of discrimination? There are few cases, with direct evidence, in which someone admits, "I'm firing you because you are black!" So, they have allowed discrimination to be proven indirectly, by *circumstantial* evidence.

Under federal law, a *plaintiff*, or the person suing, first has the burden of producing evidence that he or she is a member of a *protected class* (race, age, sex, etc.), and was terminated or rejected under *suspicious circumstances*, such as where a less qualified person got the job. Then, the burden of producing evidence shifts to the *defendant* (the employer being sued) to articulate, or state, a legitimate nondiscriminatory reason for the personnel action.

Once the employer declares its stated reason, the employee must then produce evidence that the employer's stated reason is a mere *pretext* for discrimination. The employee can do this by showing that discrimination is the real reason or by proving the employer's stated reason is false.[1] As United States Supreme Court Justice O'Conner said in one case, evidence that the employer has given a false reason "may be quite persuasive," as ordinarily the jury "can reasonably infer from the falsity of the explanation that the employer is dissembling to cover up a discriminatory purpose."[2]

Admissible Evidence

Because discrimination cases can be proven not only by direct evidence, but also by circumstantial evidence, the following types of evidence are typically admissible:

- racial, ethnic, or sexual slurs;
- stereotypical behavior;
- differential treatment of you versus others;
- past incidents of discrimination; and,
- statistical evidence.

In approximately one-quarter of the cases that are brought, the manager has made one or more derogatory slurs of a racial nature in a race discrimination case, or of a sexual nature in a sex discrimination case. Sometimes the manager did not make the statements directly, but allowed others in the workplace to make them.

Sometimes there is evidence that the manager heard the statements and expressed agreement, laughed when the statements were made, or ignored the statements. Therefore, this gives the maker of the statements tacit permission to repeat them.

In other cases, a minority worker who had complained to management about racially motivated behavior by a coworker was met with a cold reception. A management response such as "I don't want to hear it," "You handle it," or "You guys have to work out your differences" is evidence of a gross insensitivity to, if not outright acceptance of, a racially or sexually hostile atmosphere as the applicable work standard.

Depositions

Through *depositions* or statements under oath that your lawyer takes from the firing manager during the discovery phase of the case, the manager's ignorance of *Equal Employment Opportunity* (EEO) laws may be demonstrated. Through depositions of the human resources manager of the company, your lawyer may learn that there has been little EEO training in the company, that the firing manager has received little or no EEO training, or that whatever training there has been did not directly apply to your case. The human resources manager may also reveal that there have been other complaints of discrimination against the firing manager or in that manager's department. Sometimes, depositions reveal that the firing manager has been previously disciplined concerning similar acts of discrimination.

Clerical workers often know more about the workplace than anyone else. They hear things and their information is invaluable. A statement from the firing manager's former secretary may lead to information that the manager has been out to get that worker for some time or that a conspiracy has existed between that person and other managers to rid the organization of that worker.

Statements of coworkers may show that someone has witnessed the racial epithets or other hostile acts. If an employer claims that you were a poor performer, your coworkers may be called on to testify that your performance was on a par with everyone else's. Your lawyer will conduct discovery to examine specific wrongdoings that you are accused of committing, and show that you are being blamed for someone else's mistake. He or she may try to determine that others have committed similar acts and were not fired.

In some jobs, some degree of error is inevitable. For example, in the food industry, products on the shelf are coded with a date by which they must be sold. Products not sold by that date are pulled from the shelves as spoils. The fact that an employee had spoils does not necessarily indicate incompetence, because everyone has a certain amount of spoils. Yet, the company may try to blame that employee for something that is wholly outside that worker's control or for some problem that is inherent in the job because of inefficiencies in the procedures the company requires that worker to follow. Information gathered from coworkers can help put that employee's performance in perspective.

Depositions of your former managers may show that at one time you were held in high regard. This raises a question as to the validity of the evaluation of the manager who fired you. Former managers may be unhappy with their own treatment by the company. They may have been pushed out by the manager who fired you. They may even have been the victims of discrimination themselves. They may have been the superior of your firing manager at one time, and they may be in a position to testify to that person's strong and weak points, character traits, and reputation.

Documents

Your lawyer is entitled to ask the employer to produce certain documents after a case is filed. The court may compel its production if the employer refuses to cooperate. The employer's documents that typically are requested and produced include:

- your personnel file;
- the personnel files of coworkers who you claim were given preferential treatment;
- the personnel file of the manager who fired you;
- the company's personnel rules and regulations;
- any EEO training materials that the company uses;

- any past performance evaluations or critiques concerning you, not included in your file;
- any disciplinary memoranda, if any, issued to you and your comparators;
- any other complaints of discrimination against the company;
- any intracompany memoranda issued between managers about you;
- data concerning the composition of the company workforce by race, sex, or age; and,
- data concerning the race, sex, or age of the persons who were hired (in a discriminatory hiring case) or retained (in a discriminatory firing case) instead of you.

It is often the case that files about you are maintained by different managers. All must be produced by the company, including any handwritten notes by company managers that are sometimes left in the file.

Many companies give written performance appraisals to workers on a regular basis to let them know how they are doing and where they should improve. Past performance appraisals that are commendable may be used by your attorney to show that something other than your performance is the cause of a change in attitude toward you. If, for example, poor attendance was tolerated in the past, a newfound intolerance suggests that some other factor accounts for a changed attitude. (Perhaps you have protested discrimination or filed a workers' compensation claim in the interim.)

Statistics

Statistical evidence may support your case of discrimination. How this works is fairly simple. In a case of an alleged racially discriminatory hiring, when the job in question does not require special skills, the employer's workforce in that job category should reasonably resemble the applicant pool in that community in terms of racial composition. If the applicant pool in that community has 10% blacks, a *reasonable expectation* is a workforce for that employer with 10% blacks. A small variance from that number is no problem for the employer.

If the variance is large, however, an expert statistician who has analyzed the data may conclude that the variance is *statistically significant*. Thus, if 8% of the workforce is black, the variance may not be statistically significant. If only 3% of the workforce is black, the statistician may be able to say that the variance is *suspect* and that it is likely that some factor other than pure chance accounts for the variance. Usually a statistician is not prepared to provide this testimony until, after applying all of the statistical formulas to the data, the results would occur by chance five or fewer times out of 100.[3]

Stereotypes

Some cases involve discriminatory stereotyping. Comments may have been made by managers that display such stereotyping. Blacks are often stereotyped as *lazy*. Women should be home with their children. Older workers are viewed as hard to train and set in their ways. There is no empirical evidence to support these stereotypes. However, these stereotypes are sometimes used as reasons not to hire or to fire a person. Sociologists and cultural anthropologists study the phenomenon of ethnic, gender, and age stereotyping and test those stereotypes against the real world. Those studies are often used by plaintiffs' attorneys to help a judge or jury understand the fallacy of certain stereotypes about a particular class or group.

National origin discrimination cases provide a unique opportunity to explain opposition to an employee even by a member of that employee's own race, as the following case study shows.

The Case of the Upwardly Mobile Foreigner

A black man was having trouble getting a promotion. He was from French Martinique, an island in the West Indies. He was well educated and intelligent. He also had a heavy French accent. He was not only opposed by some whites, but also by some other blacks at his place of employment. Some of them thought he asked too many questions. An expert cultural anthropologist testified on his behalf. The expert had studied the cultural assimilation problems experienced by the Haitian boat people in New York City.

The expert testified that French-speaking, black, West Indians highly value education, are upwardly mobile, and are extremely vocal about their rights. He testified that they also had a certain pattern of speech in which they would restate a fact to demonstrate their understanding, which made it appear as though they were asking a question about something they were just told. The expert explained that they were opposed by whites because they were black and opposed by blacks because they were upwardly mobile.

Result: verdict for employee.[4]

Stereotyping also occurs in the context of discrimination against persons with a physical or mental impairment. Sometimes, when an employer learns that an employee has a particular health problem, that worker is presumed to be debilitated without supportive medical evidence. The employer often does not understand the limitations imposed by that health problem, and the employee is truly impaired, not by his or her physical or mental limitation, but by the *stigma* associated with the malady and the employer's unreasonable reaction to it.

For example, an employee who sees a psychologist or psychiatrist for job-related stress may be viewed as being crazy by that worker's manager and may be ostracized by his or her peers because of that misperception. The worker may be disadvantaged, not by the stress from the work, but by the handicap of not receiving proper training, supervision, or management support.

Disparate Impact

In addition to the disparate treatment theory, under Title VII, the courts allow victims of discrimination to prevail if they can prove that a *facially neutral* employment practice, such as a height or weight requirement, has a *disparate impact* on the members of a protected class.

In order to prevail under a disparate impact analysis, the plaintiff must:

- identify a facially neutral employment practice and
- demonstrate that it causes an adverse impact on the class to which he or she is a member.

Before the passage of the *Civil Rights Restoration Act* the Supreme Court recognized that sometimes when an employer makes hiring decisions on a subjective basis, that too can cause a disparate impact. Therefore, if an employer follows such a practice, that system is susceptible to the disparate impact analysis.[5] That concept was incorporated into the *Civil Rights Restoration Act*.

A disparate impact is typically demonstrated through statistical analysis, which means that the numbers of persons involved have to be large enough to lend themselves to that analysis. To accomplish this, proof of a difference that is statistically significant is required. That is to say, one which would occur by chance very infrequently. The Supreme Court, in one case, held a disparity of two to three *standard deviations* from a normal distribution was statistically significant.[6] If adverse impact is shown, the employee need not provide further evidence the employer intended to discriminate.

Once adverse impact is shown, the *burden of persuasion* shifts to the employer to prove that the practice is job related for the position in question and consistent with business necessity. (See 42 U.S.C. Sec. 2000e-2(k)(1)(A)(1).) If it fails to do that, liability is established under that section of the statute.

If the employer establishes a business necessity, the employee is given an opportunity to show there is a less discriminatory alternative employment practice available to the employer. (42 U.S.C. Sec. 2000e-2 (k)(1)(A)(ii).) The employee can also prevail by showing the employer's claimed business necessity is a mere *pretext* for discrimination.[7]

FEDERAL REMEDIES

There are two parts to every case—*liability* and *damages*. If you are able to prove you should recover something (liability), each law differs as to what that recovery can include (damages). In 1964, when it was passed, Title VII was said to be designed to *make whole* the victim of discrimination by allowing recovery of lost wages and fringe benefits and by requiring the employer to reinstate the worker. There was no right to a jury trial. This remedy was helpful to the injured party and provided some measure of justice. However, it hardly made the victim whole after having suffered the trauma and distress of losing a job. The reality that the initial remedies that were available under Title VII of the 1964 *Civil Rights Act* were inadequate provided incentive to civil rights lawyers everywhere to develop other remedies broader in scope that would compensate for the emotional distress that accompanied discrimination and displacement.

Then, after the publicity associated with the Clarence Thomas Supreme Court confirmation, Congress passed the *Civil Rights Restoration Act* to address this inadequacy. That Act provided to victims of discrimination under Title VII of the 1964 *Civil Rights Act* the right to a jury trial, limited damages for emotional distress, and punitive damages, in addition to economic loss. The scope of the remedy was designed to correspond with the size of the company in terms of numbers of employees.

Size of Company	Amount of Damages Available
Employers of 15–100	up to $50,000
Employers of 101–200	up to $100,000
Employers of 201–500	up to $200,000
Employers of 501+	up to $300,000

Therefore, employees who suffered discrimination under Title VII could recover *noneconomic damages*. Employees who suffered on-the-job discrimination, such as sexual harassment that did not lead to a termination, had meaningful, albeit limited, remedies. These remedies were also made available to victims of discrimination against under the *Americans with Disabilities Act* (ADA).

Unfortunately, Congress did not also make them available to victims of age discrimination. Even today, victims of age discrimination are limited to economic loss and cannot recover emotional distress damages. However, if a victim of age discrimination proves the violation was willful, they can recover *liquidated damages* equal to their lost *back pay* or economic loss from the time the loss first occurred to the time of trial. Likewise, persons who have been discriminated under FMLA have no right to recover noneconomic damages.

PROCEDURAL HURDLES

Before you can get into federal or state court on a federal discrimination claim, you must first exhaust your administrative remedies. You do this by filing an *administrative complaint of discrimination* with the appropriate federal and state enforcement agency. At the federal level these are the regional offices of the Equal Employment Opportunity Commission (EEOC). (See Appendix A for a listing of the regional offices of the EEOC.)

Many states have their own civil rights enforcement agency as well. Where a state has an enforcement agency, the federal government may defer to the local state agency to initially conduct the investigation and make a determination whether substantial evidence of discrimination exists. Once a determination is made, the EEOC, if requested, will independently review the case to see if a violation of federal law occurred.

If there is no deferral agency in your state, you have 180 days to file an administrative complaint of discrimination with the EEOC. If there is a deferral agency in your state, you have 300 days from the date of discrimination or 30 days from dismissal of the state proceeding, whichever is earlier, to make such a filing under federal law. Be aware that, under your state laws, you may have a longer or shorter period to file a claim. These state law limitations periods vary from thirty days to three years. If you are a government worker, you may also have a separate tort claims notice filing requirement. So do not delay getting advice concerning the amount of time you have to file your claim. You may get such advice by speaking with a lawyer.

Once you file your complaint, the appropriate administrative agency will investigate it. At the conclusion of the investigation, it will make a determination. If the matter is not settled in *conciliation* at the agency level, you will be given what is known as a *right to sue* letter. This gives you a certain amount of time to file an action in court. An EEOC Right to Sue letter gives you ninety days from your date of receipt to do that. If you did not already have a lawyer, that ninety-day period will give you an opportunity to find one to independently review your case and decide whether it merits a court filing, regardless of what the agency determined.

STATE LAW PROTECTION

Almost all states have passed some form of statewide discrimination statute. However, the scope of those statutes wildly differ. For example, Alabama only prohibits discrimination on the basis of age. Mississippi's discrimination laws regulate public but not private sector employment.

In addition to the categories protected under federal law, many states also prohibit discrimination based on marital status or change in marital status. Many also provide statutory protection against retaliation for filing a state civil rights or workers' compensation claim. Persons who serve in the state military are typically protected. Eighteen states have created ancestry as a protected class—in addition to national origin. While the two categories together would protect against discrimination if you or your parents were born in a foreign country, Vermont's even broader statute, which prohibits discrimination based upon place of birth, bans discrimination against persons born in other states.

Eight states have included creed as a separate category in addition to religion to broaden protection based upon one's beliefs. Not all states that prohibit other forms of discrimination outlaw disability discrimination. On the other hand, some states have broader statutory disability protection. Washington state bars physical, mental, and sensory disability discrimination. New Mexico extends its health-related protection against discrimination to persons with serious medical conditions. California, as well, protects against discrimination based on medical condition, which it restrictively defines as relating to a history of cancer or genetic characteristic. Hawaii and Oregon extend legal protection to employees who are associated with a disabled person in order to reach situations in which an employer may think itself burdened by the cost or distraction associated with an employee's disabled dependent.

Age, likewise, is given widely differing treatment by the states. Some states follow the age 40 and over requirement before offering protection. Very few states, such as Minnesota, New Jersey, and Oregon recognize that there are some situations in which a person may experience discrimination because he or she is too young, and thus provide legal protection to persons who have attained majority.

While there is no federal law banning sexual orientation discrimination in the private sector, thirteen states (California, Connecticut, Hawaii, Maryland, Massachusetts, Minnesota, Nevada, New Hampshire, New Jersey, New Mexico, Rhode Island, Vermont, and Wisconsin) and the District of Columbia have made sexual orientation discrimination unlawful by statute.

Pro-family legislation has created even more protected classes at the state level. A handful of states and the District of Columbia prohibit family relationship discrimination of one form or another in order to prohibit termination because a family member works or used to work for the employer. Alaska prohibits parenthood discrimination. The District of Columbia has taken it a step further and prohibits discrimination against persons who have discharged family responsibilities, which the Act leaves undefined. Mothers who breast-feed or express milk at work are protected in Oregon, Hawaii, Minnesota, New Mexico, and Tennessee. In North Carolina, the employer cannot discriminate against an employee for participating in court-ordered parental duties, or for taking up to four hours leave per year to attend activities at a child's school. The importance of education is acknowledged in the District of Columbia in its ban on discrimination for matriculation.

Privacy concerns have stimulated other local legislation. Five states bar discrimination against persons who have lawfully used lawful products off the employer's premises during nonworking hours. A few others specifically protect persons who lawfully use tobacco. Minnesota prohibits discrimination against employees who fail to contribute to charity.

In addition to those statutes aimed to protect private activity, other statutes protect private information. Seven states now prohibit discrimination on the basis of genetic information or condition. One state, New Jersey, outlaws such discrimination for atypical cellular or blood trait. Three states make it illegal for discriminating against someone who has received public assistance. Two states prohibit discrimination on the basis of one's criminal history. Massachusetts prohibits discrimination on the basis of a person's mental commitment history.

Two jurisdictions regulate discrimination purely on physical characteristics. Michigan bans discrimination based on height *or* weight. The District of Columbia, creating probably the most wide sweeping of all protected class categories, bans discrimination based on personal appearance.

The number of employees in the employer's workforce required to activate the legal protection afforded also differs from state to state. For example, in Missouri, the employer must have at least six employees. In Virginia, the employer is regulated only if they have between five and fifteen employees. In Oregon, the number is six for disability discrimination, but one in most other cases.

In most states, an administrative agency has been established to enforce state civil rights laws. In some states, no independent claim may be pursued outside the administrative process. (For a detailed listing of the notable discrimination statutes in each state and contact information for each available state enforcement agency see Appendix B.)

As you now understand, virtually everyone is a member of at least one protected class. (For more on your rights under those laws, see Chapters 6 through 10.)

RIGHTS OF REJECTED APPLICANTS

The laws prohibiting discrimination extend to the hiring process. If you are a rejected applicant for employment, you have the legal right not to be discriminated against for your membership in a protected class (race, age, sex, etc.). That means that while you can be rejected as an applicant even though you are a minority or a woman, you cannot be rejected because of that status.

The hiring process is complicated and discrimination can occur at any number of the various stages of it. Some of the things to be on the lookout for include the following.

- Any minimum qualifications imposed by employers must be job related and consistent with business necessity. For example, height and weight requirements for police and fire candidates stimulated much litigation in past years because of their adverse impact on women.
- Similarly, college degree requirements for some jobs have been found to have an unwarranted adverse impact against some minority groups.
- An employer leaves itself open to liability if its recruitment policies have resulted in an underrepresentation of women or minorities in its workforce (*i.e.*, a percentage of that protected class that is significantly less than the available labor pool).
- Any screening devices employed by the employer must not have an adverse impact (*i.e.*, disqualifying women or minorities in disproportionate numbers). Employers must take care that their criteria are objective and relate to the requirements or qualifications for the position.

Thus, even before interviews are conducted, an employer may have already discriminated against you by: imposing a minimum qualification that has an adverse impact against your protected class; targeting its recruitment efforts so that it intentionally avoids generating interest for its openings amongst women or minorities; or, screening out applicants on the basis of impermissible considerations, or those that do not relate to the qualifications for the position.

Discriminatory Interview Questions

Contrary to popular belief, with the exception of the Americans with Disabilities Act, most federal discrimination statutes do not specifically prohibit certain questions from being asked on applications and in interviews. However, if questions are asked that seek disclosure of one's race, color, religion, sex, national origin, or age, that may later serve as evidence of bias in a case brought by a rejected applicant who is as equally qualified as the successful candidate.

Questions that could serve as evidence of bias in particular cases include the following.

- Religious Discrimination:
  - Are you available to work on weekends?
- Race, Color, or National Origin Discrimination:
  - What is your credit record?
  - Do you own your own home?
  - Are you a U.S. citizen?
- Sex Discrimination:
  - Do you have children under age 18?
  - How many?
  - How old are they?
  - What arrangements will be made for child care?
  - Are you married, single, divorced?
  - Are you known as Ms., Mrs., or Miss?
  - Are you pregnant?
  - Do you plan to have children?
- Age Discrimination:
  - How old are you?
  - What is your date of birth?
  - When did you graduate from high school? From college?
- Disability Discrimination:
  - Do you have a disability?
  - What is the nature or severity of your disability?
  - Have you ever been hospitalized?
  - Have you ever been treated for mental illness?
  - Do you have a physical or mental impairment that may prevent you from performing the job?
  - How often would you require leave for treatment for your disability?
  - Have you ever filed a workers' compensation claim?

Even if impermissible questions are asked, that does not mean you will automatically win your discrimination case. You still must prove that your protected class status was a motivating factor. That may be hard to do unless you are also able to show you were, objectively, at least as qualified as the successful candidate. However, the fact that impermissible questions were asked will raise a red flag and serve as some evidence your nonselection was a product of unlawful bias.

Other Interview-Based Discrimination

Interviews can be discriminatory in ways other than with respect to the questions that are asked. They may be perfunctory. You may have been selected for an interview only because the hiring manager wanted to tell his or her supervisor that the interview pool included minorities or women. Factors that may show this include the length of the interview, its setting, or by the coolness and disinterest shown to you by the interviewers. In some cases, words of discouragement about your qualifications for the position, assertions that the position is not a good fit for you, or statements about your poor prospects for selection—even before your interview is over or all other candidates are interviewed—will establish that you were treated differently in the interview from other candidates.

Damages

A final complicating factor to consider in the case of a rejected applicant is that in addition to proving you were the best qualified candidate and also proving that your protected class status was the reason for your nonselection, you must also prove the amount of your damages. Sometimes, that can be difficult. Whereas a long term employee can show from years of acceptable performance the likelihood that successful performance in that position would continue, a rejected applicant may lack a track record of performance in similar positions that would show to the satisfaction of a jury that the applicant would have successfully performed for a substantial period of time. In order for your discriminatory hiring case to have value, your lawyer will need to prove that whatever damages you are seeking are based on assumptions relating to your continued employment that rest on more than mere speculation.

This book discusses all aspects of the understanding of the term *wrongful discharge*. It will discuss terminations that are wrongful in the sense that they violate a *discrimination statute*, a *whistleblower law*, a *term of a contract*, or were wrongful in the manner in which they occurred. This chapter, however, is devoted to the more specific meaning of the term, the *public policy tort* of wrongful discharge.

PROTECTION FOR PRIVATE EMPLOYEES

The United States is unlike the countries of Western Europe and Canada that recognize that employees in the *private sector* generally have a *property right* to employment. Many public employees in the United States have been afforded property right protection in this country through the civil service system. Similarly, union workers may only be discharged for just cause. But workers in the private sector have traditionally been referred to as employees at-will who can be terminated without cause—for any reason or no reason at all.

The stark contrast in this country between the protections afforded to workers in the public sector and union workers on the one hand and everyone else on the other, brought home to judges the vulnerability of the nonunion worker. In 1959, a union business agent was terminated one day after he refused to give false testimony to a state legislative committee. A California appellate court held that he could sue for wrongful discharge because his termination was against public policy. (*Petermann v. International Brotherhood of Teamsters*, 344 P.2d 25 (Cal. App. 1959).)

For almost fifteen years after that case was decided, no progress was made in the development of the tort. After passage of the Civil Rights Act of 1964, the workplace began to be viewed as no longer untouchable by the courts. It took developments in other areas of law, most notably in commercial law between merchants and in insurance law that honored the *reasonable expectations* of the parties. As judges observed other abuses in the workplace outside the protection of the civil rights laws, this new willingness to intervene led to the creation of additional remedies for terminated employees.

–3–

WRONGFUL DISCHARGE

Around the country, the American rule of *at-will employment* came under assault. In New Hampshire, a court ruled in 1974 that an employee who was dismissed for refusing to date her supervisor was wrongfully discharged.[8] In Oregon, in 1975, the Oregon Supreme Court ruled that an employee who was dismissed for reporting to jury duty was wrongfully discharged.[9] In Massachusetts, in 1977, a salesman with twenty-five years of service, who was discharged the day after the company obtained a $5,000,000 order on which he would have received a $92,000 bonus, was held to have been wrongfully discharged.[10]

In 1980, in Michigan, a court ruled that a discharge without cause in violation of an *employee handbook* that had been distributed to the employee by the employer was wrongful.[11] In that same year, a California court held that an employee who was discharged after eighteen years' service, allegedly without good cause and for union activity, could bring an action against the employer in contract and tort for wrongful discharge because the termination offended the implied covenant of *good faith and fair dealing* that attended the employment contract.[12]

The stage was set for something big to happen. In rapid fashion over the next few years, most states developed their own rule recognizing a small exception to at-will employment. The public policy tort of wrongful discharge was created.

PUBLIC POLICY

Since 1975, the great majority of states have accepted wrongful discharge as an additional legal tool a terminated employee can assert—but only under limited circumstances. In most cases, in order to assert the claim, the employee has to show that he or she was terminated contrary to public policy. Typically, this requires the employee to show he or she was terminated for doing something or refusing to do something. Thus, in most states, the claim will lie only if the termination was in *retaliation* for the employee's conduct.

In a few jurisdictions, however, including Delaware, Maryland, Vermont, Virginia, and the District of Columbia, the courts have said that a purely discriminatory discharge on the basis of protected class status is just as contrary to public policy as any other, and therefore, do not require the element of retaliation. But in all states that have recognized the tort, there must be a public rather than private interest that is implicated by the termination. An individual terminated for acting to protect his or her own personal interest is insufficient. In each case, the court's concern is whether a public policy will be thwarted if protection is not afforded. The struggle has been about how to define what public policy is.

States differ over what courts may look to in discerning whether a public policy exists that is deserving of protection. In some states, like California and Missouri, the courts have decided they will look to constitutional and statutory provisions and administrative regulations.[13] In other states, including West Virginia, New Jersey, and Ohio, courts are not so restrained and they will look to not only those sources, but also to judge-made common law.[14] In Utah, in somewhat of a slight to public administrators, the Supreme Court has said it will look to constitutional provisions, statutes, and judicial decisions, but not to administrative regulations.[15] Still in other states, the courts have held that public policy may be found even in a private professional code of conduct.[16] Some, but not all, will consider federal law in declaring state public policy.

In some states, such as Illinois, New Hampshire, and Oregon, the courts have not felt compelled to hold that an enunciation of public policy be specific. In Illinois, for example, an employee who was discharged for reporting the crime of a coworker to the sheriff was given protection despite the absence of any statutory authority because the court said that public policy favored citizen crime fighters.[17]

In Oregon, there was a case in which a bank employee was discharged for refusing to disclose confidential customer financial information. The court held that for a public policy wrongful discharge to lie, it was not necessary to identify a particular statutory or constitutional provision had been violated. It is sufficient that the public policy the plaintiff relies upon for protection is reflected in a common concern by one or more statutes, so that the policy would be thwarted if the discharge could stand with *impunity*.[18]

By historical standards, the tort is in its infancy and has not been universally accepted. Georgia has thus far refused to recognize the tort, citing traditional adherence to the rule of at-will employment.[19] Florida has refused to recognize it, apart from one case in which it begrudgingly acknowledged clear statutory authority to bring it.[20] In a few other states, it has remained remarkably underdeveloped.

Some states have adopted it very restrictively. In Texas, for example, the tort is recognized only if an employee is discharged for refusing to engage in illegal activity.[21] Therefore, in Texas, while employees who refuse to perform an illegal act are protected, it has been held that merely questioning an employer about the legality of its practices will not be given protection.[22]

The narrowness of the application of the tort may also be seen in the decisions of the District of Columbia, where protection has been given to an employee who refused to violate the law,[23] but not for reporting the illegal conduct of a coworker.[24] In other states, such as Pennsylvania, the claim will not lie at all if there is an available statutory remedy.[25]

Application of Public Policy

No standard has been uniformly applied as to the categories of activity that will be protected. Generally, however, where the tort is recognized, it has been applied to cases in which an employee has refused to engage in illegal activity,[26] for reporting illegal activity,[27] for performing a public duty (like reporting to jury duty[28]), or for pursuing an employment right or benefit made available by statute, such as filing a workers' compensation claim.[29]

Even within these well-recognized categories, however, there is debate. In reporting illegal activity, for example, some states, including Arkansas, Connecticut, Minnesota, Nevada, New Jersey, Oklahoma, Pennsylvania, Utah, and Texas, appear to require a report to an appropriate law enforcement or regulatory agency outside the employer.[30] About the same number, however, including Arizona, California, Connecticut, Illinois, Kansas, Maryland, Massachusetts, and Oregon, afford protection whether or not the report was made outside the employer.[31]

Similarly, most states that have decided the question, have held that an employee need not prove the actual unlawfulness of the employer's conduct they were reporting, just his or her good faith belief that it was unlawful.[32] In Pennsylvania though, if the employer's conduct was not in fact illegal, the employee has no claim.[33] On the other hand, an employee who complains of conduct that is not thought to be unlawful, but just amounts to unscrupulous business practices, is not given legal protection by this tort in any state.

The public policy tort of wrongful discharge is illustrated in the following cases.

The Case of the Honest Renegade

A group of businessmen in a company allegedly devised a scheme to promote illegal price-fixing. An employee allegedly refused to go along with the scheme and was fired in retaliation.
Result: recovery allowed.
(*Tameny v. Atlantic Richfield Co.*, 610 P.2d 1330 (Cal. 1980).)

The Case of the Modest Employee

An employee was requested to engage in *mooning*, but refused the request and was terminated.
Result: recovery allowed. The public policy against indecent exposure supported the claimed right not to expose himself.
(*Wagenseller v. Scottsdale Memorial Hospital*, 710 P.2d 1025 (Ariz.1985).)

The Case of the Curious Landlord

An employee was instructed to enter a tenant's apartment and search the tenant's belongings without permission. The employee refused and was terminated.

Result: recovery allowed. An employee should not be required to invade someone else's privacy to keep his or her job.

(*Kessler v. Equity Management, Inc.*, 572 A.2d 1144 (Md. 1990).)

The Case of the Stubborn Environmentalist

An employee was told to alter pollution reports, refused to do so, and was terminated.

Result: recovery allowed. It would be contrary to public policy to allow employers to be able to coerce such false reporting.

(*Trombetta v. Detroit, Toledo & Ironton R. Co.*, 265 N.W.2d 385 (Mich. 1978).)

The Case of the Pesky Nurse

A nurse observed that a patient's health was failing because of what she believed to be poor medical care. Though she was told to stay out of it, she reported her feelings to the patient's family and was terminated.

Result: recovery allowed. Laws regulating nursing care would require her to be honest in giving advice to the family about the patient's medical condition.

(*Kirk v. Mercy Hospital Tri-County*, 851 S.W.2d 617 (Mo. App. 1993).)

The Case of the Inquisitive Employee

An employee was discharged for seeking information about insurance coverage she was promised and threatening to obtain legal counsel to obtain it.

Result: recovery allowed. To terminate an employee for consulting with a lawyer regarding an issue that affected promised employee benefits violated public policy.

(*Chapman v. Adia Services*, 688 N.E.2d 604 (Ohio 1997).)

NOTE: *See Appendix C for a listing of some of the notable cases recognizing the tort in each jurisdiction.*

PROVING WRONGFUL DISCHARGE

Wrongful discharge is proven by the very same evidence that lawyers use to prove discrimination. Your attorney will look for evidence of a *causal connection* between the *protected activity* that you engaged in and the *termination*. As with proof of discrimination, that evidence may be either direct or circumstantial. Sometimes the timing of events alone suggests that linkage. A change in attitude toward how you and your performance are regarded, before and after the protected activity, may suggest the connection. (Typically, you will not be required to show that the protected activity was the sole factor in your discharge, just that it was a substantial or determining factor.)

WRONGFUL CONSTRUCTIVE TERMINATION

Employees frequently ask: "Is it possible to sue my employer if I resign?" It may be that an employee is about to resign because his or her employer has been harassing the employee because of his or her protected class status or for some kind of protected activity they have undertaken. Most employers are not stupid. Neither are their lawyers. They do not want to set themselves up for liability. They know that if they outright terminate someone, that person will have an easier case to prove than if that person leaves on his or her own. So, often the employer intentionally engages in conduct with the purpose of making it so awful the employee will surely resign. Sometimes, though, the employer may not intend to be mean, but cannot help itself, and behaves in a way the employer should realize would lead to a resignation if that conduct continued.

In the early days of employment law, the employee who resigned was out-of-luck, as most remedies that had developed were for terminated workers. As years went by, courts were presented with too many cases in which it would be unjust to leave the employee without a remedy whose termination was precipitated by the employer. Courts began to allow recovery under limited circumstances to employees who resigned. The federal courts led the way, and in interpreting Title VII allowed recovery to workers who resigned where the work atmosphere had become objectively *intolerable*.

Eventually, the various state courts were faced with the issue. In most of the states that have decided the issue, the courts have held that there will be limited circumstances in which the employee will be allowed to sue if the employee has resigned. They have held that if those narrow circumstances exist, even though the employee resigned, the law will deem that a termination occurred as a fictional legal construct. Thus the term *wrongful constructive termination*.

The law of the states differ, however, as to what those circumstances are. To discourage fraudulent suits, the standard has invariably been a strict one. In harassment type cases, the law will typically require that the intolerability be objectively determined. That means that even though you may subjectively feel the employer's conduct toward you is horrible and that you can't take it anymore, a judge or juror will be able to second guess you later on. If they believe that you were hypersensitive or that you jumped the gun, you may lose the case. It is absolutely critical, therefore, that you consult with a lawyer *before you resign* to avoid or minimize the risk of harming an otherwise good case.

REMEDIES

In almost all states that have recognized the tort, damages are available. Those damages include what are known as *compensatory damages* for such things as *emotional distress* and *economic loss*.

Emotional distress follows the trauma of most firings. To recover emotional distress damages, typically you will not need to see a doctor, psychiatrist, or psychologist. The shock, humiliation, embarrassment, anxiety, nervousness, depression, loss of appetite, and sleeplessness that may follow a wrongful discharge are among the many and varied forms for which terminated employees seek damages for emotional stress. The trial judge will instruct the jury that there is no fixed standard for awarding such damages. Jurors are merely told they may award whatever damages they believe to be fair and reasonable.

Economic loss will include both past and future economic loss. Past loss is measured from the date of termination to the date of trial. Future economic loss includes the damages from the date of trial forward. This does not mean that you will be entitled to receive an award of future economic loss free of any obligation to look for replacement work. A plaintiff in an employment case is expected to use reasonable efforts to mitigate (lessen) the loss they are claiming by looking for other substitute employment.

Tort damages may also include *punitive damages* if you are in a state that allows them. Whereas compensatory damages are awarded to compensate the plaintiff for harm suffered, punitive damages are awarded to punish the guilty party. Rather than look at the harm done to the injured person, the court instructs the jury that in awarding punitive damages, it should examine:

- the nature of the act that was committed;
- the likelihood the employer will repeat its acts;
- the wealth and income of the employer; and,
- the amount of money that would be required to deter the employer and others similarly situated from repeating the offense.

Punitive damages are sometimes called *exemplary damages* because they are awarded to set an example for the employer and others not to do it again.

Some jurisdictions regulate wrongful discharge by statute. In Montana, a state statute (Mont. Code Ann. Sec. 39.2.602) requires an employer to have good cause to terminate a worker. In that state there is no tort of wrongful discharge any longer. No other state has followed suit. Nebraska has codified, or specified by statute, the categories of public policy exceptions to at-will employment it will accept in a wrongful discharge claim. (Neb. Rev. Stat. Secs. 48-1101 to 48-1125.) Virginia has passed similar legislation. Talk to an attorney in your state to find out if what you are doing constitutes protected activity.

• • • • •

As the tort of wrongful discharge develops in the United States, there are relatively few cases of unfair termination that will fall within one of the public policy wrongful discharge exceptions. The recognition, though, that employers were engaging in violations of public policy in terminating employees, and the reluctance of some courts to expand the law quickly, led some legislators to step in and adopt statutes to expressly provide legal remedies for persons who were wrongfully terminated.

Employment lawyers, frustrated by the narrow scope of the tort, applied continuing pressure on the courts to recognize employee rights in other areas of civil law. The next two chapters on tort claims and employment contracts will show you how that pressure translated into the development of positive law.

—4— TORT CLAIMS

For a number of years, the at-will employment rule was so deeply entrenched that courts viewed the relationship between employer and employee as practically untouchable. But as courts became used to intervening in that relationship in civil rights cases, lawyers pressured the courts to broaden the remedies that were available to employees.

This chapter discusses the areas of law that once were available only to right wrongs in civil cases between total strangers or business associates, but are now available to right wrongs between employers and employees.

Termination is not included in this list. If you are defamed, your privacy is invaded, or your supervisor commits some outrageous act toward you, you do not have to lose your job to have one of these claims. At the same time, an unlawful termination is often accompanied by conduct that the employer has committed in the course or manner of the termination.

You may have an *unlawful termination plus* situation in which one or more of these claims will exist, in addition to the discrimination or wrongful discharge claim. The courts require a plaintiff in a civil case to include as many claims as exist in one lawsuit. It is not uncommon to see a complaint in an employment case with multiple claims.

INTENTIONAL INFLICTION OF EMOTIONAL DISTRESS

Sometimes we hear about or experience an event that is so far outside the bounds of acceptable conduct in our society that it can be fairly categorized as outrageous. In some states, this type of event has been recognized as the tort of *intentional infliction of emotional distress*. Generally, where it has been recognized, you must show:

- that the employer either acted intentionally to cause you to suffer emotional distress or in *reckless disregard* (*i.e.*, "I don't care") of whether you would suffer such distress;
- that the conduct was so far outside the bounds of accepted conduct it was outrageous; and,
- that the conduct has resulted in severe emotional or mental distress.

The tort is sort of a catch all for highly unusual cases that defy categorization. It is not favored in the courts. Most trial judges require extreme facts before they will allow this claim to go to trial. It is often said that the facts have to pass the *Oh, my God! test*. This high bar is intended to prevent people from suing for the mean, rude, or insulting conduct that is often part of everyday life. It is thought that without the requirement of a showing of outrageousness, the courts would be overburdened with such suits.

Just as there is no limit to the ways in which an employer could conceivably be abusive, there is no one type of case in which the tort applies. It has frequently been applied in cases involving abusive investigations, shocking behavior, highly offensive physical contact, highly unusual and extreme forms of retaliation, and horrendous treatment of the infirm. Ordinary workplace harassment will not qualify. The following cases exemplify its application.

The Case of the Drill Sergeant Supervisor

Two employees were harassed daily over a two-year period by a supervisor who was a former U.S. Army sergeant. The harassment included grossly abusive, threatening, and degrading conduct that included daily yelling, screaming, cursing, and

repeated physical assaults in which he would actually *charge* at the employees in a threatening manner to terrorize them.
Result: recovery allowed.
(*GTE Southwest, Inc. v. Bruce*, 998 S.W.2d 605 (Tex. 1999).)

The Case of the Acrophobic Photographer

A photographer, who everyone knew was afraid of heights, was assigned a new supervisor. The supervisor assigned him to jobs requiring photography at great heights despite knowledge of his disability and the distress that it caused.
Result: recovery allowed.
(*Brown v. Ellis*, 484 P.2d 944 (Conn. 1984).)

The Case of the Miserly Employer

The day before an employee was to go in for cancer surgery, the employer notified her it was cancelling her insurance coverage because it would be *too great a burden* on the employer.
Result: recovery allowed.
(*Clifton v Van Dresser Corp.*, 596 N.E.2d 1075 (Ohio App. 1991).)

The Case of the Deviant Owner

A waitress was sexually harassed by the owner of a coffee shop. His harassment of her included putting his hands on her waist, leg, and breasts. He would try to kiss her. He would pin himself up against her. Once he exposed his genitals to her. He continued this behavior though he knew it was unwelcome, caused her distress, and aggravated an abdominal disorder he knew she had.
Result: recovery allowed.
(*Priest v. Rotary*, 634 F.Supp. 571 (ND Cal 1986).)

The Case of the Shameful Sham Offer

An employer repeatedly misrepresented to a thirty-two year employee that if he resigned his position and signed a release, he would be eligible for a transfer to a different facility. He was told that if he did not sign the release, he would be fired anyway. He signed the release and traveled to the site of the supposed other job only to learn that it had never been available. The employer had deceived him merely to induce him to sign the release. When this fraud caused him to suffer a disabling depression, the employer tried to interfere with his receipt of disability insurance.

Result: recovery allowed.

(*The Kroger Company v. Willgruber*, 920 S.W.2d 61 (Ky. 1996).)

This tort is relatively new and its application to employment cases is particularly recent. No one can tell its limits at this point. However, in the past few years, it has been applied in the following ways:

- in a case of retaliation for reporting sexual harassment;[34]
- in cases of racial epithets and racial harassment;[35]
- in cases of abusive investigations, particularly ones that include false accusations, threats of criminal prosecution, or *gestapo-type tactics*;[36]
- in some cases of retaliation for reporting illegal activity, if the conduct is sufficiently outrageous;[37] and,
- in a case when the employer circulated false rumors that the employee was stealing in an effort to force the employee to resign.[38]

As can be seen, the courts will look to the subject matter or content of the conduct. Thus, unlawful sexual or racial harassment will be more likely to be the type of conduct the courts will find sufficiently beyond the realm of social toleration than abusive conduct generally. Further, the courts will also consider the duration and severity of the conduct.

Intentional infliction of emotional distress is an intentional tort. In most states, the intent requirement will be met either when the actor desires to inflict emotional distress, or when the actor knows that such distress is certain, or substantially certain, to result from his or her conduct.[39]

Although the courts require proof in the case of this particular tort that the plaintiff's emotional distress was severe, in most states, no medical testimony is required to establish the connection between the defendant's actions and the resultant distress. One court in Missouri, however, held that the distress be medically diagnosable and significant.[40] In most states, awards are based on evidence of crying, loss of sleep, reclusiveness, humiliation, and anguish, that is more than transitory.[41]

Montana has barred such claims in its *Wrongful Discharge from Employment Act*, as the quid pro quo for its grant of for cause termination protection.

In extreme cases, the tort of intentional infliction of emotional distress will be important in vindicating employer violations. The very limited nature of its application, however, caused employment lawyers to seek even more legal tools to vindicate employee rights.

FRAUD

When someone promises you something and then does not fulfill that promise, that is *breach of contract*. When that person knew at the time the promise was made that the promise would not or could not be fulfilled, intending that you act in reliance on that promise anyway, that is *fraud*. Fraud can also be based on a representation made with reckless disregard as to its truth or falsity. In the law of misrepresentation, it means making a promise without knowing whether it can be performed.

An employee may claim fraud in the recruitment process in connection with the promises made regarding the nature of the work, the compensation for that work, or the circumstances in which the work will be performed. For example, when a worker is recruited for a position and agrees to take that position, but is never given that position, and the employer knew at the time the worker was recruited that the worker would not receive that position, that is fraud.

Similarly, when a worker is promised $10 per hour plus vacation pay, sick leave, and retirement benefits, but reports to work and is paid only $8 per hour with no fringe benefits, that is fraud if the person making the representation either knew it to be false at the time or made the promise in reckless disregard whether or not the statement was true. The following cases illustrate this tort.

The Case of the Secret Plant Closure

An employer recruited engineers and others around the country to join its workforce in Eugene, Oregon. Plaintiffs were four recruits and their wives. During the recruitment process, the recruits were told about the advantage of living in Eugene and how the company in Eugene would be *ramping up* their workforce. They communicated these statements to their wives.

The plaintiffs alleged that unbeknownst to them and to local management in Eugene, the company's parent corporation back east had already decided it would close its Eugene subsidiary, upon the happening of certain conditions likely to occur. The Eugene plant was closed soon after the plaintiffs were hired.

Result: claims for both recruits and their spouses were allowed to proceed to trial. The court held that an employer who tells a half-truth is obligated to tell the whole truth, and in that event, must divulge all likely material contingencies to its recruits.

(*Meade v. Cedarapids, Inc.*, 164 F.3d 1218 (9th Cir. 1999) (applying Oregon law).)

The Case of the Disappearing Project

A former employee alleged that when she was recruited by the company to manage a project, she was told the company was financially secure and that the project she was hired to manage had a bright future. In fact, the company had serious financial problems, and the project was in jeopardy and was soon abandoned.

Result: recovery allowed.

(*Berger v. Security Pacific Inf. Systems, Inc.* 795 P.2d 1380 (Colo. App. 1990).)

The Case of the Bogus Promise of Permanent Employment

An employer led the pilots it had inherited to believe that its plan was that if they continued to work for the employer and remained with the company through the transition period, they would be permanently retained. As a result, the employee agreed to work for the company as a pilot and completed the transition period only to find that he and some of the others who lasted through the transition period were not retained. He alleged it had never been the plan to retain them at all.

Result: recovery allowed.

(*United Parcel Service v. Rickert* 996 S.W.2d 464 (Ky. 1999).)

The representation need not be made to the employee directly. It may be made to an agent of the employee or, as in the Meade case, a third party (the spouses) with the intent that it be communicated to and acted upon by the plaintiff.

Employees have used misrepresentation as a theory of recovery in other similar cases. Some examples include:

- concerning an employee's working conditions;[42]
- concerning the living conditions associated with an out-of-state work assignment;[43]
- concerning the employee who was tricked into signing a form of resignation, by a representation that if the employee did not sign he would be terminated anyway;[44]
- concerning an employer's representation as to how long the employee's employment would last;[45]
- concerning the employer's statements about the company's financial health;[46]
- concerning alleged recklessness in a promise by an employer not to retaliate, made to induce an employee to give information about an executive's illegal activity;[47]
- concerning the employer's failure to inform the employee both of its difficulties in developing the system he was hired to perform and its then existing intention to terminate him if the adversities it foresaw came to pass;[48] and,

- concerning the employer's alleged fraud in failing to disclose that at the time of the employee's hiring, a corporate reorganization was being negotiated when the reorganization might eliminate the employee's territory.[49]

Misrepresentation has taken an important foothold in employment law. It has only begun to develop as a powerful tool to encourage honest communication in workplace settings.

INTENTIONAL INTERFERENCE WITH ECONOMIC RELATIONS

In the commercial context, if a competitor of yours uses unfair competition to injure your relationship with a customer, you can sue your competitor for third-party *interference with economic relations*. In their quest to find additional remedies for employees, lawyers tried to apply the same principle to the workplace. The idea being, if a manager lies about the employee's performance, why shouldn't the employee be able to sue the manager for doing that? Moreover, since the manager was performing his or her duties as manager at the time, (acting within the scope of employment) why shouldn't the employee be able to sue the company that the manager was serving as well?

This effort has been met with mixed results. In some states like Pennsylvania,[50] both the supervisor and the employer may be sued for such interference. In many states, the tort will not lie either against the company or the manager unless the manager was acting completely on his or her own and not on behalf of the company (*i.e.* outside the scope of his or her employment for the company). This could happen, for example, if the manager has a personal grudge against you or someone with whom you are associated.

There are some cases in which it makes sense to consider holding the individual liable. For example, if a nonprofit corporation has no means to pay a judgment, but its CEO who terminated you egregiously is personally able to compensate you.

In most states, to state a claim for intentional interference with economic relations, the employee must prove:

- the existence of a business relationship;
- intentional interference with that relationship;
- involvement by a third party;
- involvement accomplished through improper means or for an improper purpose; and,
- that damages were caused.

As stated, it is not enough that the employee prove the CEO/supervisor acted solely for his or her own purposes. Those acts also must be proven to be improper under the law for the action to lie. In most states, there are two ways that those actions could be considered legally improper—if the CEO/supervisor is acting by *improper means* or for *improper purposes*. These have included the following situations.

- A supervisor induced an employee's termination by saying she was "dissatisfied with her employer and the department," when that statement was knowingly false.[51]
- A CEO induced the employer to breach its obligations to the employee under a severance agreement.[52]
- A president terminated the employee comptroller in order to force out a major shareholder.[53]
- An employee was terminated soon after she refused the request of a supervisor to submit some, but not all, files to state authorities, and after her refusal the supervisor threatened to quit if she was not fired.[54]
- An employee was fired by bank officers who induced her termination by making negative statements about her that she alleged were false, made knowingly false, and made intentionally and maliciously in an effort to justify the termination of her employment.[55]
- A former employer complained that an employee's hiring was in violation of a noncompete agreement it knew was invalid, causing his termination.[56]

The following case illustrates the application of the tort.

The Case of the Retaliating Anesthesiologist

A nurse anaesthesiologist was terminated after she testified in a malpractice trial against physicians who practiced at the hospital. She sued, alleging that the physicians against whom she testified procured her termination in retaliation for giving that testimony.

Result: recovery allowed.

(*Sides v. Duke Hospital*, 328 S.E.2d 818 (N.C. App. 1985).)

INVASION OF PRIVACY

Under the common law of most states, with the notable exceptions of New York, Minnesota, Louisiana, and Virginia, each person is entitled to protection from unreasonable invasions of privacy. Generally, an invasion of privacy can occur in one of four different ways:

1. *appropriation* or use of another's name or likeness without their permission;
2. *unreasonable intrusion* upon the private affairs or seclusion of another;
3. *public disclosure* of private facts; or,
4. placing another in a *false light* in the public eye.[57]

In the employment context, an employee's privacy is most often violated by intrusion into the employee's private affairs or concerns, but cases involving all four species of the tort can be found.

Invasion by Intrusion

In the great majority of states, an employer who unreasonably intrudes into your private affairs or concerns after you are employed will be liable to you for invasion of privacy. In each case of alleged unlawful intrusion, a balancing test is applied in which the employee's interest in privacy is weighed against the employer's need to know. To succeed in a claim of invasion of privacy by intrusion, an employee must typically show an *intentional intrusion* (physical or otherwise) upon the employee's private affairs or concerns, that would be offensive to a reasonable person.

There are numerous examples in which the tort has been applied.

- An employer tested employees for pregnancy, syphilis, and sickle cell anemia without their consent.[58]
- An employer searched an employee's locker and purse without her permission—where the lock was her property.[59]
- The employer allegedly engaged in secret videotaping of employee restrooms through two-way mirrors.[60]
- An employee's personal mail at work was opened and read without her authority.[61]
- A flight attendant's personal medical file containing gynecological information was disclosed to her male flight supervisor, who had no compelling need to know.[62]
- The employer allegedly accessed an employee's home telephone records while investigating the employee's activities during disability leave.[63]
- An employer sexually harassed an employee. The harassment included inappropriate touching, requests for sexual intercourse, and highly offensive intrusive questions about her sexual practices.[64]
- An employer required an employee to take a polygraph exam under threat of losing his job.[65]
- An employer discussed an employee's confidential medical information with an independent physician it had retained to examine the employee, when permission was required under its own policy to release that information.[66]

The following case illustrates the application of the tort.

The Case of the Lascivious Supervisor

Female employees alleged that their supervisor would invite some of them to swim nude with him in his pool; told one of them his hands were cold and asked if he could put them in her pockets; said he wished they would come to work braless; told one of them if she had not stayed up all night

having sex, she could do her work properly; and, attempted to follow one into the bathroom.
Result: claim could proceed to trial.
(*Busby v. Truswal Systems Corp.*, 551 So.2d 322 (Ala. 1989).)

Public Disclosure of Private Facts

With respect to the tort of invasion of privacy known as *public disclosure of private facts*, the two problematic requirements are: the facts be private and they be publicly disclosed. The degree of publicity that is required has given the courts the greatest trouble. For example, disclosure in a private setting to just a few coworkers is ordinarily not enough. The following cases illustrate this type of tort.

The Case of the Employer Who Told too Much
An employee consulted with the employer's resident nurse concerning a mastectomy she was to undergo. She learned that the employer released that information to her fellow employees.
Result: claim could proceed.
(*Miller v. Motorola, Inc.*, 560 N.E.2d 900 (Ill. App. 1990).)

The Case of the Zealous Personnel Director
An employer, in an effort to verify a former employee's military status while the employee was appealing the termination, wrote to the Army reserve. The employer made uncomplimentary statements about the employee in a letter, including that the employee was disloyal, had used his reserve status in an abusive and manipulative manner, and was dismissed because of abandonment of duties and dereliction of supervising responsibilities.
Result: case could proceed to trial.
(*Beaumont v. Brown*, 257 N.W.2d 522 (Mich. 1977).)

DEFAMATION

For most people who work, their marketability is their most important asset. Nothing bears on a person's marketability more than their reputation. The law has long recognized that a person has a legal interest in his or her good name. The law of defamation provides a remedy for persons whose reputation has been damaged by injurious communications.

Not every unkind word is actionable. Only *defamatory communications* give rise to liability. Traditionally, communication is defamatory if it tends to subject the person to hatred, contempt, ridicule, or tends to diminish the esteem, respect, goodwill, or confidence in which the person is held by a substantial minority of the community.

A defamatory communication can be *libel* or *slander*. In common law, libel was based on written communications and slander was based on oral communications. Today, defamatory television and radio broadcasts are considered to be libel.

The law of defamation is the same in employment cases as to libel and slander except on the issue of damages. Common law proof of *special damages* is required in slander cases, except in certain special categories called *slander per se*, that commonly include statements that impute:

- the commission of a crime;
- unfitness to perform duties of employment;
- a loathsome disease; or,
- unchastity.

Examples of defamatory statements are illustrated in the following cases:

- statement that the employer had strong evidence the employee was involved in a car theft;[67]
- statement by a pastor about a church secretary that charged her with misappropriation of funds at a church meeting;[68]
- statement by a former employer that an employee was discharged and that he had questionable loyalty and ethics;[69]

- statement about a microcomputer expert that he had erased computer files;[70] and,
- statement that the employee was terminated *for cause.*[71]

In order to be actionable, the defamatory communication must be published or communicated to a third person. That means to someone other than you. It is not actionable if you are the only one who hears it. On the other hand, in most states, a communication between employees within the same company is sufficient to satisfy the third-party communication requirement. A few states require the publication to be to a person outside the corporation.

Speaking the Truth

You cannot bring an action for defamation against someone who has merely told the truth about you. The American tradition favors freedom of speech and permits the circulation of damaging communications about a person unless the statements are false. Further, a statement of opinion is neither true nor false. Statements of pure opinions are ordinarily not actionable unless a person could reasonably conclude they were based on undisclosed facts. Generally, a statement of fact will be considered true if the gist or sting of the statement is true, even though the statement contains slight inaccuracies. If a statement is true, the defendant is said to be absolutely privileged to make it. That is, there are no circumstances in which the privilege to speak the truth can be lost. It is ordinarily the defendant's burden to prove the truth of a defamatory statement.

Privileged Communications

Beyond truth protecting statements, other privileges exist in the law to permit defamatory communications. Statements made during *legislative* or *judicial proceedings*, for example, are absolutely protected. Comments made during these proceedings will not subject the speaker to prosecution.

Qualified privileges. Most other privileges to speak are not absolute, but are termed *qualified*. They are said to be qualified or *conditional privileges* that can be lost under some circumstances. For example, your supervisor may be allowed to tell others in the company what he or she thinks about your performance. When your supervisor does so, he or she is said to be qualifiedly privileged to speak. In so doing, supervisors can say what they think about your work, even if they are wrong, so long as they have a reasonable belief that what they are saying is true. However, if they do not have reasonable grounds to believe the statement is true, the privilege is said to have been abused and thus lost. Generally, a jury is given the power to ultimately decide that question.

A qualified privilege can be abused or lost in any of four different ways:

1. if the speaker does not believe that the statement is true or lacks reasonable grounds to believe it is true;
2. if the statement is made for a purpose other than that for which the privilege is given, as where someone takes the opportunity to speak ill of you when they do not have to, and are doing it because of a secret personal vendetta;
3. if the statement is made to a person not reasonably believed to be necessary to accomplish the purpose, as where the person broadcasts the defamatory matter to a *broader audience* than necessary to hurt you; or,
4. if the statement includes defamatory matter not reasonably believed to be necessary to accomplish the purpose, as where the supervisor goes out of the way to volunteer derogatory information that does not relate to the topic of discussion at hand.

Abuse of the qualified privilege is illustrated in the following case.

The Case of the Public Posting

An employee was terminated. The employer then posted a memorandum on the bulletin board and subsequently distributed the memorandum throughout the department that stated that the employee was terminated for "alcoholism, inefficiency, and unreliability."

Result: a jury could determine whether the employer had over-publicized the statement and thereby abused the privilege. (*Welch v. Chicago Tribune Company*, 340 N.E.2d 539 (Ill. App. 1976).)

Cases in which the qualified privilege was lost include ones in which:

- the employer was reckless in failing to verify the information;[72]
- the statements were made in anger to prevent future employment;[73]
- the statements were published without reasonable belief in order to effectuate the employer's discharge;[74]
- the employee was accused of theft to effectuate his termination when the true reason related to the cost of his industrial injuries;[75]
- the defamatory letter was disseminated to persons who were not authorized to read it;[76] and,
- the defamatory statement was made with *actual malice*.[77]

Defamation cases present several problems. First, unless the defamation is captured in writing somewhere, the precise defamatory statement may be difficult to establish. Words are important. Witnesses to slander may not be able to remember or repeat them with certitude. Second, it may be difficult to trace a defamatory communication back to the employer as its source, as opposed to something that had been generated in the rumor mill. Third, outside parties, such as prospective employers, may be reluctant to report to you what they have heard about you from a former employer that is derogatory.

The inherent problem with defamation cases, however, is that the filing of the action itself broadcasts the defamatory charge, and some people who read it believe in the old adage that where there is smoke there is fire. Careful consideration should be given to the real need to press such a claim before it is instituted.

NEGLIGENCE

Some plaintiff's employment lawyers have had success in a few states pursuing liability against an employer on a *negligence* theory by claiming that the company failed to exercise *reasonable care* in monitoring a safe workplace.[78] Most of the cases have involved employer liability for allowing race or sex discrimination.[79] Typically, liability is based on the employer's negligence in hiring or retaining known harassers.

In one Ohio case, for example, the court said the claimed injury was foreseeable based on evidence that the harasser had a past history of and reputation for sexual harassment. In a case out of Georgia, a court allowed a claim for negligent retention of a sexual harasser to proceed because the employer knew or should have known the harasser had a propensity for sexual harassment.[80]

Five states allow a *negligent inflection of emotional distress* claim only if the victim has experienced a *physical impact*. Fourteen others require the victim to have been within the *zone of danger*.[81] (The zone of danger is the area and circumstances surrounding the physical event. How close a person has to be to the event, whether physically or emotionally, is generally determined on a case-by-case basis.)

Some states refuse to recognize negligence claims in employment cases because of the existence of workers' compensation preemption statutes. In other jurisdictions in which such claims are allowed, the courts reason that the claim is outside the scope of the workers' compensation statutes. Thus, a negligence theory may be available in an instance of violence in the workplace that an employer could have avoided through the exercise of reasonable diligence. The violence will typically not arise out of the employee's work as required by workers' compensation statutes.

Very few cases have allowed the employee to pursue a claim for negligence against a third-party provider of services to the employer, such as a doctor or a testing laboratory who have examined or taken a sample from the employee and misreported results.[82]

• • • • •

As you can see, lawyers for employees have been fairly successful in bringing legal tools to bear against employers that no one dared apply just a quarter century ago. The cloak of protection that employers once had in their conduct towards their employees is largely gone. Even so, it is not enough just to afford employees with the same protection others have in cases of egregious employer behavior. Employees are in a special and vulnerable position *vis-à-vis* employers. They need to be able to count on what employers promise about their jobs. Therefore, at the same time these tort remedies were being developed, lawyers pursued the development of new theories giving contract rights to employees on a separate track.

–5– EMPLOYMENT CONTRACTS

Not long ago when referring to private sector, nonunion employment, you would not find the words *employment contracts* in the same sentence. An employment contract and employment at will were thought to be mutually exclusive. But, while lawyers were working to expand employee rights in other areas, they were prevailing upon courts to apply the law of contracts to the workplace. When that effort first began, it was so novel that courts would sometimes reject it on the grounds that the employee had no written employment agreement.

In the last quarter century, however, courts have recognized that employment, even at-will employment, is essentially contractual in nature. The worker has something to sell, his or her labor, and the employer wishes to buy that labor on stated terms. Suppose an employer hires a worker to perform labor at $10 per hour and the worker commences performance. A legal obligation, or contract, arises that requires the employer to fulfill that promise. The employment relationship is still at will because its duration is indefinite. Even so, the worker can enforce that aspect of the relationship concerning the agreed upon price for the labor. Once it is recognized that a promise as to the price for labor may be enforced as a matter of contract, then the possibilities for the formation of other enforceable agreements, even in at-will employment, are boundless.

CONTRACT-MAKING OPPORTUNITIES

Even for at-will employees, opportunities abound for making legally enforceable obligations. Some stages in the employment relationship are more likely than others to provide contract-making opportunities.

The Recruitment Phase

Recruitment can be a troublesome period for the employer. Often, an employer will make some representations to a potential employee to induce him or her to become employed, particularly when necessary to induce an employee to leave a current employer. These representations may relate to compensation, job title, duties, future advancement, working conditions, job security, or any other items that typically concern employees. They may come in oral and/or written form during the initial contact or in follow-up interviews. They may be prepared statements or they may be responsive to the questions the employee puts to the company representative.

The Orientation Phase

During the first few days of an employee's tenure, the employer typically provides information to introduce the employee to the company and in the ways the employer does business. Orientation checklists sometimes compel personnel staff to present the new employee with loads of company informational materials. These materials are given to the new employee, in part, because management wants to put the employee at ease and give him or her a sense of security.

As a result, various materials are disseminated, such as employee handbooks, procedure manuals, and employee benefit materials. These materials contain language of promises. That language may relate to such things as promises of fairness, a particular disciplinary system, or a layoff system. Promises are also verbally made by the new supervisor or the human resources representative confirming that what the employee heard during the recruitment process is true. New promises are made to the employee about the help, support, and training the employee will receive. Also, promises may be made concerning its nondiscrimination policy, and its *open-door policy*.

The Honeymoon Phase

The first few months of employment is usually characterized by praise for the employee by those who participated in his or her selection because they like to confirm their own good judgment in having chosen the employee. During this period, the praise may be accompanied by meetings and power lunches at which the employee hears the company's game plan that will involve the employee as a key player. Such statements will only lead to probing by the employee for more specific details, which, when provided, may very well be specific enough to enforce.

The Development Phase

During the course of the development of the employment relationship, the parties reach understandings to address needs and resolve problems. Previous promises relating to training, equipment, tools, labor, performance reviews, and the like may have been violated. New assurances may be sought and given. For example, "I can't meet these quotas without some help." "Ok, we'll get you some." Or, "Why can't I go to Denver for that training? Max went." "Ok, we'll send you next time." Successful performance may breed promises of better compensation or promotion. Ongoing performance evaluations and goal statements will establish the standards by which future performance will be judged.

The Termination Phase

Even when the employment relationship is doomed, the employer makes promises regarding how it will deal with the employee. Letters of warning may specify the criteria by which performance during a probationary period will be judged. It may also detail the procedures that will be followed if the employee's performance is not improved.

Many employers have what is known as a *progressive discipline* system, whereby they will give ascending degrees of discipline. In most cases, when the employer tells the employee that a system will be followed—if broken—can serve as the basis for a lawsuit.

ENFORCING CONTRACTS

Over the last twenty-five years, the courts in most states have accepted that promises made by at-will employers to their employees are as entitled to legal enforcement as any other. Further, they have recognized that agreements can arise *expressly* or by *implication*. If you and your employer agree, for example, that the terms of a progressive discipline policy contained in the employee handbook will govern your employment, that is an express agreement.

On the other hand, if nothing is expressly stated but the handbook containing such provisions is given to you to read and follow, the courts in most states have recognized that under those circumstances an enforceable contract may be implied. The understanding is that your employer will be bound by the handbook as well.[83]

Surprised by the number of decisions in which courts enforced the statements in handbooks, lawyers for employers then began to couch handbook language in softer, less definite language of intention (*i.e.*, Ordinarily we will follow this procedure). What once were touted as due process procedures the employee could count on as a matter of procedural fairness (akin to what a unionized or civil service workforce would enjoy), became watered down guidelines in which management retained discretion whether or not to follow.

Another tactic was for the employer's attorney to insert what became known as *disclaimers* at the beginning of the handbook that said that the handbook was not an employment contract, that nothing in the handbook was intended as a promise, and that the relationship was at will. In addition, employees were required to sign acknowledgments that they read and understood the handbook provisions. The practice became so widely followed that today a defense lawyer who does not insert such a disclaimer in the handbook is probably committing malpractice.

Despite these efforts, *contract liability* has continued to be generated. During the recruitment phase, there is no way to inoculate the employer from liability because so much of the contact with the prospective employee is verbal. Representations relating to compensation, title, or job security during the recruitment phase have continued to serve as a hotbed for litigation. During employee orientation, questions prompted by handbook provisions generate responses that are outside the shroud of a protective disclaimer. Internal memoranda distributed to employees after employment commences frequently do not contain a disclaimer. The validity and adequacy of the disclaimer itself may be suspect.

Similarly, the bulk of statements made during the honeymoon and development phases of the relationship will be verbal or in writing without a disclaimer. In such cases, most courts will hold that the at-will employment relationship has been modified by a subsequent written or verbal understanding. Finally, as illustrated below, some implied contract cases have been decided, based not upon any single statement that would be susceptible to a disclaimer, but upon the parties' entire course of dealings.

EMPLOYEE HANDBOOKS

Most states accept the general proposition that whether a *personnel manual* or *employee handbook* gives rise to implied contractual obligations is a factual question to be discerned from the totality of the parties' statements and actions.[84]

In dealing with the effect of a disclaimer on the enforceability of the handbook, sometimes the courts will refuse to enforce disclaimers in the face of other, more specific language in the handbook that appears to contradict the disclaimer. One federal circuit court held that when the employee was terminated contrary to the personnel manual's promise that all terminations needed to be approved by senior management, a question of fact existed as to whether the company breached an agreement with the employee notwithstanding the existence of a disclaimer. The requirement in the handbook to obtain senior management approved was mandatory and specific.[85]

Even where an employee manual stated it was a guide only, some courts have found such language to favor an implied contract, reasoning that it suggests that a policy be followed.[86]

Other courts have held that if the employee has been required to sign a statement agreeing to be bound by the handbook, that is a factor in favor of finding the handbook to be binding on the employer as well.[87]

Still, other courts enforce handbooks as implied contracts and decide the validity of a disclaimer and whether the language of the disclaimer is sufficiently conspicuous or clear.[88]

Enforceable promises contained in employee handbooks can take many forms, such as:

- promises of fair treatment;
- promises of warnings before termination;
- promises of progressive discipline;[89] and,
- a promise it has an open door policy.

As for the last category, employers often have an *open-door policy*, meaning, if an employee has a complaint or concern, they are encouraged to report it. Sometimes there is an express promise that if the policy is exercised, no retaliation will follow. Even where no express promise is given, such a promise is implied. If the policy is exercised, all too often the employer begins to view the employee as a troublemaker. Sometimes confidentiality is breached and the manager about whom the report is made learns of it and retaliates, setting up litigation over the breach of promise not to retaliate.

Another source of contract litigation has been the employer's publication of its own nondiscrimination policies. In one case, a federal court applying Colorado law affirmed a $500,000 jury verdict against an employer for breach of contract for violating its EEO policy not to discriminate on the basis of sex.[90]

PAST PRACTICE

Many courts will examine all of the facts and circumstances to determine if the at-will relationship has been modified by the past practices of the parties. In those cases, as stated by the Ohio Supreme Court, the courts will look to such things as the employee handbook, company policy, and oral representations.[91]

For example, in one case in which a judge upheld a jury verdict for an employee who had contended that the employer had breached an implied contract, there was evidence that the employee was not treated in accordance with the company's routine policy of rating each employee before deciding on layoffs. The court held that *routine practice* could serve as the foundation for an implied contract claim, despite the existence of a disclaimer in the employee handbook.[92]

DURATION OF EMPLOYMENT

Some employees have successfully asserted that, because of the dealings between the parties, the at-will aspect of the relationship is modified so that employment can only be terminated at or after a particular time. In one Colorado case, it was held that in view of the specific promises made during the recruitment phase in response to specific questions about job security, there was a promise to keep the employee for a reasonable time. The company had promised it would provide sufficient backing to the office in question, in order to give it time to ensure its survival. Instead, the office was closed two months after the employee was hired. The court held the promise gave rise to an obligation to retain the employee for a reasonable time and that the employee's request for one year's pay was not unreasonable.[93]

The principle is illustrated in the following case.

The Case of the Tenacious Trainer

Before Mike Tyson turned professional, his manager, Mr. Gus D'Amato, promised Mr. Kevin Rooney that if Mr. Rooney agreed to train the young Mr. Tyson free of charge until he turned professional, he would be able to train him thereafter "for as long as [Mr. Tyson] fought professionally." Mr. D'Amato died and Mr. Tyson allegedly authorized his new manager to repeat the commitment to Mr. Rooney.

Mr. Rooney continued to work as Mr. Tyson's trainer for three years, until he and Mr. Tyson had a falling out and he was terminated. Contending that Mr. Tyson breached the agreement, Mr. Rooney sued.

Result: decision for Mr. Rooney. The New York Court of Appeals held that the verbal promise was a contract for a *definite duration* and was binding.
(*Rooney v. Tyson*, 697 N.E.2d 571 (N.Y. 1998).)

In other cases the courts have held that the premise for which the employee was first hired may limit the ability of the employer to terminate at will. Thus, assurances of employment as long as we have production to run was held by a court in Oregon to be a promise of a job as long as the work he was able to do was needed. Further, as the employee in that case was 55 years old at the time, the court held that was evidence that supported a jury's verdict that the contract was for permanent employment.[94]

Other courts have enforced assurance of security as a promise of permanent employment. In Massachusetts, in 1993, a contract for permanent employment was enforced, based upon a promise that if the plaintiff accepted employment, he would spend the rest of his working career with that employer.[95]

Still, other courts have found an employer was precluded by its promise from terminating an employee because of the happening of some event. In Utah, a court held that where a company president told the employee to "take all the time he needed" to recover from his illness, the company breached its *implied in fact contract* when it terminated him for that absenteeism.[96] A court in New Mexico reached the same decision in a case where a female employee was told to take all the time she needed to take care of her medical condition.[97]

For Cause Terminations

Some cases have held that because of the existence of special circumstances, an employee is not terminable at will, but only *for cause*. In one New York case, the employee was told the firm's policy was not to terminate without *just cause* and the court enforced that promise.[98] In another case, the Kansas Supreme Court held that it could consider *tenure*, or longevity with the employer, as one factor in determining whether a mutual intent existed to employ the plaintiff as long as he did his job satisfactorily.[99]

Similarly, the California Supreme Court held that evidence of personnel policies or practices, longevity of service, and actions and communications by the employer that reflected assurances of continued employment were all factors that supported an implied contract by which the employer could only terminate the employee for *good cause.*[100] In that case, there was evidence the plaintiff was repeatedly told he would be retained as long as his performance remained adequate. Since that case, however, the California Supreme Court has retreated somewhat from that position. They have held that the mere passage of time alone cannot form an implied in fact contract. Therefore, the employment is no longer at will, because it said longevity, raises, and promotions are their own rewards for the employee's continuing valued service.[101]

The principle that at-will employment is susceptible to modification is illustrated in a case out of New Mexico that follows.

The Case of the Set-for-Life Employee

An employee was talked out of accepting a job offer with a competitor by being told about the competitor. "He's the type of person who will walk into your office without warning and fire you on the spot. You never have to worry about that happening here." In addition, he was told, "Your career is secure with me…When I sell the magazine you are going to be set for life."

Result: recovery for employee. The court held those promises created an implied contract that the employee could only be discharged for cause.

(*Ettenson v. Burke*, 17 P.3d 440 (N.M. App. 2000).)

Similarly, in a case in Indiana, an employee who was being recruited from a long career with the state police told the prospective employer he would not leave that permanent employment unless he had assurances of similar job security. The prospective employer told him he would have the same security. He left his job with the state police and sued after he was subsequently terminated.

The court held the promise of a permanent job with the new employer meant that he could only be discharged for good cause.[102]

Likewise, in a Connecticut case, the employer told the employee he would *take care of him* if the employee did a good job, and hoped he would stay forever. In addition, at the time the employee was first employed, the employee handbook specified employment could only be terminated for cause. However, a handbook without that promise was later distributed prior to the termination. The court held the employee could be terminated only for cause, notwithstanding the issuance of the second handbook.[103]

Arguments that an employment relationship is not at will can be enhanced if facts like the following exist.

- The employee handbook refers to developing a career with the company.
- In the initial interview, the participants had discussed this as a career opportunity and had outlined a career path up the corporate ladder.
- The employer designs its employee benefit plans so that the benefits are enhanced with longevity to induce employees to stay with the employer.
- The employer requires an employee to complete a *probationary period* before the employee becomes a regular employee and during probation, the employee is not entitled to warnings before termination.
- The employer, as a past practice, has not terminated employees without good cause.

Still, even if all of these factors apply, it will be difficult to avoid the strong bias in favor of employment at will. Unless special factors exist, the truth is that you may not be any more secure in your job in your twentieth year of service than you were in your first.

CONTRACTS IMPLIED BY LAW

Sometimes the courts will supply the terms of an employment relationship. For example, in most states the law will not allow an employer to terminate a worker just before receiving a commission in order to deprive the worker of the commission that otherwise would have been received.[104]

THE COVENANT OF GOOD FAITH

Whether express or implied, there is an implied duty of good faith in the performance of every contract.[105] In some states, depriving an employee of a benefit that would otherwise vest has been treated as a breach of the implied covenant of good faith and fair dealing.[106] In other states, where an employment at-will contract has been modified by the dissemination of a policy, it has been held that a employer may be liable for breach of the implied covenant of good faith if it attempts to manipulate the policy to its own advantage. That is illustrated in the following case.

> ***The Case of the Misleading Statistics***
>
> An employer had an attendance policy that required at least 95% attendance over a given period. When the employer calculated the employee's absentee rate over a shorter period than that, the attendance rate fell below the 95% target.
>
> *Result:* Employee prevailed. The employee's allegation that a shorter period had been used to result in the lower rate stated a claim for breach of the implied contract of good faith.
>
> (*Elliott v. Tektronix*, 796 P.2d 361 (Or. 1990).)

THE PROBLEM WITH CONTRACT CLAIMS

There is a big problem with contract claims. In almost all states, in almost every situation, the only recoverable damages for breach of contract is *economic loss*. That means no matter how egregious, intentional, or outrageous the breach—no emotional distress or punitive damages are recoverable. An employment case is unlike a personal injury case in which permanent physical injuries have been sustained. In contrast, a worker who has been terminated will eventually find replacement work in most cases. If the only recoverable damage is for the economic loss that occurs during the interim period, few cases will be feasible to prosecute. The amount of the loss may be so small that an attorney cannot accept the case on a contingent-fee basis. Even if work is obtained at a lesser rate, any interim earnings will offset the loss the terminated employee can recover against the employer.

In most cases then, it is imprudent to embark on litigation that has resulted in a few months' lost income where the only theory of relief is based on breach of contract. The limited utility of contract claims in most cases sparked the development of the tort law remedies discussed in Chapters 3 and 4, so that employees could recover emotional distress and punitive damages. In some cases, however, particularly those in which an older worker has suffered a career ending termination, contract claims can be quite powerful.

NEGOTIATED, WRITTEN CONTRACTS

Some employees are able to negotiate a written employment contract with the employer. This rarely happens, and when it does, often the employer presents the employee with a standard form that the employee has no leverage to change. If, however, you are one of the few to be able to obtain and negotiate an employment contract, you will want to pay attention to the points discussed below.

TERMINATION PROVISIONS

The single most important thing the executive wants to pin down, besides compensation, is how long the contract will last. They want a three- or five-year minimum deal. However, all too often, a five-year employment contract, on careful review, is merely illusory because the employment is permitted to be terminated in different ways and for all sorts of reasons before the expiration of that period. The contract often provides a laundry list of situations to justify termination before the extended period expires, including:

- good cause;
- misconduct; or,
- thirty days prior written notice.

So, if employment for a particular minimum period is important to you, be sure to communicate that to your attorney.

An employment contract that contains termination provisions may provide a false sense of security. Termination provisions often begin by giving the employee just cause protections, but end up by defining just cause to include a laundry list of objective and subjective criteria ending with, "for any other breach of this agreement."

Just Cause

If your agreement has *just cause* protection, your lawyer will make sure that term is defined in the agreement, because there is no fixed meaning of the term *just cause* in the law. From your perspective, you want to objectify that term. For example, rather than accept the rather vague provision that allows termination for "dishonesty," it would be better to use "conviction of a felony involving theft of company property of substantial value for personal gain." Instead of accepting the language "inability to perform the duties of the position," it would be better to use the language "willful failure to substantially perform the duties of the position causing demonstrable injury and damage to the company."

Warnings and Notices

If the termination for just cause is performance-based (due to poor performance rather than dishonesty or some similar conduct problem) your lawyer will insist on a system of progressive discipline. Therefore, you can be terminated for poor performance only if the company has done all it should to call perceived performance problems to your attention and has also given you a fair opportunity to correct those problems before termination. The usual procedure calls for an oral warning and at least one written warning before termination.

COMPENSATION

Complete terms of compensation often are omitted or not clearly expressed in employment contracts. Base salary is only one aspect of a total compensation package. The employer may have made promises about the array and value of other benefits during the recruitment phase. These promises should be reduced to writing. Other details pertaining to compensation need to be specified.

Fringe Benefits

Any representations that the employer may have made about the type, amount, and value of stock options, profit share plans, bonus programs, and other fringe benefits should be put into the employment agreement.

If the employer did not mention fringe benefits and you did not ask, do not be surprised if you do not have the same deal as a coworker. If it is important that you receive the same benefits (or more) as others, then it makes sense to ask how the benefits that are being offered to you compare with benefits that are being offered to others at your level.

Do not forget noncash benefits such as athletic club and country club memberships, auto allowances, and tickets to athletic events or the symphony. Your employment may require high community visibility. If you believe that these items are part of what it takes for you to achieve the desired level of market penetration, it is better to negotiate that before you sign the employment agreement. Any questions should be answered up-front about what happens to those benefits at the end of employment.

Pay and Position Advances

Often times, during recruitment, the employer makes representations about when the next pay increase will take place and in what amount. These representations should be reduced to writing.

Sometimes a person is placed in a lesser position for a training or trial period before assuming the duties the person was recruited to fill. Without documentation of the overall long-range plan in the agreement, the employee can be left high and dry in a lesser position, particularly after a change of management. If future advancement is promised, your lawyer will make sure that the title, department, job duties, and pay range of the promised position are included in the employment agreement, if possible.

Accrual of Benefits

The employment agreement should specify whether vacation accrues from year to year and whether it is earned on a *pro rata* basis during the year.

Also, the agreement should specify whether sick leave accrues, and whether unused sick pay, like unused vacation pay, is to be paid on termination.

Severance Pay

In our age of downsizing, mergers, and leveraged buyouts, severance pay is very significant. Employees often assume there is some severance plan when there may not be any.

If you are recruited from an existing job, particularly to a newer company, your attorney may suggest requiring the employer to promise to pay one to two years' additional severance pay if you are terminated within two years from the date of hire in the event of merger or acquisition. This protects you if you are ousted after a corporate takeover.

Vacations and Sabbaticals

If you have a certain time requirement for vacations each year (for example, you need four weeks and always the week after Christmas due to your kids' vacation schedules) it may be important for your lawyer to specify these requirements in the employment agreement.

If your employer has a paid sabbatical program, that should be specified as well.

Other Earnings

You may have other income-generating activities or sources of income that you need to protect in the agreement. Your attorney will ensure that the employment agreement specifies that you may continue these activities without running afoul of any *moonlighting* or *best efforts* clauses. Even if you do not engage in any activities like that now, you may want to do so in the future. If in doubt, it is best to allow yourself the freedom to work and consult outside the company and to retain the earnings from those activities.

Expense Reimbursements

If expenses are reimbursable, your employment agreement should specify the types of reimbursable expenses and allowances that are available, along with the procedure for obtaining reimbursement. It is important to pin down the proper procedure for recording and presenting claims for reimbursement so that a trumped-up false expense account charge is not later asserted against you as a ruse to cause your termination.

SPECIAL CLAUSES

Every employment situation is different. Yours may call for consideration whether to add, delete, or modify one of the types of provisions that follow.

No Transfer Clauses

You may be interested in working for this employer, but only if you are never, ever transferred to its Aleutian Islands warehouse facility. For example, if you want to restrict the ability to transfer you to another geographic area or to realign your duties, be sure to instruct your lawyer to include that restriction in the agreement.

Property Rights

You may be involved in creating and developing new properties. Unless your attorney negotiates joint or exclusive ownership or licensing rights, you will not have any. The employment agreement should specify to whom that property belongs and what will become of it when either you or the company terminates the employment relationship.

Covenants Not to Compete

You may be asked to sign an employment agreement that contains a *covenant not to compete* with the employer for a period of time after employment. In most jurisdictions, such clauses are valid if reasonable. They are barred or restricted in about a dozen states. Typically, the covenant must be reasonable in its restriction as to time and geographical area. It is possible that the employer will not require you to sign such an agreement if you are in a job title that does not carry the threat of competitive injury, such as a staff accountant or human resources professional.

But if your employer insists that you sign one, discuss your situation with your lawyer. He or she will try to negotiate a deal that you could reasonably live with in the event of early termination. Perhaps the time or geographic restraints can be narrowed. Perhaps the definition of competition can be restricted or certain lines of work or specific employers excepted. Sometimes a penalty is set out in the event of a violation of the clause. Your attorney will try to ensure the penalty is not excessive.

Arbitration Clauses

Some employment contracts require all disputes to be decided by an *arbitrator* whose decision is *final and binding*. Talk to your lawyer about whether it is advisable to sign such an agreement. Sometimes it will be acceptable. Generally, though, employees want juries, not arbitrators, to decide their cases. It is not often that employees, other than senior executives, are able to negotiate the terms of their employment.

—6—
A CLOSER LOOK AT TITLE VII

As discussed in Chapter 2, the modern civil rights era in employment began with the passage of *Title VII* of the *1964 Civil Rights Act* that bars discrimination in employment based on race, color, religion, sex, and national origin.

RACE DISCRIMINATION

Discrimination against many minority groups can and does occur.[107] The critical question in the context of discrimination law is whether a person is being treated differently because of his or her race. A person is also protected by the law if he or she is being unfavorably treated because of his or her association with a racial member.[108] Title VII also bars race discrimination between members of the same racial minority.[109]

As stated in Chapter 2, however, liability can be premised on differential treatment in many ways—differential training,[110] differential failure to renew a contact,[111] and differential treatment in promotional opportunities.[112]

One concept that is still evolving relates to the definition of *race* itself. In one case, the Supreme Court held that being of Arab ancestry qualified as a racial class for purposes of the *Reconstruction Era Civil Rights Statute*. (42 U.S.C. Sec. 1981.)[113] It noted that the definition of race at the time that statute was enacted in 1870 was much broader than modern thought. Also, the legislative history of that Act contained references to numerous ethnic groups that were considered distinct races in the nineteenth century, including Chinese, Latins, Mexicans, Scandinavians, and Germans.

The Court concluded that if a distinction is based upon ancestry or ethnic characteristics, as opposed to place of origin, a racial class may be asserted. It specifically held that a *distinctive physiognomy* is not essential to qualify for protection under that statute.

Reverse Discrimination

Title VII prohibits all racial discrimination in employment, without exception, for any group of particular employees.[114] Caucasians, therefore, are as entitled to protection against disparate treatment because of race as any other racial group.[115] Thus, *reverse discrimination* is prohibited in cases where, for example, a Caucasian is punished to avoid prompting litigation by a racial minority.[116] Some courts require plaintiffs in reverse discrimination cases to establish *background circumstances* that will justify applying to a majority plaintiff, the same presumption of discrimination afforded to a minority plaintiff, such as evidence that the employer tended to discriminate against persons of that race.[117]

NATIONAL ORIGIN DISCRIMINATION

Protection is afforded under Title VII to persons who are discriminated against on the basis of national origin whether or not they are citizens of the United States.[118] Protection is afforded on bases broader than country of birth and includes cases in which the person has the *physical, cultural,* or *linguistic characteristics* of a national origin group. (29 C.F.R. Sec. 1606.) It includes persons discriminated against because they are married to or associated with a person of a national origin group. It includes cases in which a person is identified with a particular national origin group by virtue of attendance at schools, churches, temples, or mosques. (29 C.F.R. Sec. 1606.1.) In such cases, evidence of adverse treatment because an employee speaks with an accent or evidence of resentment towards foreigners who take jobs from U.S.-born workers has been held to support the claim.[119]

Reverse Discrimination

With the globalization of the world's economy, foreign corporations now employ large workforces domestically. Title VII cases are available to U.S.-born workers who claim to have been discriminated against because the foreign corporation favors or prefers to promote workers from the county of origin of the corporation.[120] However, sometimes the foreign employer has successfully invoked the protection of a *Friendship, Commerce, and Navigation Treaty* that permits discrimination on the basis of citizenship for accountants and other technical experts, executive personnel, attorneys, agents, or other specialists so long as the employer is truly a foreign company and not a wholly owned American subsidiary.[121]

GENDER DISCRIMINATION

Since the advent of the Civil Rights Act of 1964, great advances have been made to abolish sexually segregated job classifications and provide women access to all echelons of what formerly were unreachable positions in the private and public sector. Challenges still remain. Enclaves of institutional resistance still exist in many occupations, most notably the construction trades. Women still find themselves hitting the *glass ceiling* in some corporations. The average earnings differential that remains between women and men has been well publicized. People still use and abuse power in sexually harassing others. But at least, as Title VII developed, employers found the courts were making it near impossible for them to justify hiring males only into a particular job as a *bona fide occupational qualification.*[122]

Pregnancy

One type of gender discrimination is *pregnancy discrimination.* In 1978, Title VII was amended to specifically bar discrimination on the basis of pregnancy, childbirth, or related medical conditions by the *Pregnancy Discrimination Act.* According to the Act, it is illegal for an employer to discriminate against a woman because she is pregnant.[123] Since then, a claim was even held that alleged the employee was discriminated against because of her potential or intended pregnancy.[124]

Because of those amendments, employers are now prohibited from maintaining a mandatory maternity leave policy unrelated to the employee's ability to do the work.[125] Women cannot be barred from certain jobs based on a fetal protection policy.[126] Equality in fringe benefits for pregnancy and pregnancy-related medical conditions is required.[127]

As with *race discrimination* cases, it is now recognized that Title VII protects all persons, female or male, who are treated adversely because of their gender.[128] Male employees enjoy the same comprehensiveness of coverage as female employees.

SEXUAL ORIENTATION DISCRIMINATION

In addition to whatever legal protection has been given to gays and lesbians at the state and local level, some protection is afforded directly or indirectly by the federal government, though Congress has not thus far amended Title VII to add sexual orientation as a protected class.

Executive Order 13087, which is a presidential order that is binding on federal employees, provides a uniform policy that prohibits discrimination based on sexual orientation in civilian, nonmilitary employment in the federal government.

Civil Service Reform Act of 1978 (CSRA)

The *Civil Service Reform Act of 1978* (CSRA) prohibits federal employees from discriminating against applicants and employees on the basis of race, color, sex, religion, national origin, age, disability, marital status, or political affiliation, and from discriminating against an applicant or employee on the basis of conduct that does not adversely affect the performance of the applicant or employee. That Act has been construed by the Office of Personnel Management (OPM) to bar discrimination based on sexual orientation. Therefore, *federal civilian employees* who believe they have been discriminated against on the basis of sexual orientation may file an EEO complaint within their agencies. Grievance procedures for such complaints may also be available under their collective bargaining agreement.

If you have a question about sexual orientation discrimination in the federal civilian labor force, you should contact the Office of Special Counsel at 202-653-7188 or the Merit System Protection Board at 202-653-6772. Those are the agencies that are assigned to enforce the provisions of the CSRA.

Same-Sex Sexual Harassment

Prior to 1998, the scope of Title VII was less certain in protecting against *same-sex sexual harassment*. The Seventh Circuit had indicated that same-sex sexual harassment was always actionable, so long as it was sexual in nature.[129] The Fourth Circuit had held a claim that male on male harassment would lie, so long as the harasser was homosexual.[130] The Fifth Circuit had precluded any action where both the victim and the harasser were male.[131]

Then in 1998, in *Oncale v. Sundowner Offshore Services, Inc.*, 523 U.S. 75 (1998,) the Supreme Court unanimously decided that Title VII's prohibition of discrimination *because of ... sex* applied to a case of same-sex sexual harassment of a male. In this case, the plaintiff alleged that while employed as a roustabout on an oil-rig as a member of an eight-person crew, he was subjected to sex-related humiliating actions against him by three of the crew members, two of whom physically assaulted him and threatened him with rape. He further alleged that his complaints to supervisory personnel produced no remedial action. Finally, he had to quit out of fear he would be raped. The Court made it clear that Title VII prohibits sex-specific conduct regardless whether the gender of the harasser and the victim is the same.

It discussed that conduct could be undertaken because of sex and thus be proscribed by Title VII not only where the individual sexually desires the victim, but also where the harasser displays a hostility toward the presence of a worker of a particular sex in the workplace.

Since *Oncale*, courts in several of the circuit courts of appeal have discussed their willingness to rule that if an employer discriminates against a man because he did not meet stereotyped expectations of masculinity, it will constitute a violation of Title VII.[132]

The Ninth Circuit, in one case, for example, held that verbal abuse, including references to a gay male as "she," taunting, saying that he walked and carried his tray "like a woman," and derisive comments about his not having sex with a woman, were held to be conduct because of sex, as it reflected a belief that he was not acting in conformance with a male stereotype.[133]

More recently, the Ninth Circuit held that an openly gay plaintiff who pleaded that he was sexually harassed because of his sexual orientation nonetheless stated a Title VII claim, because sexual orientation neither provides nor precludes a claim for sexual harassment. Rather, it said a claim is made out under Title VII upon evidence that the harasser engaged in severe or pervasive unwelcome physical conduct of a sexual nature, regardless of one's sexual orientation.[134]

RELIGIOUS DISCRIMINATION

Under Title VII of the 1964 Civil Rights Act, it is unlawful for an employer to discriminate on the basis of an employee's or applicant's religion or to fail to reasonably accommodate an employee's religious practices.

Title VII defines the term *religion* to include all aspects of religious observance and practice, as well as belief. It bars such discrimination unless an employer demonstrates that it is unable to reasonably accommodate an employee's or prospective employee's religious observance or practice without undue hardship on the conduct of the employer's business. (42 U.S.C. Sec. 2000e-(j).)

Thus, religious discrimination cases fall into two distinct types—discriminatory treatment because of the religious beliefs of the victim or harasser and failure to accommodate.

Disparate Treatment

In cases of religious discrimination based upon *disparate treatment*, courts have adopted the conventional discrimination framework to require the following proof:

- plaintiff is a member of a protected class because of his or her religious affiliation or beliefs;
- plaintiff informed the employer of the religious beliefs;
- plaintiff was qualified for the position;
- plaintiff suffered an adverse employment action; and,
- similarly-situated employees outside of the plaintiff's protected class were treated differently or there is other evidence giving rise to an inference of discrimination.[135]

As with other Title VII cases, after the plaintiff establishes a *prima facie* case, the burden then shifts to the employer to articulate some legitimate nondiscriminatory reason for its action. If the employer satisfies this standard, then the burden shifts back to the employee to show that the stated reason was a pretext for discrimination.

Discrimination on the basis of religion that creates a hostile or abusive work environment is also a violation of Title VII.[136] By analogy to other Title VII cases, to be actionable, the harassment must be sufficiently severe or pervasive to alter the conditions of the victim's employment and create an abusive working environment.[137] In determining whether the conduct is sufficiently severe or pervasive, the plaintiff must establish, from the *totality of the circumstances*, both that the employee subjectively felt the conduct was abusive and that a reasonable person would feel the conduct was abusive.[138]

In a disparate treatment case, threatening an employee because of his or her religious beliefs is evidence of religious discrimination.[139] Comments such as that the employee did not "fit in" have been held to be some evidence of discrimination. As the court said in one such case, "It requires a logical leap of the smallest kind to conclude that [the supervisor] was referring to [the plaintiff's] religion, while demanding a resignation, when he opined that [the plaintiff] did not fit in."[140]

Liability may also be based on *religious harassment*. In one case, two Russian-Jewish employees based their claim on evidence that their supervisor kept a coffee mug that prominently displayed a swastika in plain view in his office and nothing was done about their complaints.[141]

Liability may also be based on adverse treatment from the employee's *failure to conform* to the employer's religion. In one case, for example, the "born again" owners of a private manufacturing corporation generated liability by requiring employees to attend mandatory devotional services at work during work hours.[142] Even more extreme cases can be found, as the next case illustrates.

The Case of the Proselytizing Police Chief

A police chief, who referred to the workplace as "God's House," pressured a radio dispatcher to engage with him in religious dialogue. He urged her to entertain his religious beliefs and play by "God's rules," to worship at his church, and to choose "God's way" over "Satan's way," or else risk losing her job.

Result: she could proceed with her claim of religious discrimination.

(*Venters v. Delphi*, 123 F.3d 956 (7th Cir 1997).)

Religious Accommodation

To establish a *prima facie* case of failure to accommodate religious beliefs, a plaintiff must establish that:

- he or she had a *bona fide* religious belief, the practice of which conflicted with an employment duty;
- the employee informed the employer of the belief and the conflict; and,
- the employer threatened the employee with or subjected the employee to discriminatory treatment because of the employee's inability to fulfill the job requirements.[143]

Once the employee establishes a prima facie case, the employer must establish that it initiated good faith efforts to accommodate the employee's practices.[144]

The employer is relieved of the duty to accommodate only if it can show accommodation would be an undue hardship.[145] The Supreme Court held, in one case, that an employer did not have to accommodate the plaintiff by hiring a replacement on the Sabbath at overtime pay. It said that would be an undue hardship, as it would involve more than a *de minimus* cost to the employer.[146] The employer is only required to offer the employee reasonable accommodation, not necessarily the form of accommodation preferred by the employee.[147]

—7—
SEXUAL HARASSMENT

Sexual harassment is a type of sex discrimination. It is prohibited by both state and federal law. Both men and women are legally protected from sex discrimination.[148] Same-sex sexual harassment is also prohibited.[149]

As a matter of a working definition, *sexual harassment* is any verbal or physical conduct of a sexual nature that is unwelcome and is both objectively and subjectively offensive. In other words, it is an act or condition a reasonable person would find offensive and one the victim found offensive as well.[150]

While there is no law against sexual activity in the workplace that is welcome, the Supreme Court has said that conduct can be unwelcome for Title VII purposes even though the victim submits to it.[151] The Supreme Court has recognized that to submit to sexual advances out of fear of losing one's job does not make the conduct welcome. Thus, the issue in a sexual harassment case is whether the harassment is unwelcome, not whether the victim consents.

It does not necessarily need to be verbally expressed that the conduct is unwelcome. Courts will take into account nonverbal communication such as ignoring or walking away from the harasser. Further, it can be unwelcome even though the victim formerly participated in the conduct, so long as its unwelcomeness was later communicated.

Sexual harassment can result in liability not only when you are terminated, demoted, or refused a pay increase or promotion because of it, but also where it creates a *hostile working environment*.[152] However, the Supreme Court has made it clear that not every act of a sexual nature that is unwelcome and offensive will be actionable. It has been said that offhand comments, simple teasing, and isolated incidents, unless extremely serious, will not amount to liability.[153]

In order for there to be liability for creating a hostile working environment, the harassment must be sufficiently severe or pervasive as to alter the conditions of the victim's employment and create an abusive work environment.[154] In order to determine whether that standard has been met, the court will examine the totality of the circumstances, including the frequency of the conduct, its severity, whether it is physically threatening or humiliating or a mere offensive statement, and whether it interferes with an employee's work performance.

SUPERVISORS

In holding employers liable for supervisor sexual harassment, the Supreme Court differentiates between cases of sexual harassment that have resulted in a *tangible employment action* and others. A tangible employment action is one, for example, that has resulted in a termination, denial of a raise or promotion, or undeserved reassignment. As developed by the Supreme Court, the rule is that under Title VII, the employer is liable for the acts of a supervisor that involves a tangible employment action.[155] But in a case of a hostile work environment where no tangible employment action has occurred, the employer may escape liability if it can prove:

- it exercised reasonable care to prevent and correct promptly any sexually harassing behavior and
- the victim unreasonably failed to take advantage of any preventive or corrective opportunities provided by the employer, or to otherwise avoid the harm.[156]

That is why it is so important to report the harassment. Otherwise, you may let the employer off the hook altogether.

COWORKERS

The employer is liable for the acts of coworkers that it knows or should know is occurring, but is not responsible for acts of coworkers of which it is reasonably unaware. Therefore, if the employer has knowledge of prior incidents of sexual harassment by your harasser, it may be liable for that coworker's harassment of you. Once you report the harassment, the employer is placed on notice and it may be liable for subsequent acts committed against you. Similarly, the employer may be liable for the acts of nonemployees in the workplace the employer knows or should know are occurring.

Once the employer has notice of the sexual harassment, certain responsibilities follow. It must take immediate and appropriate corrective action designed to end the harassment. While the courts give the employer a great deal of latitude to decide what action to take, the Ninth Circuit Court of Appeals, for example, has said the action must take some form of discipline.[157]

IDENTIFYING SEXUAL HARASSMENT

As stated earlier, it is important to report sexual harassment when it occurs. Otherwise, the harassment may continue. If it does and the employer knows nothing about it, the employer may not be legally responsible for what follows. Understandably, however, it is not something that is easy to do. In fact, it is not always easy to know when to report sexual harassment or even whether it is occurring.

In the beginning stages of the classic case of boss sexual harassment of a female, the victim first feels off-balance by the overture and unsure of, not only how she should respond, but also whether she even heard it right. Sexual predators are usually smart enough to mask their predatory intent behind words and conduct that are capable of double and triple interpretations, at least one of which is innocent. The victim does not want to appear to impute evil intent where there was none. So silence is the usual result.

The predator not having heard a "no" usually repeats the advance. Again, the victim is either reluctant to draw the worst conclusion or is reluctant to cause embarrassment to either party. She knows that if she restates the disguised advance in more direct terms and then rejects it, "If you mean will I go out with you, the answer is no," this leaves her open to the comeback, "That's not what I meant at all." She also knows that if she rejects the overture, she may be candidly communicating her position, but may embarrass the inquirer and risk reprisal. So silence again seems the safe bet.

Feelings of guilt are also usually present. She usually wonders what she is doing to provoke these verbal and physical assaults. She usually blames herself and concludes she must be doing something to invite them. She may modify her behavior by wearing baggy clothes or less makeup or by distancing herself from the aggressor. During this process of self-examination, she again spares herself the trauma of confrontation.

At some point, however, she reaches the unequivocal conclusion—*it's not me; it's him*. She may reach the conclusion through conversations with a friend, coworker, relative, lawyer, psychologist, or simply by process of elimination. Usually, by this time, the probing and prodding has interfered with her work; has upset her emotionally; and, probably, has become an item of some discussion and debate at work. She has modified her behavior by learning to communicate her displeasure of the advances with nonverbal conduct. At first she ignored him. Then when he made a sexual remark, she would give him a dirty look or make a "tsk, tsk" noise. Now she gets up and walks away.

Her boss grows impatient with what he views as her game-playing—she will not say yes, but she has not said no. His attitude changes. He tends to be short with her; his tone of voice hardens; his instructions become quick; and, he tends to look for mistakes and more frequently calls them to her attention. There may be interludes of peace during cordial lunches in which he speaks of future advancement. These dangling carrots are usually followed by renewed sexual advances. When the advance is rejected, the retaliation intensifies. In this classic example of boss sexual harassment, the victim faces a constantly escalating upward spiral of tension and hostility.

If the foregoing sounds familiar, it may be that you are being subjected to sexual harassment. As stated, ordinarily you should communicate your displeasure early on, first to your boss and if the boss does not desist, to his or her supervisor, or to the human resources manager. How you choose to solve the situation is less important than that you do it.

As a practical matter in sexual harassment cases that are taken to court, the conduct of the offender is so egregious and offensive that the unwelcomeness of the conduct is not even an issue. To stop sexual harassment in its beginning stages, however, it is important to make known that you are not receptive to the overture being made.

Reporting Harassment

An initial reaction of many people who find themselves the target of sexual harassment is, *If I accuse my boss of sexual harassment, why would anyone believe me*? However, if you do not report the problem, the harassment may continue, intensify, and you may be forced to eventually leave. If you report the harassment, at least you will have gone on record and given the employer a chance to do the right thing.

An investigation normally follows. The investigation will give you some respite temporarily after the harasser learns of it and goes on his or her best behavior. During the investigation, the harasser may deny the charge, although sometimes he or she may admit it. Afterwards, even if the result is not in your favor, the fact that you demonstrated your willingness to report it, may deter future harassment. Therefore, in terms of giving yourself relief, it is less important that people believe your story than that you make your position known.

Usually, some corroborating evidence will support your story. You probably are not the first victim of this person's behavior. If the sexual harasser denies that he or she has sexually harassed you because he or she would never harass an employee, another employee's story may contradict the harasser's and tip the balance in your favor.

Furthermore, harassers engage in certain behavioral characteristics as part of their pattern of harassment that involve wider numbers of players. For instance, although he may have asked only you to accompany him on that weekend trip to the Bahamas, he may have been giving back rubs, neck rubs, hugs, and kisses to others. Other people in the office may have been witnesses to sex jokes, which require an audience, or of the boss' retaliation after your rejection, by humiliating you in public because the boss desires an audience to heighten the mortification.

In addition, if the harasser is questioned by human resources about the reasons for a poor evaluation or discipline against you, the rationale for that action may not stand close scrutiny. That only supports the theory that some other motive accounted for it.

Finally, the harasser may share personal and sometimes intimate information or details with the victim that the victim would only know if the harasser had informed the victim of them. If he did not propose sex with her, for example, how did she learn that he had access to the president's penthouse that weekend? Whether he did or not is objectively verifiable. He may also share intimate details about his marital problems and his wife's treatment of him. Even a comment like "my wife is out of town" would be told to a file clerk only under very limited circumstances and is objectively verifiable.

If you report, you may be surprised how readily others will believe your story, or at least reserve judgment, regardless of your position at work.

Retaliation for Reporting Sexual Harassment

If you are terminated for reporting or resisting sexual harassment, the law provides even broader remedies. In most states, you would be entitled to sue for common law wrongful discharge. That would entitle you to recover damages for economic loss, emotional distress, and, in some cases, punitive damages without regard to the caps on damages under Title VII. Even if you do not lose your job, retaliation for reporting sexual harassment would be unlawful under Title VII and most state discrimination statutes. (For more on retaliation, see Chapter 10.)

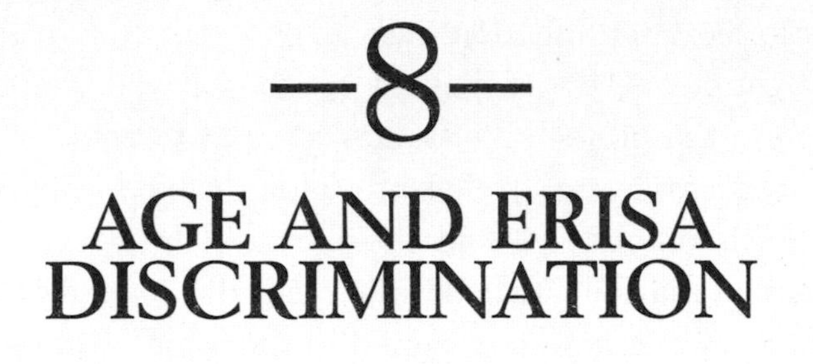

—8— AGE AND ERISA DISCRIMINATION

Older workers are granted some additional legal protections from discrimination. One such protection comes in the form of the *Age Discrimination in Employment Act* (ADEA). In addition, a separate act, the *Employee Retirement Income Security Act* (ERISA), protects older workers and others who are terminated in order to deprive them of benefits.

AGE DISCRIMINATION

The Age Discrimination in Employment Act (ADEA) prohibits an employer from discharging, refusing to hire, or otherwise discriminating against an employee in the terms or conditions of employment because of the employee's age when the employee is 40 years or older. (29 U.S.C. Sec. 623.) However, in *Kimel v. Florida Board of Regents* (528 U.S. 62 (2000)), the Supreme Court held that ADEA suits may not be maintained by employees against a state government employer because of the states' sovereign immunity.

Required Proof

The conventional discrimination formula controls the burden of proof in a disparate treatment age discrimination claim. A *prima facie* case of age discrimination is typically established where a plaintiff establishes that he or she:

- was a member of the protected class (*i.e.*, over 40);
- was performing his or her job in a satisfactory manner;
- was discharged; and,
- was replaced with a younger employee.[158]

As the Supreme Court noted in one case, a plaintiff can prove a *prima facie* age-discrimination case even when the plaintiff was replaced by someone 40 years of age or older as well.[159] The fact that one person in the protected class has lost out to another person in the protected class is thus irrelevant, so long as he or she has lost out because of his or her age, said the Court.[160] In a layoff case, the fourth element may be satisfied if the plaintiff can prove that one or more younger workers were retained in the same position.[161]

Under federal standards, once the employer states a legitimate nondiscriminatory reason for the action, the employee must produce enough evidence to allow a reasonable fact-finder to conclude either:

- that the alleged reason for [plaintiff's] discharge was false or
- that the true reason for the discharge was a discriminatory one.[162]

Factors to consider in determining pretext include what information is known to the employer at the time of the adverse employment decision; the plausibility of the explanations offered in light of the evidence; and, any inconsistencies within the explanations offered.[163] Overscrutiny of an employee's work is also evidence of pretext.[164]

As the Supreme Court noted, "It is the very essence of age discrimination for an older employee to be fired because the employer believes that productivity and competence decline with old age."[165] Thus, evidence of repeated age-related comments made by supervisors and coworkers directed at the employee or other older workers is evidence of discriminatory intent.[166] So, in one federal court case, a statement by a supervisor that he was planning to "get rid of older employees to create a new team" was held to be direct evidence of discrimination.[167] In another case, the statement, "When you get that age, those things happen to you in our company," was held to be such evidence.[168] Similarly, the statement, "old dogs won't hunt" was held to be admissible evidence of age discrimination in another.[169]

Likewise, evidence that the employer treated the employee differently than it did younger employees in the employee's position and held the employee to unattainable goals supports the claim.[170] Other proof can include an employer's failure to follow company policy in its handling of the plaintiff, including its policy of helping employees overcome deficiencies.[171]

Even if the only proof the employee can muster is to prove that the employer's stated reason for the adverse personnel action is false, the Supreme Court has held such proof alone will ordinarily raise an inference of discrimination.[172]

EMPLOYEE'S REMEDIES

The ADEA was not included in the *Civil Rights Restoration Act of 1991*, and therefore a violation of age discrimination will be limited to back pay and front pay where reinstatement is inappropriate. (29 U.S.C. Sec. 626.) Therefore, no emotional distress damages are recoverable. A prevailing plaintiff is also entitled to an award of attorney's fees. (29 U.S.C. Sec. 216(b).) An ADEA plaintiff is entitled to a jury trial. (29 U.S.C. Sec. 626(c)(2).)

Front Pay vs. Reinstatement

The decision whether to order *reinstatement* or to award *front pay* or *future lost income* is a decision for the court. When the court concludes that reinstatement is not feasible, the jury determines the amount of the front pay award. Reinstatement is not feasible where there is evidence of hostility between the parties, even where that hostility has developed because of the litigation. In one case, the court held that the trial judge did not abuse his discretion in awarding the plaintiff front pay, rather than reinstatement. This is because there was evidence that some hostility had developed between plaintiff and his former employer during the litigation, despite the former supervisor's testimony that he still considered the plaintiff a friend.[173]

Penalties

Under the ADEA, a plaintiff is entitled to liquidated damages equal to twice the backpay award where a plaintiff establishes a willful violation of the Act. (29 U.S.C. Secs. 216(b), 626(b).) A willful violation is established where a plaintiff proves that a defendant has shown a knowing or reckless disregard for whether its conduct was prohibited by the ADEA.[174]

ERISA DISCRIMINATION

Closely related to age discrimination is discrimination associated with an employee's actual or presumed cost relative to a pension or welfare benefit plan. Section 510 of the *Employee Retirement Income Security Act* (ERISA) prohibits employers from interfering with the receipt of benefits covered by that Act. When an employee was turned away by the Supreme Court in one case where he claimed that to terminate him just shy of vesting a pension was age discrimination, the Court stated that while what happened to him was not age discrimination (because age and tenure were not related in that case) it could be discrimination under ERISA.[175]

Thus, in one federal court case, an employer was held to violate Section 510 whose computer program was designed to automatically cause the closure of plants when the average age of plant workers rose to a certain level to avoid pension liability.[176] Similarly, where a worker was terminated just four months short of qualifying for enhanced pension benefits, the unexplained timing was said to create a *prima facie* case of liability under Section 510.[177] Another court held that an individual who left employment just prior to vesting his benefits due to a hostile work environment that he alleged was being maintained to force him to quit could maintain a claim.[178] Another case was decided in favor of an employee who was reclassified to an independent contractor to avoid paying her pension benefits.[179]

ERISA protection extends beyond mere interference with pension or retirement benefits. The Act also regulates employee *benefit plans* for active employees, including health insurance plans and other employee welfare plans to which such participants may become entitled. (29 U.S.C. Sec. 1140.) Thus, many cases have found violations of ERISA when an active employee used or was about to use a welfare benefit and was terminated.

In one case, for example, an employee alleged he was discharged for the purpose of depriving him of continued participation in the company-provided medical insurance plan in violation of ERISA.[180] In another case, an employee was discharged soon after he was injured on the job, reported his injury to the employer, and requested that his injury be reported to the ERISA plan administrator. This was considered evidence that he was discharged to prevent him from eventually using his company-sponsored medical and disability insurance in violation of ERISA.[181]

While under ERISA an employer may reserve the right to discontinue a welfare benefit plan, it may not otherwise discriminate against or discharge workers for the purpose of interfering with their anticipated right to receive benefits.[182] In one case, the wife of a deceased employee stated a case when she alleged that the employer interfered with her deceased husband's right to obtain benefits under the company-sponsored health plan by terminating him during his illness before his death because it was concerned about its increased costs of health coverage by his use of services.[183] Similarly, in another case, a claim was stated where it was alleged an employee was fired in retaliation for his former wife's use of the company's group health insurance plan.[184]

Cases of discrimination under ERISA are procedurally distinct from age-discrimination cases. There is a different administrative exhaustion requirement. So do not think that if you file an age-discrimination complaint with the EEOC, it will satisfy the procedural requirements under ERISA as well. Talk to a lawyer soon after any event that causes you to think an ERISA violation may have occurred.

• • • • •

While it is beyond the scope of this book, given the Enron scandal, you may ask what happens if the pension fund is raided by the employer or the company goes under altogether and your stock becomes worthless. ERISA itself has inadequate bonding requirements to guard against such losses. It does, however, impose statutory responsibilities on plan fiduciaries, and creates remedies against plan trustees, for example, who breach their fiduciary duties.

The *Sarbanes-Oxley Act of 2002* creates additional remedies. Beyond that, people who are damaged in such debacles must resort to lawsuits against company officers or professionals who have rendered services to the company, such as accountants or lawyers, under traditional common law theories, like negligence and misrepresentation.

—9—

FEDERAL RIGHTS OF DISABLED WORKERS

Thirty years ago, disabled persons had no civil rights. Absolutely nothing prevented an employer from refusing to hire a person in a wheelchair because the person could not get in the front door or up the stairs—even if the person could do the work. Similarly, if you became injured on the job and your physical capacity to lift, for example, was curtailed, nothing prevented the employer from terminating you before investigating whether your work could be modified in some way to allow you do it. As a result, a lot of people who were injured on the job were fired. Their status as *injured workers* made them used or damaged goods that the employer wanted to throw away.

In 1973, we abandoned the concept of the *shut in* or the *disposable employee*. At the federal level, Congress enacted the *Rehabilitation Act of 1973*, forbidding discrimination in employment against handicapped workers. In the summer of 1990, Congress enacted the *Americans with Disabilities Act* (ADA), which broadened the scope of federal protection to include most employees working in the private sector.

THE REHABILITATION ACT

The federal Rehabilitation Act of 1973 did not seek to reach all private employers. Instead, it only applied to federal contractors and local and state governmental agencies. Section 503 of that law applied to federal contractors and required them to take affirmative action to employ and promote handicapped workers. That section is enforced by the *Office of Federal Contract Compliance Programs* (OFCCP) of the United States Department of Labor. Section 504, the other principal section of that law, prohibited discrimination against handicapped persons by governmental bodies who received federal financial assistance.

THE AMERICANS WITH DISABILITIES ACT

The Americans with Disabilities Act (ADA) prohibits discrimination against disabled workers in *terms, conditions,* and *privileges of employment.* It covers both employees and applicants for employment. It protects persons with either physical or mental impairments. But it does not protect those who cannot do the job in question. It only protects persons who can do the work involved with *reasonable accommodation.*

Not every person who has an impairment is protected. The law protects persons who have impairments that are *substantially limiting.* On the other hand, the law protects persons from discrimination who may not have a physical or mental impairment, but are erroneously perceived to be disabled by the employer. The Act applies to employers who employ fifteen or more persons.

Ability to Do the Job

You must be a *qualified* individual with a disability. In other words, if you cannot do the work, no matter what, the ADA does not protect you.

The Act does not require the employer to keep you around if you cannot be productive. Nor does the employer have to lower its production standards to suit your disability. With few exceptions, you have to perform to the standards that are generally applied to others, so long as they are job-related and consistent with business necessity.

If your disability prevents you from performing some aspect of the job, you still maybe have protection. The law requires that you must be able to perform the *essential functions* of the job. There is no legal definition of essential function, and what it turns out to be will vary with the evidence in each case. However, that term is intended to refer to the core duties of a position. The law gives deference to the employer's judgment in defining the essential duties of the position, but its definition is not conclusive.

If you cannot perform an essential function, the question becomes, can you perform it with some reasonable form of accommodation? If so, then you should be allowed to perform it. However, if no reasonable accommodation exists to allow you to perform it, you are said to be an unqualified person.

Disabilities Covered

The ADA does not have a comprehensive listing of *covered disabilities*. Rather, so long as a physical or mental impairment substantially limits a major life activity, it can qualify with certain enumerated exceptions.

The Equal Employment Opportunity Commission (EEOC) gives examples of *major life activities*. Major life activities are functions such as caring for oneself, performing manual tasks, walking, seeing, hearing, speaking, breathing, learning, and working. Thus, the list of major life activities is not exhaustive. The Supreme Court has held that reproduction is a major life activity.[185] Courts around the country have found that other activities qualify as well. For example, the First Circuit Court of Appeals has held that the list includes lifting.[186] The Ninth Circuit held the list includes engaging in sexual relations and interacting with others.[187] Thinking has been held to be on the list.[188] As cases are decided, that list will grow and become clearer.

The Act specifically excludes protection for persons engaging in the illegal use of drugs, transvestites, homosexuals, bisexuals, and persons suffering from most sexual disorders, compulsive gambling, kleptomania, and pyromania.

Substantially Limited

In order to be protected, however, you must be substantially limited. That means unable to perform the major life activity in question or significantly restricted in your ability to perform it, as compared with an average person in the general population.

If your only limitation is that you cannot perform some aspect of your job, you probably are not substantially limited. In 2002, the Supreme Court in *Toyota Motor Manufacturing, Kentucky Inc. v. Williams*, 534 U.S. 184 (2002) held that if the major life activity in which the employee contends he or she is substantially impaired is working, the employee must show more than a substantial limitation in the performance of some job-related tasks in a particular job. The employee must demonstrate that he or she is unable to perform tasks central to most people's daily lives in a broad range of jobs, not just in a single job. In addition, said the Court, the limitation must be permanent or long-term.

If you take medication to control your condition, and when medicated you have no limitation, you will not be considered disabled under the Act. In 1999, the Supreme Court held that your degree of impairment is to be evaluated in your medicated condition. (*Sutton v. United Air Lines, Inc.*, 527 U.S. 471 (1999).) In that case, two persons who applied to be pilots for United Airlines were nearsighted, but were correctable to 20/20 with glasses or contact lenses. The Court held that the language of the Act required the person to be presently, substantially limited, and if a person's impairment was corrected by medication or other measures, he or she did not have an impairment that presently, substantially limited them.

Reasonable Accommodations

If you are substantially limited in a major life activity because of a physical or mental impairment, the law does not allow the employer to just toss you out on your ear because of that disability, even if it impacts your ability to do the work. First, there must be consideration given to whether something reasonable could be done to allow you to perform it. The law requires the employer to give you reasonable accommodation.

No book defines what a reasonable accommodation is. It is to be determined on a case-by-case basis in consideration of all the attendant circumstances. Accommodation can take many forms, including:

- making facilities accessible;
- job restructuring;
- modifying work schedules;
- modification of equipment; and,
- reassignment to a vacant position. (The EEOC takes the position that reassignment is an accommodation of last resort.)

It is often the case that an employer can accommodate a production worker, for example, who has a lifting restriction by either obtaining a work aid for him or her, such as a hoist. An employer can also reassign his or her lifting duties to others, modify the employee's schedule so he or she avoids the heaviest lifting, or modify his or her job so he or she only works on the lighter machines. In addition, a leave is one possible form of accommodation.[189]

However, there are limits to the reasonable accommodation obligation. Accommodation is not required where it would pose an *undue hardship*. Undue hardship means an action requiring significant difficulty or expense for that employer, in consideration of factors such as:

- the cost of the accommodation;
- the resources of the employer;
- the employer's size; and,
- the effect or impact of the accommodation upon the operation of the facility.

The larger the employer and facility in question, the easier it would presumably be for that employer to accommodate a disability.

Seniority Systems

In *U.S. Airways, Inc. v. Barnett*, 535 U.S. 391 (2002), the Supreme Court held that an employer ordinarily is not required to violate the terms of its seniority system in order to reasonably accommodate the disabled worker. Therefore, if jobs are awarded by seniority, you may not be entitled to reassignment to a job desired by a more senior person.

Safety Threat

In *Chevron U.S.A. Inc. v. Echazabal,* 536 U.S. 73 (2002), the Supreme Court held that an employer may exclude an employee or applicant from a job not only if he or she poses a direct threat to the health or safety of others, but also because of a direct threat to his or her own health or safety.

Requesting Reasonable Accommodation

In order for an employer to be liable for refusing to reasonably accommodate you, it must be aware of the need for accommodation. Individual state requirements may differ, but under federal law no magic words are required. Some courts hold that all that is necessary is that the employer receives information that would cause a reasonable employer to recognize a need for accommodation. Others require you to prove you requested accommodation. To remove any argument about it, your attorney will probably advise you to request it and to document your request.

Once an accommodation has been requested, you and your employer must engage in an *interactive process* to cooperatively attempt in good faith to arrive at a solution to reasonably accommodate your disability.[190] That process would ordinarily require the employer to meet with you, request information about the condition and limitations, and to consider the accommodation you are requesting.[191] Reasonable accommodation is a continuing duty on the part of the employer. If one accommodation fails, the process of accommodation must begin anew.[192]

Perceived Disability Discrimination

The ADA provides protection in cases where, for example, even though you are not presently limited by an actual disability, the stigma associated with having had a health problem or the employer's belief that you do leads to discrimination. Therefore, Congress prohibited discrimination against persons who have a record of impairment or who are regarded by the employer as having an impairment. (42 U.S.C. Sec. 12102 (2) (B) and (C).)

–10–

WHISTLEBLOWING AND RETALIATION STATUTES

Nearly everyone has seen one Hollywood movie or another, such as *The Insider*, that deals with the subject of retaliation against an employee *blowing the whistle* on an employer for engaging in some kind of illegal activity.

Recall from Chapter 3, if you are terminated for reporting the illegal activity of your employer, in most jurisdictions you will be able to sue your employer for wrongful discharge.

In addition to the common law remedy that developed, many federal and state statutes prohibit retaliation and give protection to *whistleblowers*. Many of those statutes provide protection whether you are formally reporting discrimination to an outside agency or simply reporting to your employer that you are being discriminated against. Most of them also broaden your legal protection to include retaliation that occurs on the job that does not lead to termination.

OPPOSITION STATUTES

Title VII of the *1964 Civil Rights Act* (42 U.S.C. Sec. 2000e-3(a)), which bars discrimination on the basis of race, color, national origin, sex, and religion; the *Age Discrimination in Employment Act*, (29 U.S.C. Sec. 623(d)); the *Americans with Disabilities Act* (42 U.S.C. Sec. 12203); and the *Family and Medical Leave Act* (29 U.S.C. Sec. 2615) all bar retaliation against employees who report or oppose unlawful discrimination. *Opposition statutes* are whistleblowing statutes that apply in the discrimination context.

Opposition takes many forms. You do not have to stand up on a soapbox and say, "I oppose this discrimination." On the other hand, remaining silent or simply excusing yourself from a discussion without more will not provide enough of an objective signal about where you stand on the matter to suggest opposition and provide you with legal protection.

Everyone understands that a good employee tries at first to be cooperative with the employer and finds subtle ways to express concern. The employee need not be caustic, belligerent, or self-righteous in dealing with those situations. However, if the employer allows sexual harassment of its female workforce to continue despite your first subtle expressions of concern, further overt steps on your part, such as a report to human resources objecting to the conduct and characterizing it as discrimination, may be necessary to ensure your protection under the statute. Otherwise, the employer may ultimately be able to defeat your claim by proving that despite your knowledge of the practices, you did nothing significant enough in opposing them to justify legal protection.

Protection is afforded under those opposition statutes, not just to those who complain they are being discriminated against, but also to those who oppose discrimination against others.

If you have opposed specific mistreatment of a black worker, for example, you will be viewed by the employer as that person's supporter and the employer may presume that you would be opposed to any further distress to that worker. The employer may also wish to be rid of you, too when the black worker is fired because of your anticipated reaction. The employer may also resent the challenge to its authority. If that challenge was publicly made, a manager may feel that he or she has lost face or has been insulted. In such cases, once you have registered objection, you are protected from retaliation under these opposition statutes.

Indeed, the opposition statutes spread this protection to persons who are witnesses on the victim's behalf. The employer often views employees as either for them or against them. When someone who is a female or minority challenges the employer and files a complaint of discrimination, the employer may become defensive and count the likely number of persons the challenger will be able to rely on for support. Sometimes the employer will use preemptive strikes to weed out that support or to weaken that support by setting an example. A person who has provided information to an EEO investigator that in any way confirms the challenger's report or disputes the employer's will be a likely target for retaliation. In such cases, the opposition statutes provide protection.

Federal Laws outside the Discrimination Context

Other federal laws deal specifically with affording legal protection for reporting other kinds of illegal activity. *The Occupational Safety and Health Act* (OSHA) (29 U.S.C. Sec. 660(C)) bars retaliation against a person who has made a complaint about health or safety with the employer or with OSHA.

The federal *Whistleblower Protection Act* (5 U.S.C. Sec. 1212), which applies only to employees of the federal government, bars retaliation against federal employees who report unlawful activity, gross management, a gross waste of funds, abuse of authority, or substantial or specific danger to public health and safety.

Federal law also protects whistleblowers from retaliation who file claims on behalf of the federal government against federal contractors for fraud under the *False Claims Act.* (31 U.S.C. Sec. 3730(h).)

A host of other federal statutes protect persons from retaliation who have engaged in whistleblowing activities. These include reports of violations of federal laws that regulate the environment, such as the *Clean Air Act* (42 U.S.C. Sec. 7622); employee health, such as the *Coal Mine Health and Safety Act* (30 U.S.C. Sec. 815(C)); and public safety, such as the *Toxic Substances Control Act.* (15 U.S.C. Sec. 26220.)

In 2002, in the aftermath of the Enron scandal, Congress passed the *Sarbanes-Oxley Act* that demands greater corporate accountability for financial reporting. It includes whistleblower protection for persons providing information or assistance for acts reasonably believed to be violations of that Act, the rules of the Securities and Exchange Commission, or any law relating to fraud against shareholders. Protection is given where information or assistance is provided, not only to federal regulatory or law enforcement agencies, but also to employees of the corporation whose job it is to stop such behavior or even to the employee's own supervisor. (18 U.S.C. Sec. 1514A.)

STATUTES RELATING TO PROTECTED ACTIVITIES

In addition to protected class status, other federal statutes prohibit discrimination for engaging in either protected activities, like reporting for military service, pursuant to the *Uniformed Services Employment and Reemployment Rights Act* (USERRA) (38 U.S.C. Sec. 4301), or for reporting for federal jury duty (28 U.S.C. Sec. 1875.) Section 8(a)(4) of the *National Labor Relations Act* bars retaliation against a person who engages in union activity. Section 215(a)(3) of the *Fair Labor Standards Act* bars retaliation against a person who makes a wage claim under that statute.

STATE LAWS

Many states have whistleblowing laws of one form or another. Many have opposition statutes that prohibit retaliation for reporting or opposing discrimination. Many also have other antiretaliation provisions. For example, sixteen states have a statute that bars retaliation for filing a workers' compensation claim. About a dozen have statutes that bar retaliation for taking family leave. Connecticut bars any employer from retaliating against an employee who exercises his or her free speech rights under the United States or Connecticut constitutions, so long as that activity does not substantially interfere with the employee's bona fide performance or the working relationship between the employee and the employer. (Conn. Gen. Stat. Sec. 31-519.)

Many states have also adopted statutes that protect persons from retaliation who have reported other forms of illegal activity. But just as courts have differed from state to state as to the details of such protection, so too have legislatures similarly differed. They differ as to the gravity of the offense that is being reported. Misconduct that does not rise to the level of a violation of law, gross mismanagement, or abuse of authority is typically not covered. They differ in their requirement of whether conduct being reported is actually illegal. For example, to afford protection against retaliation, Iowa requires only a reasonable belief that the conduct was unlawful. (Iowa Code Sec. 19A.19.) New York, on the other hand, affords no protection unless an actual violation of law existed. (NY Lab. Law Sec. 740(2)(a).)

In the same vein, some statutes including those in Florida and Texas, afford protection only if the whistleblower makes his or her report to a government agency. (Fla. Stat., Sec. 112.3187(b); Tex. Rec. Civ. Stat. Ann. 6252-16(a), Sec. 2.) The statutes of other states, like the one in Kansas, provide protection even in cases of internal reports to the employer. (Kan. Stat. Ann. Sec. 75-2973.)

In Maine and New York, no protection is afforded unless the whistleblower first gives the employer a chance to remedy the situation. (ME Rev. Stat. 26 Sec. 831-836; NY Lab. Law Sec. 740, 20-C.)

Outside the discrimination context, state whistleblower statutes in many states, including Alaska, Arizona, Colorado, Delaware, Florida, Kansas, Kentucky, Maryland, Missouri, Nevada, South Carolina, and Texas protect only state employees or public employees generally, but not private employees.

As each state statute is different in terms and requirements and in the ways their terms have been interpreted, it is advisable to immediately consult a practiced employment lawyer in your state to see whether your state whistleblower law applies to your situation.

• • • • •

One thing about retaliation cases is that they are typically easier to win than the underlying discrimination suit. All you have to prove is that you were retaliated against because you engaged in the protected activity. You do not also have to prove that the firing manager was a bigot. It is always difficult to prove bias or prejudice because direct proof of one's state of mind is rare. That is why discrimination is permitted to be proven indirectly through circumstantial evidence. Retaliation cases are much more straightforward. While it is true that a *retaliatory state of mind* must be shown, usually the timing between the complaint and the retaliation and a sudden change in treatment or attitude toward the employee suggests the causal connection.

The difference in treatment after the protected activity tends to be more pronounced in a retaliation case than in the ordinary discrimination case because of the difference in the emotions at work in each. Whereas a supervisor may be biased against a woman and tend to associate negative stereotypes to her performance, he may not become personally angry with her until after she reports him for sexual harassment. That anger is often difficult for the employer to camouflage.

—11—

EMPLOYEE BENEFITS AND WORKING CONDITIONS

Over the years, a host of federal and state legislation has been passed that regulate terms and conditions of employment in the United States. From the earliest child labor laws to the most recent family leave requirements, those laws touch upon every facet of the workplace. This chapter presents a few of the most important statutes that afford you benefits and protection.

THE FAMILY AND MEDICAL LEAVE ACT

Since 1990, state and federal legislators have enacted pro-family legislation to allow persons who work for certain employers to remain at home after the birth or adoption of a child, or for medical reasons. The rights are conferred only to persons who work for employers having over a certain number of employees. There are conditions to asserting these rights. The leave periods are of limited duration. The employer is not required to pay the employee who takes a leave. However, existing benefit rights, such as vacation or sick leave, may be applied during the leave period.

Basic Provisions

On August 5, 1993 the *Family and Medical Leave Act* (FMLA) took effect. This legislation requires employers having fifty or more employees to allow leave to employees under certain circumstances. In states that have state leave laws, the employee is entitled to whichever benefit is greater under the two laws, although the leave period may run concurrently.

FMLA grants eligible employees up to twelve work weeks of leave during a twelve-month period for the following purposes:

- to care for a child following the birth of a child or the placement of a child for adoption or foster care;
- to care for a family member (spouse, parent, or child) of the employee when the family member has a serious health condition; or,
- when an employee has a serious health condition that makes the employee unable to perform the functions of the position of the employee. (29 U.S.C. Sec. 2612(a)(1).)

An *eligible employee* under FMLA is an employee who has been employed for at least twelve months by the employer. The employee must have worked for at least 1,250 hours of service with the employer during the previous twelve-month period. The employee must also work at a worksite where the employer employs fifty or more employees within seventy-five miles. (29 U.S.C. Sec. 2611(2).)

A *serious health condition* under FMLA is defined broadly to include illness, injury, impairment, or physical or mental condition. These must involve either inpatient care for any period or continuing treatment by a health care provider for a period of incapacity of more than three consecutive calendar days; for any period of incapacity due to pregnancy or for prenatal care; or, that is related to a chronic serious health condition. (29 U.S.C. Sec. 2611.)

Notice to the employer is required, in accord with employer policy, not to exceed thirty days' notice in cases where the need for the leave was anticipated and as soon as practical in other cases. (29 C.F.R. Sec. 825.302 and following.)

Under FMLA, an eligible employee may take leave intermittently for the employee's own serious health condition when the leave is medically necessary for treatment by or under the supervision of a health care provider. (29 U.S.C. Sec. 2612(b)(1).)

Upon conclusion of the leave the employer is required to reinstate the employee to the position held at the time the leave was required or to an equivalent position. (29 U.S.C. Sec. 2614.) An equivalent position is one that has the same pay, benefits, working conditions, and similar duties and responsibilities.

Under FMLA, it is unlawful for an employer to interfere with or deny the exercise of the right to medical leave. It is also unlawful for an employer to discharge or otherwise discriminate against an employee for opposing an unlawful employment practice under FMLA. (29 U.S.C. Sec. 2615.)

FMLA allows a successful plaintiff to recover monetary damages and appropriate equitable relief, including reinstatement. (26 U.S.C. Sec. 2617(a)(1).) The monetary damages are equal to:

- the amount of compensation denied or cost to employee because of the employer's violation; plus,
- interest on that amount; plus,
- an additional penalty, equal to the sum of the damages and interest; and,
- a successful plaintiff is also allowed recovery of attorney's fees and costs. (29 U.S.C. Sec. 2617(a)(3).)

Interaction between FMLA and the ADA

Sometimes employers mistakenly believe FMLA supercedes instead of works in conjunction with the Americans with Disabilities Act (ADA). They mistakenly believe that if an employee exhausts his or her FMLA leave and is still unable to return to work, the employee may be terminated at that point. However, even after the employee takes his or her twelve weeks of FMLA leave, if he or she is disabled, an additional leave of absence from work may be a reasonable accommodation under the ADA. (*Nunes v. Wal-Mart Stores, Inc.*, 164 F.3d 1243 (9th Cir. 1999).)

Alternatively, an employee who is covered by the ADA may be entitled to part-time work or a modified work schedule after FMLA leave has been exhausted, as one form of reasonable accommodation. Conversely, an employee may be entitled under FMLA to intermittent leave that is medically necessary due to a serious health condition, even though it would be an undue hardship under the ADA.

It is easy to confuse the ADA and FMLA since they both work in tandem in some respects. For example, an employee's request for FMLA leave because of the employee's serious health condition may also constitute a request for ADA reasonable accommodation and trigger the employer's duty to engage with the employee in an interactive process to determine the need for and type of reasonable accommodation necessary. (see Chapter 9.)

The employee should not be confused into thinking that a serious health condition under FMLA is necessarily a disability under the ADA. The two are not necessarily the same. (29 C.F.R. Sec. 825.702(b).)

RETIREMENT LEGISLATION (ERISA)

Federal legislation known as the *Employee Retirement Income Security Act* (ERISA) not only regulates the maintenance of retirement benefits, but also grants protection to employees who may become entitled to them. (see Ch. 8.) Section 510 of the Act prohibits an employer from terminating or discriminating against a worker who exercises any right under an employee benefit plan. It also prohibits an employer from interfering with the attainment of any right to which a worker may become entitled under any such plan. The plans referred to include not only retirement plans, but also health insurance plans and severance plans.

In an ERISA case, an employee need not prove that the employer's sole purpose in taking adverse action against the employee was to interfere with the attainment of the benefit, just that it was a motivating factor. Some courts have held that timing alone can raise an inference supporting an employee's case. Conventional discrimination law analysis will apply to test the articulated reason of the employer for the adverse action, to see if it holds water. (See Chapter 8 for cases that illustrate ERISA discrimination under Section 510.)

COBRA RIGHTS

The *Consolidated Omnibus Budget Reconciliation Act* (COBRA) requires certain employers to offer health plan continuation coverage to employees and their dependents who would otherwise lose their group coverage due to certain *qualifying events* such as termination, divorce, or death of the employee. A termination for *gross misconduct* is disqualifying.

Not all employers are covered. Employers having fewer than twenty employees are exempt. However, for purposes of COBRA, independent contractors are included in the count.

Following a qualifying event, the employer is required to give notice to the eligible participant of his or her rights under COBRA. The employer must notify the plan administrator within thirty days of an employee's termination or other qualifying event. The plan administrator must notify the participant of the right to elect continuation coverage within fourteen days thereafter. The notice should contain adequate information about the coverage offered and its cost. The participant must notify the employer of the election to continue coverage within sixty days of receiving notice. The notice must be given in writing.

Thereafter, the participant must pay the insurance premium that is due. The insurance that is offered must have the same coverage that the participant had before the qualifying event. Generally, COBRA eligibility lasts for eighteen months. Eligible persons who are disabled for social security purposes at the time of termination may continue COBRA coverage for a total of twenty-nine months, but at a premium rate for the additional months. There are some circumstances in which it can be extended for a total of thirty-six months, such as for a spouse or child, but never for a terminated employee.

THE FAIR LABOR STANDARDS ACT

The *Fair Labor Standards Act* (FLSA) is a comprehensive federal statute that regulates wages, hours, and working conditions. It also regulates child labor. The following is an introduction to its major provisions.

Minimum Wage and Overtime

The *Fair Labor Standards Act* regulates minimum wages and rights to overtime pay. (29 U.S.C. Sec. 201 and following.) State laws may set a higher minimum wage rate. All employers with an annual dollar volume of $500,000 are subject to the federal minimum wage laws. Working for employers having less than that dollar volume may still be covered if the workers are engaged in *interstate commerce*.

The FLSA requires that employees be paid at least the minimum wage for the first forty hours they work in a workweek, and one and one-half times their regular rate of pay for all additional hours worked. Hours worked includes any time employees are required or permitted to perform work. It also includes work not requested by the employer if the employer has knowledge of it.

Calculation of wages. Under the Act, *wages* for minimum wage and overtime calculation purposes include not just cash payments, but also the reasonable cost of board or lodging furnished to the employee and a portion of tips received by certain employees.

An employee hired to work solely *by the hour* must be paid at least the statutory minimum wage. The federal minimum wage rate can yield to higher minimum wage rates mandated by state law. An employee's fixed weekly salary divided by the number of hours worked during the workweek must equal or exceed the statutory minimum wage. Fixed monthly or biweekly wages should be convertible to a weekly wage equivalent to ascertain compliance.

Commissions. Many employees are compensated in whole or in part on a commission basis. When commissions are paid on a weekly basis, the hourly rate is determined by dividing the total earnings for the workweek by the total number of hours worked in that week. Commissions paid over a longer period are applied retroactively over that period in which the commissions were earned to compute the hourly rate.

Piecework. For employees paid on a piecework basis, the hourly rate is computed by taking the worker's total earnings for that workweek and dividing that by the total hours worked that week. The resulting number must exceed the statutory minimum.

Tips. For employees whose income includes tips, the Act provides that so long as the employer's cash wage is at least half the minimum wage, and that combined with the employee's tips equal the minimum wage, the employer can receive a credit of up to 50% of the required minimum wage for the tips received by the employee. To receive credit, however, the employer must allow its employees to retain all tips received. State laws may limit the tip credit otherwise available under federal law.

Compensable time under FLSA. Questions often arise as to what time may be included as *compensable time* under the FLSA.

Waiting time. Whether waiting time is compensable is dependent upon the facts in a particular case. Generally, if a person is *engaged to wait*, the waiting time is compensable, but if the person is *waiting to be engaged* the time is not compensable.

On-call time. Whether on-call time is compensable is also dependent upon the particular facts involved. The determination largely turns upon how free the employee is able to use the on-call time as his or her own. Factors that are typically considered include: whether the employee is required to remain on or in close proximity to the employer's premises; whether the frequency of calls is unduly intrusive; and, whether an unduly restrictive response time limit is imposed. The time is compensable if after applying all of the relevant factors, the restrictions are so burdensome that the time is spent predominantly for the benefit of the employer.

Rest and meal periods. Whereas rest periods of twenty minutes or less are compensable, meal periods of thirty minutes or longer are excluded from worktime. That is true, however, only if during the meal period the employee is not required to perform any duties.

Deductions. Under the Act, deductions that do not reduce cash wages below the statutory minimum are generally permitted, even if the employer benefits from the deduction. Some states have laws that restrict this right. Under the FLSA, however, these deductions may include those to repay loans to the employer, the cost of furnishing or maintaining uniforms, tools or equipment, or taxes the employer is required to collect from the employer. Contributions to a pension or health benefit plan may be deducted if the employee voluntarily agrees to the deduction, regardless of the effect on minimum wage requirements. Similarly, union dues may be deducted if made pursuant to a valid checkoff clause in a collective bargaining agreement.

State wage laws commonly limit deductions, diversions, and withholdings. Most states prohibit deductions unless required or permitted by law or with the written consent of the employee. Some also require that the deduction be for the benefit of the employee, not the employer.

The FLSA and state laws. The FLSA permits states to pass laws that impose restrictions on employers not found in the Act, such as requirements for meal or break periods or absolute work hour limitations.

State laws also commonly regulate the payment of wages upon termination of employment. In some states, all accrued wages must be paid on the last day of employment. In others, the payment must be made by the end of the next business day. Still others do not require payment until the next regularly scheduled payday. Some states only require immediate payment in the case of an involuntary separation.

Overtime provisions. There are numerous general exceptions to the coverage of federal overtime laws. Special legislation to benefit certain industries has created a hodgepodge of exemptions, including:

- salespersons who sell boats, trailers, or aircraft;
- salespersons, partsmen, and mechanics working in automotive or farm implement dealerships;
- employees of motion picture theater enterprises;
- employees working as seamen;
- taxi drivers; and,
- agricultural workers. (29 U.S.C. Sec. 213 (b).)

Executives and *supervisors* are exempt from minimum wage and overtime requirements under the FLSA if they are paid a salary of not less than $455 per week and meet the following test.

- The executives or supervisors regularly direct the work of two or more employees.
- They have the authority to hire and fire employees, or their recommendations regarding hiring or firing are given particular weight.
- They exercise independent judgment and discretion.
- Their primary duty is management. (29 C.F.R. Sec. 541.100.)

The *primary duty* may be satisfied through a percentage of time test (more than 50%) or in cases where it is less than 50% through a more intricate test that evaluates the duties of the employee on a qualitative base. The latter test takes into account such factors as the relative importance of the management duties and the frequency with which discretionary powers are exercised. (29 C.F.R. Sec. 541.700.)

Administrative employees are exempt if they are paid a salary of not less than $455 per week and:

- perform responsible office or nonmanual work that directly affects management policies, general business operations, or the academic administration of a school;
- they regularly exercise independent judgment and discretion regarding matters of significance; and,
- their primary duty is administrative as described above, and includes the exercise of independent judgment and discretion.

(29 C.F.R. Sec. 541.2(e).)

The independent judgment that is exercised must be real and substantial and must be exercised *with respect to matters of consequence.* (29 C.F.R. Sec. 541.202.)

Professional employees are also exempt if they:

- perform work that requires advanced knowledge customarily acquired by a prolonged course of study;
- perform work in a recognized field of artistic endeavor that is original and creative in character;
- teach in a school system or educational institution; or,
- perform work that requires highly specialized knowledge in computer systems analysis, programming, or software engineering. (29 C.F.R. Secs. 541.300, 303, 400.)

Professional employees must also meet the following criteria for exemption to apply.

- They consistently exercise discretion and judgment.
- Their primary duty is the performance of professional duties.
- They are paid on a salary basis. (29 C.F.R. Secs. 541.300, 301.)

Additional categories of works that are exempt include:

- outside salespersons (29 C.F.R. Sec. 541.500);
- certain commissioned retail employees (29 U.S.C. Sec. 207 (i));
- drivers and certain other workers employed by a motor carrier (29 U.S.C. Sec. 213 (b)(1)); and,
- certain computer professionals. (29 U.S.C. Sec. 213 (a).)

Those who are subject to the Act, and not exempt, are to receive one and one-half times their regular rate of pay for hours worked in excess of forty hours in a work week. (29 U.S.C. Sec. 207.) This is required regardless of whether the employees are paid on an hourly, salary, or piece basis. A workweek is a seven day period of consecutive days set by the employer. The workweek is to begin at the same time and on the same day each week.

Child Labor Laws

The FLSA also prohibits *oppressive child labor*. What that is in any particular case is determined by considering both the child's age and the work the child is required to do. The Secretary of Labor by rule has defined what that is by industry and occupation. Generally, however, employment of persons under age 16, unless specifically exempted and persons ages 16–18 in certain *particularly hazardous* occupations is prohibited. Fourteen and fifteen-year-olds may be employed in occupations other than mining and manufacturing under guidelines adopted by the Secretary.

Exemptions for children below age 16 are specifically given for persons employed in agriculture, theatrical fields, newspaper deliveries, and certain work at home. Except for the Secretary's exceptions and exemptions, 16 years of age is the minimum age of employment of children in nonhazardous occupations. The list of hazardous occupations include such things as coal mining, logging, driving motor vehicles, and operating certain power machines.

THE DAVIS-BACON ACT

A different law, the *Davis-Bacon Act*, regulates prevailing wage rates. (See 40 U.S.C. Sec. 276(0).) That Act requires employees who are contractors on federally funded projects, defined to include only those where 25% or more of their funding is federal, to adhere to prevailing wage rates set by the U.S. Department of Labor. Those employers who do not comply may face contract payment hold backs, contract termination, and criminal penalties for submission of falsified payroll records.

PLANT CLOSURE LEGISLATION

Employers having at least 100 employees must give their employees and unions sixty days advance notice of a plant closing or mass layoff, pursuant to the *Worker Adjustment and Retraining Act* (WARN). (29 U.S.C. Sec. 2101.)

A *plant closing* means the permanent or temporary shutdown of a single site of employment or of one or more facilities or operating units within a single site of employment.

A *mass layoff* means a reduction in force that results in a loss of employment at a single site of employment during any thirty-day period of at least fifty employees, excluding part-time employees. However, it must constitute at least one-third of the workforce at that facility. Regulations govern circumstances in which separate facilities may be counted together. The Act does not apply to the closing of a temporary facility or the cessation of work on a project that employees were told would provide temporary work only.

Employees or their union may enforce the provisions of the Act. Damages include back pay, benefits, attorneys fees, and a fine of $500 a day, unless employees are paid within three weeks of the closure or layoff. The employer may reduce damages if it proves it acted in good faith.

OCCUPATIONAL SAFETY AND HEALTH ACT

In 1970, Congress passed the *Occupational Safety and Health Act* (OSHA). Its purpose was to establish national standards for workplace safety and health. (29 U.S.C. Sec. 651 and following.) The Act applies to practically all employers, regardless of size.

Under the Act, every employer is required to become familiar with all OSHA standards applicable to the employer's establishment. The employer is required to adequately communicate in *plain English* its safety policies to its employees. Records of workplace illnesses and injuries must be maintained. In addition, the employer must ensure that employees have access to and properly utilize personal protective equipment whenever required.

OSHA also prohibits retaliation or discrimination by employers against employees who have exercised rights under the Act. (29 U.S.C. Sec 660(c).) The Act protects not only those who file complaints against employers, but also those who testify or are about to testify in any OSHA proceeding.

Complaints of discrimination or retaliation should be filed with your local OSHA area office. Any such complaint must be filed within thirty days of any alleged violation.

WORKERS' COMPENSATION LAWS

In the nineteenth century during the industrial revolution, if a worker became injured on the job there was nothing coming to the worker in the way of any continuing pay, payment of medical bills, or other compensation unless the worker could prove in a lawsuit that the employer was at fault.

Early in the twentieth century, however, states began to pass *workers' compensation legislation* to provide such benefits without a showing of fault. In exchange, those acts provided that, with few exceptions, the workers' exclusive remedy would be the prescribed benefits under the worker's compensation system, which typically were more restrictive than that which were available in a lawsuit. Today, all states have some form of workers' compensation system. In addition, federal legislation has been enacted that provides more liberal benefits to some workers in interstate commerce, most notably railway and longshore workers.

UNEMPLOYMENT COMPENSATION

An unemployment compensation program has been established in every state and the District of Columbia. Benefits are restricted to *employees*, but that term may include persons called *independent contractors* if the applicable requirements are satisfied. Labels are not determinative. Each state has its own test, though the principal factor tends to be the employer's *right to control* the person and the person's work.

Each state has its own eligibility rules. In all states, people are eligible only if they earn a required minimum amount during the *base period*. The base period is defined in most states to include the first four calendar quarters of the last five full quarters before the claim filing. Most also require the employee to be employed for a minimum time during that period, typically at least two of the calendar quarters during the base period.

Unemployment compensation is designed to provide assistance only to those who are ready, willing, and able to work. Therefore, if a person is ill or disabled and cannot engage in any work, they are not eligible. They also must be actively seeking work to remain eligible.

A person is disqualified from receipt of benefits in all fifty states and the District of Columbia if terminated for *misconduct*. That term is variously defined. It does not include mere *inadequate performance*. It typically requires evidence of *willful* behavior. Sometimes it is defined to also include repeated acts of negligence, despite repeated warnings. In some states, the disqualification is only for a period of weeks, unless the misconduct was particularly *gross*. In most states the disqualification is for the duration of the period of unemployment.

In all fifty states and the District of Columbia, a person who voluntarily resigns his or her position forfeits the right to benefits if the resignation was without good cause. In most states, an employee who resigns without good cause loses his or her benefits during the whole period of unemployment. In most states, the employee who resigns with good cause is still ineligible unless the employee is able to prove the good cause was attributable to the employer or was connected to the work. In those states, a purely personal reason won't be deemed sufficient justification.

DRUG TESTING LAWS

Except in a very few states, drug testing (random or otherwise) is permitted in the private sector. Public sector employees, however, have used the Fourth Amendment's prohibition against unreasonable searches and seizures to restrict drug testing except where *reasonable* under the circumstances. Generally, such searches in the public sector will be permitted where there is probable cause to believe someone is working under the influence of drugs or alcohol, and in other circumstances where considerations of public safety or security are at issue. However, courts in a few states including California, Massachusetts, Louisiana, and West Virginia have used state constitutional right to privacy provisions to provide a remedy to private-sector employees who have been subjected to or refused a drug test. Currently, there is activity in other states to reach similar results. However, in most states, private-sector employees are still subject to drug testing at any time.

EMPLOYEE POLYGRAPH PROTECTION ACT

The *Employee Polygraph Protection Act* (EPPA) (29 U.S.C. Sec. 2001 and following) prohibits most private employers from using polygraphs to test employees or applicants unless they reasonably suspect the employee was involved in theft or caused other economic loss or injury to the employer's business. Government employers and certain private security companies are permitted to use them, but only according to the procedures that are prescribed in the Act. In addition, most states and the District of Columbia have laws that prohibit the use of polygraphs in the private sector as a condition of acquiring or continuing employment. State statutes vary widely in regulating their use in other cases.

HEALTH INSURANCE PORTABILITY AND ACCOUNTABILITY ACT

In April 2003, new federal regulations came into effect under the *Health Insurance Portability and Accountability Act* (HIPAA) to restrict access to the use of an individual's health information. Detailed standards for the protection of health information govern how providers use, maintain, and disclose protected health information. Health information is defined to include all medical records and other individually identifiable health data held or disclosed by the covered entity.

Employers are not covered entities, but are termed *plan sponsors* and their ability to use health plan data is restricted. A plan sponsor who requires protected health information must not disclose it except where permitted by law, must provide and account for disclosures, must destroy all health information that is no longer needed, and must ensure that firewalls have been established to protect against disclosure. For more information on the Act go to the Department of Health and Human Services website at **www.hhs.gov/ocr/hipaa**.

GARNISHMENT

Title III of the *Consumer Credit Protection Act* prohibits discrimination against a worker whose wages have been garnished. The Act further restricts a creditor's ability to garnish a worker's earnings. With few exceptions, no more than 25% of a worker's weekly disposable earnings may be garnished. *Disposable earnings* are those left after deduction of any amount withheld by law. Exception is given to the 25% limit in the case of support orders, orders from a bankruptcy court, and debts due for federal or state taxes. State law generally governs the procedures to follow in garnishment circumstances.

IMMIGRATION LAWS AND THE WORKPLACE

The *Immigration Reform and Control Act* (IRCA) makes it a crime for an employer to hire illegal immigrants. However, if you are a legal immigrant, the Act also prohibits discrimination against you in hiring and firing because of your lack of citizenship status or your national origin.

IRCA is narrower than other discrimination laws in that it does not bar discrimination in other employment actions, like wages or promotion. If you believe you have been discriminated against because of your citizenship status or national origin, this law is enforced by the *Special Counsel for Immigration-Related Unfair Employment Practices* of the Department of Justice. A complaint of discrimination may be filed with that office. IRCA also bars retaliation against you for filing a complaint under the Act.

If you are an illegal alien who wishes to attain legal status, and no amnesty period is currently offered, as it was under IRCA in the mid 80s, it is beyond the scope of this work to provide you with any guidance. However, there are lawyers who specialize in immigration law in most major cities. Some recommended ones are listed in the peer review publication, *The Best Lawyers in America* and they may be found online at **www.bestlawyers.com**. Look for those attorneys with the *AILA* designation *(American Immigration Lawyers Association)*.

RIGHTS TO UNIONIZE

The *National Labor Relations Act* provides that employees can determine for themselves whether they wish to be represented by a union. (29 U.S.C. Secs.151-169.) It provides that a majority of employees within an *appropriate bargaining unit* can vote to designate a labor organization to represent them for *collective bargaining* of compensation and other terms and conditions of employment.

A key issue in deciding whether a group of employees will be an appropriate bargaining unit is whether a community of interest exists among the employees who seek to be represented. The *National Labor Relations Board* is available to decide that issue if the parties are unable to decide it on their own. Similarities in the method of wage payment, hours of work, benefits, supervision, skills, training, qualifications, and job functions are some of the factors that are considered in that determination.

The Act prohibits employers from interfering with employees' rights to organize. It also prohibits discrimination and retaliation against any employee for the purpose of encouraging or discouraging union membership or for other union activity. Complaints of discrimination for engaging in union activity must be filed with the National Labor Relations Board. It has regional offices across the country.

–12–
EMPLOYEE PRIVACY

With the advent and widespread use of computers, new questions of law have arisen concerning an employer's right to monitor, intercept, or read employee emails and other communications.

EXPECTATION OF PRIVACY

Except in a few states, you have a common law *right to privacy*. An action for invasion of privacy by intrusion will lie where a *reasonable expectation of privacy* exists and an intrusion would be *highly offensive to a reasonable person*. Analyzing whether you have reasonable expectation of privacy in your emails, voice mails, and telephone calls will depend upon the particular circumstances of your case.

As for whether you have a reasonable expectation of privacy in your emails, for example, ask yourself the following questions.

- Does your employer provide your password or is it your own?
- If it is your own, does your employer require you to divulge your password for its use?
- What is the understanding as to the circumstances in which your employer may use the password to access your computer?
- Are those circumstances understood to be limited, such as when you are away from the workplace?
- Is your system one in which the employer is permitted to bypass the password to access the system?
- Who is doing the monitoring and for what purpose?
- Was the monitoring that occurred consistent with that purpose?
- Were you informed such monitoring would occur?

All of these questions bear on whether there was an intrusion into your private affairs or concerns because there was a reasonable expectation of privacy and whether the intrusion was offensive to a reasonable person.

The Case of the Backstage Fashion Show

Twelve models were hired to put on a fashion show at the St. Louis Convention Center. They used a makeshift dressing area backstage to change. Unbeknownst to them, the security guards who were employed by the security company at the convention center watched them change backstage during the show through the use of television surveillance cameras.

Result: recovery for the models. Each could recover for invasion of privacy by intrusion.

(*Doe v. BPS Guard Services, Inc.*, 945 F.2d 1422 (8th Cir. 1991).)

The Case of the Bathroom Exposure

An employer concealed video cameras and audio listening devices behind two-way mirrors in its restrooms at one of its terminals to detect any drug activities by its employees. Employees discovered the surveillance equipment when a mirror fell off the men's restroom wall, exposing a video camera.

Result: the court ruled the claim for invasion of privacy could proceed. However, not every case in which someone is captured on videotape leads to liability. The key question will be if there is a reasonable expectation of privacy.

(*Cramer v. Consolidated Freightways, Inc.*, 255 F.3d 683 (9th Cir. 2001).)

The Case of the Unsuspecting Tamperer

A security investigator noticed that some papers in a locked drawer in his desk had been tampered with. He received permission from the company to monitor the desk with a hidden video camera. The next night they caught the employee picking the lock of the desk drawer with a paper clip and flipping through the files. When the employee found out he had been videotaped, he sued for invasion of privacy.

Result: the court held the employee had no claim because he was being videotaped in an open office area and could have no reasonable expectation of privacy.

(*Marrs v. Marriott Corp.*, 830 F. Supp. 274 (D. Md. 1992).)

Therefore, in the case of video monitoring, obviously visible cameras that are operational may raise no reasonable expectation of privacy, so long as you know they are being used. Such an expectation might arise if hidden surveillance cameras are employed in nonpublic areas, particularly if:

- they are not being used for legitimate business reasons;
- the reason they were initially installed has disappeared; or,
- the operators of the cameras are abusing their use of the taped product.

The courts have approached audio taping in a similar manner. *Aural privacy* is a relative, rather than absolute concept in the workplace. An office need not be sealed to offer its occupant a reasonable expectation of privacy, as illustrated in the case on the following page.

The Case of the Mistrustful Chief

A city's police chief ordered one of his lieutenants to direct two police officers to bug the office of the assistant chief. The two did so by means of a briefcase in which a tape recorder was stored. One of the assistant chief's conversations was monitored in this fashion.

Result: the court held that even though the door to the assistant chief's office was open and his secretary was only fifteen feet away, he could have a reasonable expectation that the conversation in question was private.

(*United States v. McIntyre*, 582 F.2d 1221 (9th Cir. 1998).)

As stated in a different case, the reasonable expectation of visual and aural privacy in the workplace depends not only on who might have been able to observe the subject interaction, but also on the means of intrusion and identity of the intruder.[193]

TELEPHONE MONITORING

Employees being videotaped or recorded are more likely to have their privacy invaded than those having their telephone monitored. However, with respect to telephone monitoring, invasion of privacy claims may lie, unless the employer is careful to ensure the following.

- There is a legitimate business reason for the monitoring.
- Employees have notice that the monitoring will occur.
- That monitoring will terminate once personal calls are identified.
- Employees are put on notice either that:
    - they are not to make or receive personal calls;
    - personal calls are to be limited to certain times or extensions;
    - that the employer may be monitoring all calls placed or received with employer equipment; or,
    - that the monitoring policy is regularly republished and steps are taken by management to enforce it.

The Case of the Overscrutinized Employee

An employee alleged her employer kept her under close observation, informed other employees her telephone privileges had been revoked, and routed her incoming calls through her supervisor.

Result: the court ruled for the employer, noting that the monitoring that was occurring was limited to the employee's business calls and that there was no invasion of her personal solitude or affairs.

(*Smith v. Colorado Interstate Business Co.*, 777 F. Supp. 854 (D. Colo. 1991).)

The Case of the Unannounced Recordings

An employer installed telephone monitoring equipment to monitor business calls by its customer sales representatives (CSRs). The CSRs were not told that personal calls were not to be made at their desks. Their supervisors knew that personal calls were being made and received at their desks. The CSRs learned that blanket monitoring of all their calls, both business and personal, took place for a given period.

Result: the court held that though the CSRs could not claim intrusion with respect to the business calls, they could assert a claim for intrusion as to unannounced recording of personal telephone calls.

(*Ali v. Douglas Cable Communications*, 929 F. Supp. 1362 (D. Kan. 1996).)

A similar result has been reached in cases under the *Omnibus Crime Control and Safe Streets Act*, otherwise known as the *Federal Wiretapping Act* (18 U.S.C. Sec. 2510), that requires employers to obtain the prior consent of one party to lawfully monitor calls.

The Case of the Eavesdropping Supervisor

A company that sold Yellow Page advertising had an established policy whereby it would monitor solicitation calls by its employees as part of its regular training program. It also told employees that they were permitted to make personal calls on company telephones and that those calls would not be monitored except to the extent necessary to determine if the call was of a personal or business nature. However, an employee's supervisor monitored a personal call with a friend about an employment interview the employee just had with another company. After a blowup about the call, the employee was terminated.

Result: the announced program to monitor business calls did not give the employer prior consent to monitor personal calls; and that it did so was a violation of the *Federal Wiretapping Act*.

(*Watkins v. L. M. Berry & Co.*, 704 F.2d 577 (11th Cir. 1983).)

Similarly, in another case, a court held that an employer could not claim the *prior consent* exception when, although it had warned the employee it might monitor her calls, it never explicitly told her it would do so. The owner of a store who had suffered a burglary and suspected a clerk of the crime installed a recording device on an extension line that would activate if a call was made. Even before the burglary, the clerk was asked to cut down on her personal calls and was told they might resort to monitoring if she did not. After the device was installed, the owner recorded twelve hours of her conversations (much of which were of a sexual nature) with a person with whom she was having an illicit affair. The owner was held liable for a violation of the Federal Wiretapping Act.[194]

The expectation of privacy is a relative matter. If coworkers share space, such as a shared work station, then an employee's conversations could theoretically be overheard by a coworker. Even so, in one case under such circumstances, a court held it was a question of fact for a jury to decide as to whether an employee had a reasonable expectation that his or her conversations would not be intercepted by supervisors.[195]

EMAIL MONITORING

Emails are theoretically protected, but most often receive no protection from employer monitoring. The *Electronic Conversation Privacy Act of 1986* (ECPA) amended the *Federal Wiretapping Act* to expand its scope to include all electronic communications transmitted by wire, radio, electromagnetic, photoelectric, or photo-optic systems, thereby including email. However, Section 2701 of ECPA permits entities to access stored, private communications if the entity provides the wire or electronic communications system. Thus, federal statutes do not prohibit an employer from monitoring email communications on its own system.

Employers may become liable for invasion of privacy in monitoring employee email particularly if:

- they permit personal use of email;
- they have no significant interest in reading their employee's email;
- they provide no notice that monitoring will occur; and,
- the subject monitoring that occurred was not undertaken for a purpose related to the employer's business.

• • • • •

When it comes to workplace privacy, the employer is generally in the driver's seat. It is in position to dispel any notion that any aspect of the work environment is private by providing sufficient notice to the employee to that effect. If it has not provided such notice, the notice is inconspicuous, or the notice is stale and monitoring has not recently occurred, then liability may be generated. It is not inconceivable that an employer will fail to do all it needs to do to avoid liability because employers do not automate such notice.

Further, the persons who make employer policy are sometimes loath to completely dehumanize the work environment by providing the requisite notice in such prominence, number, and frequency, as to assure such protection. They do not want to establish a *Big Brother* environment. Indeed, many wish to establish just the opposite atmosphere, characterized by the feeling and thought that some measure of privacy is preserved to the employees in their work space and surroundings.

–13–

DISTINCT EMPLOYEE GROUPS

Two groups of persons deserve special mention—*government* (or *public)* employees and *union* employees. These employees are special in the sense that their legal rights evolved earlier than and different from those of persons who are employed in the nonunion private sector.

GOVERNMENT EMPLOYEES

If you are a nonmanagement public employee, you are both blessed and cursed by that status. You are blessed in the sense that for decades *merit systems* or *civil service laws* have protected you from discharge, except for cause, after completing a probationary period.

You are also the beneficiary of federal and state constitutional provisions that limit state action. For example, the First Amendment guarantee of free speech is a restriction on actions by the federal government. The Fourteenth Amendment applies that guarantee to the states, so that no state may interfere with those free speech rights. This restriction applies to public employers, generally. Therefore, over the years, many public employees who have been terminated for speaking their minds on matters of public concern have used the First and Fourteenth Amendments to protect their employment status. In contrast, with few exceptions, there are no free speech rights in the private sector. Except in very few states, an employer in the private sector may fire someone for taking a particular stand on a political issue.

Public employees with for cause or other similar protection that give them a reasonable expectation of continued employment, are said to have a *constitutional property interest* in their job that may not be taken away from them without *procedural due process*. That right entitles them to receive notice of the charges against them and an opportunity to be heard about those charges before a termination may be effected. Similarly, if they are falsely accused of serious wrongdoing, their *constitutional liberty interest* is impinged and a similar right to a hearing—to clear their name—springs into action. The Fourteenth Amendment has been a powerful weapon over the years to protect public employees.

On the other hand, public employees are cursed by myriad procedural obstacles and limitations on damages that apply in the public sector. In most states, public employees who sue under state law must comply with the procedural restrictions of that state's tort claims act. It used to be that the state could not be sued at all under the doctrine of sovereign immunity (the king could do no wrong). As holes in that theory developed, pressure mounted to abolish it altogether. The king reluctantly agreed, but only on certain conditions. First, there is typically a top limit placed on each state law claim.

The second condition is that the employee may be required to give the state notice of the tort claim within a certain period of time after the act giving rise to the claim. The actual starting date for that computation may be complicated. If you have a claim, you should entrust its calculation to a professional.

There are also requirements concerning the content of the claim and to whom it should be addressed. The requirement is typically so technical that an attorney should be consulted for the purpose of perfecting it. Other procedural limitations often stand in the way of obtaining complete relief for public employees. Federal employees are particularly subject to provisions that limit available relief, condition it on the giving of proper notice, or ban it altogether.

Modern Federal Civil Rights Legislation

It was not until May 24, 1972, that Congress extended the protection of *Title VII* of the *Civil Rights Act of 1964* to state and local government employees or applicants for employment. Two years later, Congress voted to make the *Equal Pay Act of 1963* and the *Age Discrimination in Employment Act of 1967* equally applicable. While the extension of Title VII to state and local governments was held to be constitutional,[196] the Supreme Court has since held that Congress' attempt to apply the *Age Discrimination in Employment Act*[197] and the *Americans with Disabilities Act*[198] was invalid. Therefore, state employees who believe they have been discriminated against because of age or disability must rely on some other state or federal constitutional, statutory, or common law theory for redress.

The Reconstruction Civil Rights Acts

The *Reconstruction Civil Rights Acts of 1866 and 1871*—long dormant because of restrictive court rulings—have become a real force in the protection of civil rights. They are usually presented in tandem with other civil rights claims, typically under *Title VII*, and interject different elements in the discrimination case, due to different rules as to administrative exhaustion, right to jury trial, and damages.

The Supreme Court has held that these Acts and Title VII are not mutually exclusive and, in fact, provide independent bases for potential liability against discriminating employers.[199]

Civil Rights Act of 1866 (42 U.S.C. Sec. 1981). This Act was adopted pursuant to the Thirteenth Amendment and was intended to afford all persons the same rights as white citizens. The thrust of the Act is to prohibit *racial discrimination*. Both white persons and black persons are protected by the Act.[200] As construed, the Act provides that blacks and whites have the same rights to make and enforce employment contracts.[201] Section 1981 protects employees from racial discrimination in both the public and private sectors.[202]

Civil Rights Act of 1871 (42 U.S.C. Sec. 1983). This Act was promulgated as part of the *Ku Klux Klan Act of 1871* to redress violations of federal rights by persons who purport to act under the authority, or *color*, of state law. As construed, Section 1983 has been applied to review the actions of state officials, counties, cities, and other municipal governments.

Section 1983 reads:

> *Every person who, under color of any statute, ordinance, regulation, custom, or usage, of any State or Territory or the District of Columbia, subjects, or causes to be subjected, any citizen of the United States or other person within the jurisdiction thereof to the deprivation of any rights, privileges, or immunities secured by the Constitution and laws, shall be liable to the party injured in an action at law, suit in equity, or other proper proceeding for redress.*

Under *Monell v. New York City Department of Social Services* (436 U.S. 658 (1978)) and its progeny, cities and other local governmental bodies are suable as persons. However, they are suable only when the act of the public official is pursuant to an express policy, custom, or usage of the municipality, or pursuant to a *de facto* policy of inaction evidenced by deliberate indifference to the rights of inhabitants by the municipality.[203] Actions that make policy on behalf of the municipality by persons with authority may also be within the scope of Section 1983.[204] States and state agencies are not *persons* suable under Section 1983.[205] However, *state officials* may be sued in their individual capacities for actions they undertake under *color of state law.*[206] Municipalities are immune from liability for punitive damages under Section 1983.[207] Punitive damages are recoverable against individual defendants.[208]

Application of Section 1983 to discrimination cases. In relation to employment cases, the Equal Protection Clause of the United States Constitution this law has applied to various types of unlawful discrimination, including cases of race discrimination,[209] sex discrimination,[210] age discrimination,[211] and discrimination on the basis of religion.[212]

The advantage of a Section 1983 claim for the employee in a discrimination case is that there is no administrative process that must be exhausted as there is with Title VII,[213] nor does the statute contain a statute of limitations. The courts will look to the most applicable state statute as the limitations period, which will typically be a longer period than under Title VII. Therefore, you may still have a claim under Section 1983 to assert even though your Title VII rights have expired. The final advantage is that there are no caps on damages under Section 1983, whereas damage limitations apply under Title VII.

Application of Section 1983 to First Amendment cases. Section 1983 provides relief for violators of all federal laws, not just employment discrimination laws. Therefore, a state or local government employee who is retaliated against for exercising free speech may sue the employer under Section 1983 for that violation.[214]

In *Mt. Healthy City Board of Education v. Doyle* (429 U.S. 274 (1977)), the Supreme Court established a two-part burden shifting inquiry for Section 1983 claims based upon the First Amendment. First, the employee must show that his or her conduct was constitutionally protected and that his or her conduct was a substantial or motivating factor in the employer's adverse action. Upon such a showing, the burden shifts to the employer to show that it would have reached the same decision even in the absence of the employee's protected conduct.

As for the first factor, not all speech in public-sector employment will be deemed constitutionally protected speech. Rather, such speech is protected only when it addresses a matter of public concern. Therefore, in *Rankin v. McPherson* (483 U.S. 378 (1987)), a comment by a public employee in reference to President Reagan, "I hope they get him," was held to be protected free speech. A matter that relates to the political, social, or other concern to the community has been said to be one entitled to constitutional protection.[215] So, for example, the mismanagement of a veteran's hospital has been held to be an issue of public concern.[216] However, speech that relates to the internal workings of a governmental office, even if it complains of unfairness or abusive treatment, may not be deemed protected.[217] In each case there will be a balancing of interests—the employee's interest in the speech against the employer's interest in maintaining the efficiency of public services.

The results are sometimes unpredictable. The scales have tipped in favor of protection in a case of a private complaint to supervisors to protest racially discriminatory school policies,[218] making a safety complaint,[219] a firefighting complaint about budget cuts,[220] and disclosure of possibly illegal wire taps.[221]

On the other hand, protection was not afforded in the case of a teacher who complained about class size and student discipline,[222] a professor's criticism about the internal process of selecting a university president,[223] and an employee's complaints about his or her own personal employment conditions, even though the complaints related to discrimination.[224]

Akin to the First Amendment, free speech cases are cases that claim a violation of the First Amendment's *freedom of association.* Thus, a city may not take action to ban its employees from endorsing political candidates outside of work hours.[225] Nor may a public official who is a member of one political party retaliate against a public employee because he or she is a member of a different party.[226]

Due Process

The due process clause of the Fifth and the Fourteenth Amendment to the United States Constitution limits the ability of government to impair individual property rights without *due process of law.* Employees at will, by definition, have no property rights to their position. However, because state or federal government employees have developed civil service or merit systems whereby certain employees may be removed only for cause, those employees are said to have a property right to their positions that may be taken away only after *procedural due process.*[227]

Those employees who are said to have a reasonable expectation of continued employment, based on that for cause protection, are said to be entitled to such procedural protection as is required to provide *fundamental fairness* before they may be terminated.[228] Typically, fundamental fairness requires notice of the charges and a fair opportunity to be heard prior to termination.[229] The pretermination hearing that is required, however, may be informal. The employee will not be allowed all of the procedural protections of a formal court hearing.

Good Name

Closely akin to the due process rights of certain public employees is the liberty interest they have in their *good name*. If a government employer falsely accuses an employee of theft, for example, that is said to *stigmatize* his or her reputational interest. In such cases, the employee is said to be entitled to a *name clearing hearing*.[230]

Federal Employees

The federal Civil Service Reform Act provides just cause termination protection for most federal employees. (5 U.S.C. Sec. 7501, and following.) In addition, that Act prescribes procedural requirements prior to termination that give the federal employee notice of the proposed action, an opportunity to respond, the right to legal counsel, and appeal rights—first to the Merit System Protection Board, then to the courts. If the federal worker is also a union member, the employee may opt to exercise the union grievance machinery instead.

For discrimination claims, federal employees have the most intricate internal procedural path to follow before they may seek judicial review of an agency action of any type of employee. They also have much shorter time lines to initiate action. For example, they must contact an EEO counselor within forty-five days of the act of discrimination to be timely. (29 C.F.R. Sec. 1614.105 (a).)

The Rehabilitation Act of 1974, not the Americans with Disabilities Act, applies to federal employees.

UNION EMPLOYEES

Like public employees, union employees have not had to worry about contract rights protection. Their collective bargaining agreement gives them protection. They can often be removed only for good cause. Progressive discipline may be required before termination. Labor law principles may call for their reinstatement if the punishment does not fit the crime.

On the other hand, the price for that protection has been dear. In some cases, courts have said that the contract rights under the collective bargaining agreement are all the rights the employee has.

Common law tort claims have sometimes been said to be *preempted* by the National Labor Relations Act or similar labor laws. When that is so, if the union employee misses a grievance filing deadline or has to deal with a weak union representative who cares more about the company's goodwill than the employee's rights, that person's job security may evaporate.

This predicament has been helped somewhat in the last twenty years with the development of the theory that the union owes a duty of fair representation to the employee. In extreme cases, the union member can sue the union and the employer for breach of that duty. Again, the time lines for instituting such suits is quite short, ranging from six months to twenty days.

Clearly, though, the for cause protection afforded to union employees generally gives them much more protection than workers in the unorganized workforce—most of whom are left without a remedy for an unfair discharge.

Sources of Law

Collective bargaining agreements provide good cause protection for union employees. Grievance machinery up to and usually including arbitration, are provided for in those agreements. Section 301 of the *Labor-Management Relations Act* authorizes federal courts to fashion a body of federal law for enforcement of those collective bargaining agreements. (29 U.S.C. Sec. 185 (a).)[231] Where arbitration is not provided for in the agreement, a judge will decide the dispute.

In addition, the National Labor Relations Act regulates the conduct of the parties to collective bargaining agreements in the private sector and prohibits certain *unfair labor practices* in their relationship with each other. (29 U.S.C. Sec. 160 (a).)

Employees under a collective bargaining agreement often wonder if they can go beyond that agreement in seeking remedy for employment law violations. Because there is a comprehensive legislative scheme that regulates labor management relations and the conduct of the parties to collective bargaining agreements, much of the law that has developed (as it pertains to employment rights of persons who also have collective bargaining rights) concerns the question of whether they may pursue other remedies. The concern of the courts is that the dispute is so closely related to the collective bargaining agreement that one of the applicable comprehensive federal labor laws is said to preempt other legal remedies.

In *San Diego Building Trade Council v. Garmon,* 359 U.S. 236 (1959), the Supreme Court held that employers could not sue labor unions in state court for damages for picketing. Even though the unions had not been selected by a majority of the employers they purported to represent, the subject matter of that suit related to activities that were arguably regulated by federal labor law. Since then, exceptions to that principle have eroded it. In 1966, the Supreme Court held that an employee who was defamed could bring a state court action against the employer because defamation is by nature an action that involves matters of traditional local interest.[232] Later, in 1983, the Supreme Court held that a state fraud action was similarly not preempted.[233]

Then, in 1988, the Supreme Court held that an employer's retaliatory discharge claim under Illinois state law was not preempted by Section 301 of the Labor-Management Relations Act because that issue was not *inextricably intertwined* with the provisions of a collective bargaining agreement.[234] In other words, to decide the case did not depend upon the interpretation of any provision of such agreement.

The Union's Duty of Fair Representation

A labor union is the exclusive bargaining agent for the employee. Moreover, a union employee cannot negotiate a separate contract with the employer. He or she is reliant on the union to fairly represent him or her in its enforcement. Therefore, the Supreme Court held in 1967 that a union owes a *duty of fair representation* to its members and that a member may bring an action against the union for breach of that duty for its arbitrary, discriminatory, or bad-faith conduct.[235]

It is not enough, said the court, that the union was wrong in making its decision not to arbitrate in that case. Rather, the issue is the motivation of the union and whether it acted out of personal hostility or bad faith. In such cases, the employee may sue both the employer and the union, contending that he or she was terminated without just cause, as required in the collective bargaining agreement, and that the suit is required because the union breached its duty of fair representation. Generally, before suing the employer for breach of contract under those circumstances, the employee must have exhausted the grievance process.[236]

As a result of the high legal bar imposed by the Supreme Court, mere negligence on the part of the union will ordinarily not suffice. In investigating the grievance, for example, the union is given wide latitude in deciding when and how to conduct it. It just may not be *perfunctory*.[237] However, an unexplained and unexcused failure on the part of the union to timely process a grievance may be deemed sufficiently *arbitrary* to cause a suit to lie.[238]

SECTION TWO:

Using Employment Law

The following are reflections based on more than a quarter century of experience in interviewing clients, screening, and trying employment cases. While that experience may be useful in helping explain certain tendencies in the law and behavior of people and groups, each situation is unique and dynamic. What is seen as an insight today, may be way off the mark tomorrow as it pertains to your situation.

The following chapters are not intended to be a substitute for legal advice. They are intended as a device to open your eyes to possibilities and stimulate your thinking. Any particular strategy discussed in these pages should only be attempted after coordinating with and obtaining good legal advice from a competent employment attorney in your state.

–14– REASONS FOR DISCRIMINATION

With all the laws that regulate the workplace, the comment sometimes made is that employment concerns will occupy the attention of the courts less and less. The error in that reasoning is assuming that people abide by the law.

Sadly, as long as humans are involved, we will continue to see wrongful treatment of employees. As long as humans are making employment decisions, liability will be generated. The aspects of the human factor that are brought into an employment lawsuit are numerous.

PREJUDICE

Each of us is *biased* or *prejudiced* in some matters. For example, we prefer coffee to tea, we do not approve of coffee or tea; we go to a certain church, or we do not approve of religious practices in a different church. In our country, we have the right to be prejudiced. However, in certain cases, those prejudices have turned to active discrimination in the workplace. Certain classes of people have routinely suffered as a consequence of that discrimination. Therefore, laws have been passed to provide protection to those classes of persons. The prejudice typically follows certain patterns.

Race and National Origin Discrimination

Because of the fear of the unfamiliar or the prejudices born of societal stereotyping, social segregation still prevails in the workplace between different races. Sometimes workers will still engage in racial epithets or jokes that preserve these stereotypes.

The fear of the unfamiliar is sometimes compounded when the minority worker is of foreign national origin. The worker might face stereotypes not only about race, but also about his or her country of origin. A foreign accent can heighten the sense that this foreigner does not belong here. This prejudice can be reflected in undeserved low marks on performance reviews in categories that rate communication skills.

Gender Discrimination

Women are still viewed as newcomers in the workplace. In some companies, women have not achieved management status. Newly promoted female managers who do their jobs can be seen as pushy and too aggressive. The value of their work is sometimes underrated. Occasionally, a male manager's job is reclassified to a lower level job and is filled by a woman who continues to do all the essential tasks of her predecessor. In a few cases, you still hear "that's a man's job" or "women should not be allowed out here." Women's dedication to their work as opposed to their families might be questioned more frequently than a man's. Male managers may also view women as employees who will quit the company to raise a family.

Age Discrimination

Older workers can be thought of as less productive and more difficult to train or to adapt to changing procedures compared with younger workers. If older workers are approaching age 62 or 65, managers may wonder why they do not just go ahead and retire. In making promotion decisions, managers can often be found to say such things as "let's get some new blood in here" or "why recycle the old news?"

Disability Discrimination

The array of prejudices about disabled workers are as varied as the number of disabilities themselves. A person with depression can be thought of as weak, vulnerable, and one who cannot stand the rigors of the position. A person with the AIDS virus can be treated fearfully as having a dreaded and potentially contagious disease.

RESENTMENT DUE TO AFFIRMATIVE ACTION

Workers can find themselves resented in the workplace by their managers and coworkers. This resentment may stem from who they are (their race, gender, age, etc.) or what they have done (filed a claim, received a promotion, reported harassment, etc.).

Workers who have been given protection by discrimination laws are viewed as receiving *special favors*. The prevailing attitude might be that the worker got where he or she is because of the worker's race or sex, even when *affirmative action* was not a factor at all.

In the construction industry, contractors who have government contracts must comply with affirmative action requirements. Sometimes contractors hire women or minorities only because the contractor may otherwise lose the contract. Certain trades have notoriously excluded women and blacks from active participation. Were it not for these hiring requirements, these groups would remain the victim of systematic hiring discrimination.

Sometimes, though, the woman or minority who is hired finds that to be only the first hurdle to overcome in achieving equal treatment. The contractor itself may set the stage for a hostile work environment. Sometimes when a minority or woman is hired, the contractor informs coworkers that they *had to hire one*. Sometimes the woman or minority is put on jobs away from the rest of the crew; is not given proper training, tools, or equipment; or is not given the jobs that will be longer in duration or that pay overtime.

FRUSTRATION DUE TO ACCOMMODATIONS

Under the law, a disabled person who can perform the work with reasonable accommodation must not be discriminated against. The law does not define *reasonable accommodation* and its form is varied. A truck driver with a bad back may require a cushion or special seat. A worker who is allergic to chemicals used in a manufacturing process may require special gloves or a breathing apparatus. Whatever the form, workers who must be accommodated often find themselves viewed as *damaged property* who require an accommodation that is too expensive. They get the sense from the employer that the whole process of ascertaining whether they need accommodation and accommodating them is frustrating. The energy that is directed to that process is sometimes viewed as disruptive to the efficiency of the workplace.

ANGER

Anger is very much a part of our humanity. Anger may arise from simple frustration at not being able to get our work out on time, or when someone challenges our authority, embarrasses us, or causes us to lose face. In the workplace, anger may be caused in many ways.

Coercion

It is not unusual for a worker to be coerced or pressured to engage in questionable practices for his or her employer. This may involve giving false testimony against a coworker, changing expense accounts in the boss' favor, filling out false reports to government agencies or business associates, or just standing by and failing to perform assigned duties as a watchdog. Employers who are responsible for ensuring compliance with equal employment opportunity laws, occupational health and safety laws, and other regulatory laws are often counseled to be *team players* and are admonished for blowing the whistle.

Retaliation

The retaliation that follows the anger is of particular concern to the courts. Legal protection covers whistleblowers in public agencies, persons who testify in good faith at unemployment, workers' compensation or civil rights hearings, workers who file civil rights or workers' compensation claims, workers who report civil rights violations, and workers who file wage claims.

Court decisions protect workers who have merely threatened to report health violations that the workers in good faith believe have occurred and workers who have resisted sexual harassment. The courts have indicated their willingness to take strong action against other forms of abusive retaliatory termination, harassment, or to a changed attitude toward the worker which alters his or her fortune with that employer.

GREED

Workers who are viewed by the employer as standing in the way of greater productivity are often earmarked for oblivion. For example, a disabled worker may require costly accommodations. A worker who has filed for workers' compensation may be receiving benefits. The payment of those benefits may cost the company money directly if it is self-insured, or, together with other claims, may affect the rate that the company must pay to its insurer for workers' compensation coverage.

The company may believe that a worker who is not a team player and does not cooperate in an unlawful scheme will cost the company money. As a workplace matures in age, the employer may become concerned that the elimination of older workers is desirable to save on pension benefits or the cost of health care.

FEAR

Employees who are injured are shunned by management not only because of current costs and disruption to the organization, but also because of the fear of the future cost that may be incurred. Workers who know of employer misdealings are feared because they know too much and are viewed with suspicion as to whether and when they will blow the whistle.

–15–
WORKPLACE HARASSMENT

Harassment only becomes illegal if it is committed because of race, sex, age, religion, disability, or other protected class status or activity.

Generally, laws apply to prohibit discrimination in terms, conditions, and privileges of employment, and therefore, harassment because of protected class status or activity. However, the occasions in which a lawsuit is recommended against an employer on behalf of a current employee is rare.

Juries associate damages with economic loss. The person whose focus is harassment has lost nothing economically. Unless some other act has occurred, which on its own carries an impact (such as an assault or an invasion of privacy), a jury member might resent being dragged into court to hear a case about a mean boss, when he or she faces that every day. As a result, you may find it difficult to find a lawyer willing to take your case on a contingent basis to proceed with a harassment suit that has not involved economic loss.

Instead, in most situations, the primary goal should be to end the harassment, and energy should be directed toward that end. Most employees do not want to sue. They just want to work and be left alone.

Therefore, if you go to a lawyer with a complaint about unlawful harassment, your lawyer will likely advise you of the limited legal options you have, assess whether the situation has become so bad you could claim *constructive discharge* (which will not often be the case), and counsel you about the actions you have taken thus far to stop the harassment.

REPORTING ILLEGAL HARASSMENT

The Supreme Court has ruled that an employer can escape liability altogether for on-the-job harassment that does not involve a *tangible employment action* if it can show that you unreasonably failed to follow company procedures in reporting the harassment. (*Burlington Industries, Inc. v. Ellerth*, 524 U.S. 742 (1998); *Faragher v. Boca Raton*, 524 U.S. 775 (1998).)

Apart from the legal impact of those rulings, it only makes economic sense that before quitting or suing, you give the employer the opportunity to do the right thing. So the first thing your lawyer may advise is to find out what the system is at your workplace. Find the employee handbook you were given when you were first hired. Read it. If you cannot find it, call your company's human resources department and ask for a copy. Once you read it, your lawyer may advise you to comply with its requirements. You may not have realized it at the time, but many employers require new employees to sign a statement acknowledging receipt of an employee handbook and agreeing to follow its terms.

You may have special knowledge that causes you to believe that if you report wrongdoing, nothing adverse will happen to the harasser. This may be based on the status the harasser has in the company or his or her relationship to the CEO. The harasser may even be the CEO. But in a lawsuit, the corporation is the typical defendant, not the CEO. Corporations have human resource departments to help protect them from liability, even from that caused by CEOs.

If you do not report the harassment, the corporate lawyer will be able to point that out to the judge or jury. That may prejudice your case or defeat it altogether. You may think there is no practical point in reporting harassment at the time because it would not do any good. But juries are instructed that they cannot base their verdict on guesswork or speculation. It may be that you will have to let events play out. You may have to play your part in allowing them to do so.

RETALIATION FOR REPORTING ILLEGAL HARASSMENT

To report unlawful harassment has legal significance. It expands your legal rights. Once you report unlawful discrimination, it is illegal to retaliate against you for doing so. Your company knows that as well. The company wants to avoid liability.

Many companies have a nonretaliation clause in their equal employment opportunity (EEO) policy. Most include mention of such a requirement in their EEO management training seminars. Almost all will instinctively individually counsel the manager or employee who is being reported not to retaliate.

The manager or employee whom you report will probably learn that the report was made, despite what you may hear from human resources that the employer will keep the report confidential. The problem is, it usually cannot keep the report confidential from the one person who stands to retaliate. Once a complaint of harassment is made, the employer is legally obligated to take immediate corrective action designed to end the harassment. It cannot do that before it investigates the charge. It would not be much of an investigation unless it gets both sides to the story. So it must interview the harasser.

In interviewing the harasser, the employer must give enough detail about the charge so that the harasser has something concrete to which to respond. Most human resource managers will not think it is fair to the accused to merely ask "Did you harass anybody?" Instead, they will put a charge into concrete terms. "There has been a charge against you, claiming that yesterday in the lunchroom, you called a female employee a bitch and threw a pencil at her. Did that happen?" As you can see, while the reporting employee was not named, the harasser will probably be able to identify who made the report.

COOPERATING WITH THE INVESTIGATION

It is important to report harassment. It is also important to be careful in doing so. One of the reasons for that is once you make the report, you become duty bound to cooperate with whatever investigation the employer initiates. Although you may have made an initial report to the supervisor or a particular human resources individual, the person performing the investigation may be someone else. If so, expect to have to repeat the story to the investigator. The matter may have such high visibility that a higher ranking human resources manager will also want to hear it.

Once you tell your story and the investigator interviews the harasser, he or she will come back to you for a follow-up session to get even more information. You may have to tell your story several times. Your lawyer will probably advise that at all times you must cooperate with the employer's investigation. If you do not and you are terminated for failing to cooperate, that may rob the case of the requisite causal connection between the protected class status or activity and the termination.

Because the employer knows you can be terminated for failing to cooperate, sometimes it tries to misuse the investigation as a tool to precipitate your termination on grounds that leaves it blameless. For example, a company's investigation of a woman's report of a hostile sexual environment may be twisted defensively to focus on her own conduct, under the pretense that it must discern whether the harassment was *unwelcome* to her. The investigator may question others about the sexual jokes the reporting employee told or laughed about.

The investigator may then ask the reporting employee to admit she had done the same thing. A refusal, even a rightful refusal, to make such an admission has been intentionally misconstrued as a failure to cooperate, supposedly justifying a termination. The litigation that follows turns on whether the investigation itself had become defensive and hostile and whether the person conducting it had perverted its purpose.

THE REPORTING AFTERMATH

Even if your harassment complaint is investigated and found to be well taken, once you report harassment, things are never the same. The harasser may relent. You may not feel the stress of the continued harassment. But that stress may be replaced by the stress associated with a whole host of new patterns of conduct from the harasser and his or her supporters or the employer itself.

The harasser may no longer harass you because he or she has been instructed in some fashion to watch his or her behavior around you. The harasser may have been instructed not to engage in any conduct that could even be perceived to be harassment. The accused becomes so skiddish that the result is predictable—the accused stays away from you altogether. As a result, what may have been a productive and cooperative working relationship, apart from the harassment and its report, is impaired. You may not be able to do your job as well because of that distancing. You may not be able to get questions answered. You may be left out of the loop if there are changes to the office procedures or manufacturing process.

Some postreporting crisis period exists in every case. Typically, an employee can expect to weather the storm for at least thirty days. Hopefully, things will settle back down when the harasser and his or her supporters see that you really are not interested in wanting to get anyone in trouble—you just want to work. If it does not settle down though, and you find your work is suffering for it, your attorney may advise you to go back to human resources to report the situation. At that point, human resources is given a chance to intervene and mediate a return to normalcy.

On other occasions, the harasser or his or her supporters may be more overt in their harassment. The harasser may become cold towards you or may no longer greet you in the morning. He or she may give you icy stares. Although he or she may not initially intend to interfere with your work, when he or she is not around to answer your questions, it frustrates you. If he or she comes to realize that your work is suffering because of the distancing, the harasser may try to distance further to cause further erosion in your work quality and then criticize you for it.

The harasser may start documenting your performance. It is not unusual in discovery to find that not one such paper was created until after the report of harassment was made. Then a whole slew of them follow. After the harasser believes he or she has sufficient documentation, you may be placed on formal discipline. It may not be easy to go back to human resources a second time, particularly after an unpleasant first experience, but it is usually best not to let the situation get too far down that track before you do. If you do not, having once reported the matter, the employer will be in a position to argue to a jury that the retaliation you are contending occurred is doubtful because you never reported it.

Remember, it is typically easier to prove retaliation than the underlying discrimination. You do not have to worry about proving the person is prejudiced against you because you are black, a woman, or disabled. You just have to prove that after your report, retaliation occurred. The cause and effect relationship between those acts is easier to prove from such things as timing and the absence of other factors to account for differential treatment, than a racist or sexist state of mind, for example.

COMMON QUESTIONS CONCERNING WORKPLACE HARASSMENT

Q: Should I pursue the employer's internal grievance procedure?

A: Internal grievance procedures are set up by employers out of self-interest. They help keep disputes all in the family. They do not typically result in a favorable outcome for the employee. The consequence of a favorable finding that unlawful harassment occurred could be used as an admission in any later civil proceeding that it did occur. As a result, what you often find are grievance reports that use a lot of *weasel words*. They often refuse to admit that discrimination occurred. They claim that after investigation, there was no conclusive evidence of discrimination. They may unreasonably place blame on both parties. Or, there may be no report written if its publication is thought to be too incriminating to the employer.

Even so, because of a Supreme Court precedent, the employee who unreasonably refuses to utilize the employer's grievance mechanism may prejudice his or her own case by that failure. After reviewing the particular grievance machinery in question, your attorney *may* advise you to pursue it.

Q: I don't think I can take it anymore. What should I do?

A: Your health is number one. But apart from your health interest, it is rarely in your best interest to resign. It is always easier to get employment while you are currently employed.

It may be difficult to continue to work under hostile circumstances. If you view continued employment as a tool you need to help you in the short-term to transition elsewhere for the next sixty to ninety days, that can give you a different perspective on your ability to continue. It may also prejudice your right to bring a lawsuit or to collect unemployment benefits if you quit. By all means, consult with a lawyer before quitting.

After evaluating your situation, your lawyer may be of the opinion that while the environment was not ideal, more would be needed to show that the environment you are working in is *legally actionable*. That information, while it may not control what you do, may inform you of the legal consequences of your action if you act right then. Sometimes, such advice can be sobering.

In cases in which you sense that another act of harassment is about to occur anyway and you are told that it would greatly strengthen any constructive discharge case if you did not quit until after it occurred, you may decide it prudent to ride it out for the additional time it takes for the further act to occur before resigning to remove any speculation about your employer's intent. In doing so, you would vastly improve your case and its value.

Q: I want to leave. Should I just ask for a severance?

A: Typically not. If you let your employer know you want to leave, you will have nothing left to sell. If you approach your employer and say, "I want out; just pay me a severance" the employer will be tempted to reply, "You are free to leave any time you wish."

Before tipping your hand, it is best to consult with a lawyer. After laying out the situation to a lawyer, becoming introduced to the legal principles that apply and thinking calmly and coolly outside your work environment about what is best for you, your health, your employment record, your personal finances, and your marketability, the two of you, together, can come to an agreement about what is in *your* best interest.

It may be that because you are so stressed, you would accept next to nothing to leave. The employer will not pay you a penny without a complete release from liability. You do not want to make a rash decision about releasing your legal rights while you are extremely upset.

Q: When should my lawyer get involved with my employer?

A: Generally, when you have nothing left to lose. Once a lawyer gets involved, it changes the chemistry in the workplace. All of a sudden you are viewed as someone who would sue your employer. Relationships change not only with your supervisors, but also with your peers. Word gets around that you are threatening a lawsuit. Your coworkers may avoid you for fear they would otherwise be perceived by the employer to be a witness on your behalf. While you may obtain relief in the short term from the stress of an impending termination, you may come to feel a different stress from the hostility that follows from what is taken to be a blatant act of disloyalty.

However, if you are in your late fifties, have worked in that establishment for many years, have limited skills, and that is the only place in town that provides work for people with your skills, you and your lawyer may decide you have no choice but to fight to keep the job you have—at all costs. Then a firm, factual, but respectful letter to your employer from a lawyer may be in order.

Still, if the matter is one of work-related harassment that your employer can reasonably contend it does not know is going on, your lawyer will probably ask you to put the employer on notice that the harassment is happening yourself. This is usually sound advice. You minimize the probability of retaliation if you put the employer on notice when you merely follow its request in its employee handbook that you do so, rather than by obtaining a lawyer (which is always viewed as threatening), no matter how nonthreatening the approach. That way, by reporting according to procedure, you are perceived as being merely cooperative.

Sometimes the employer is even grateful for the heads up. From a legal standpoint, in many cases the law requires such notice and generally, juries expect it as a matter of fairness.

Q: How can I negotiate a better severance?

A: Sometimes when an employee comes to my office and I conclude that the person does not have a case, I will tell the employee that he or she is in a better position to negotiate a severance than I am because there is nothing I would be able to put in a lawyer's letter to give the employer cause for concern. The employer's lawyer would read my letter, call me, and ask me, "Come on, what do you really have?" It would take him or her about two seconds to learn I do not have anything. That gives the employer's lawyer the opportunity to go back to his or her client and earn his or her fee by reporting that the employer need not pay my demand, because I do not have a case.

So, first go to a headhunter or employment agency, tell them who you are, what you do, and how much you make. Ask how long it will take for you to get work at or near what you are now earning. They will tell you it will take about x months. Then you take that information back to your employer. Tell them that you can appreciate the offer of x weeks, but that XYZ agency, the most respected in town, has told you it will take x months to replace that income. Can they enhance that offer in order to allow you to make ends meet until you land your next job?

With this approach you have not said anything about lawyers or lawsuits. In the back of the employer's mind, however, it will know that if it does not meet your needs you may have no choice but to go to an attorney. The fear that you might do so may give you greater leverage than anything your lawyer might say under those circumstances. Of course, before you know whether you have legal leverage, you must first consult with a lawyer. If you do not have a legal case, your lawyer may suggest a different approach.

—16—
SURVIVING EMPLOYER DISCIPLINE

You may currently be subject to pending *disciplinary action* by your employer. Even though you are an employee at will, most employers will adopt a disciplinary system. They do this for their own protection. They want a system in place to prevent rogue managers who are biased because of race, sex, or some other status from creating liability. Therefore, they adopt a system to generate some modicum of uniformity of treatment.

When questioned in court cases, most employers will contend that they have a policy of being fair to their employees. They will admit that towards that end they give employees notice of perceived deficiency and a fair opportunity to correct any such deficiency.

Usually a system is installed that incorporates the concept of *progressive discipline*. Under that type of system, the employee is given mild discipline at first, typically a *verbal warning*, but if the problem is not corrected, progressively ascending levels of discipline are given before termination—a written warning, a second written warning or suspension, then termination. If an employer deviates from its own personnel policies, that variance may serve as proof of differential treatment in a discrimination case.

SURVIVING PENDING DISCIPLINE

The first thing you usually can do to survive pending discipline is to respond positively and constructively. You may disagree with your supervisor that the discipline was merited. However, your supervisor is the boss and you are not. If the matter becomes a struggle over who is in charge, you will lose that battle.

By the same token, it is frequently the case that conflicts that rise to the level of formal discipline are precisely that—a struggle for authority. Your supervisor may sense that you do not respect him or her. They may be threatened by you because you are smarter, more experienced, or have greater support amongst your peers. There may be some history that you are vocal, argumentative, or simply unskilled in verbal communications and come off sounding like a smart aleck.

Instead of arguing with your supervisor about the wisdom or fairness of giving you discipline, you will be surprised by how easy it is to diffuse a potentially volatile situation by simply accepting the discipline and demonstrating your willingness to subordinate yourself to your supervisor's authority. In the vast majority of cases, once you do that, you will find that your supervisor will relent.

The most unpleasant part of any manager's job is to manage the personnel problems that come with it. If he or she can avoid having to deal with an employee with formal discipline, it will happen.

VERBAL WARNING

If you have been unable to avoid the first step in the disciplinary process—a verbal warning—your job is to immediately correct the objective behavior that is to account for the warning.

For example, if tardiness is the problem, you must take extraordinary care not to repeat the offense. If you are an employee at will, it does not matter that you were late to work for a reason beyond your control, like a freeway tie-up or an alarm that did not go off.

You will be held responsible for being at work on time, regardless whether you are at fault. On the other hand, if a health problem is to account for the tardiness, you will need to supply the employer with information sufficient to cause it to view this not as a problem in your behavior, but a problem in your health.

Further, your employer cannot be expected to rely on *your* medical opinion. It may be legally sufficient to put your employer on notice of a need for accommodation by just telling your employer that you have a medical concern. However, in order to get your employer to fully cooperate, you will need to present the employer with a note from a doctor informing the employer of the diagnosis, telling the employer that you are under treatment for the problem, and requesting some kind of accommodation.

An accommodation in such cases could be anything from a leave to undergo treatment, to a relaxation in the attendance policy for a brief period of time while you are undergoing it, or to allowing you to work from home during the treatment period. Every case is different. It depends on the type, severity, and the difficulties of the disorder. It also depends how the particular requested accommodation would affect the employer given its size, the size of its workforce at your facility, and other similar factors.

If the verbal warning is more subjective in nature (for example, a poor attitude), your task is more difficult. Again, such warnings are usually related to the employee's refusal to show respect to the supervisor. You need to show respect even when you do not respect your supervisor, in both verbal and nonverbal communications.

You can show respect by keeping disrespectful opinions to yourself when speaking to your supervisor, particularly in front of others. Even well-meant suggestions, if habitual and presented in a know-it-all way, can be construed by your supervisor to be quarrelsome behavior. However, if your supervisor believes you have a tendency to engage in such behavior, you will have to take care that your non-verbal communication is not offensive in the workplace. A disgusted facial expression, a heavy sigh of frustration, crossed arms, or a defensive stare can challenge your supervisor. If you engage in such behavior, even unintentionally, you may bait your supervisor into calling you out to say what you really think. That is never good.

Because your attitude may be difficult to change or because you find it difficult to hide your true feelings (unless your employer ordered you to keep the matter strictly confidential), look to some peer in the workplace whom you trust for advice as to whether you are displaying disrespect and in what ways you are doing that. Then, as you internalize whatever advice he or she gives, you may wish to use that person as a *coach* to ensure that you are changing the way you present yourself in the workplace.

If you disrespect a supervisor to others behind his or her back, it will be even harder not to display that disrespect in the supervisor's presence. Indeed, the source of the problem may have been that your supervisor heard that you were bad-mouthing him or her to others. Once that stops outside the supervisor's presence, the supervisor will know it. It will be easier for you to display respect to the supervisor in his or her presence when you have ceased the bad-mouthing and therefore do not feel you have to keep up appearances.

At first, check in with your coach two or three times a day for a week or so. Then daily for two to three weeks, or until the two of you are satisfied that if there is a problem, the problem is not you. Make sure that both you and your coach keep what you are doing confidential. An employer does not appreciate someone stirring up trouble by broadcasting that his or she is being unfairly disciplined.

WRITTEN WARNING

If you have been unable to stem the tide and your supervisor steps it up to the next level and issues you a written warning—do not react in anger. Whatever you do under the influence of anger will probably be wrong and damaging to your career. Again, particularly in cases of persons with long, distinguished careers, the problem is not one of performance. The supervisor in such cases is usually new, feels threatened by that person's superior expertise, or feels that the person is resistant to change and stubbornly insistent on clinging to the old ways of doing things. If you become incensed and challenge your supervisor for having the nerve to give you such a thing, that will only tend to make the supervisor think that he or she cannot work with you. Therefore, do not react immediately, take time to reflect before you do.

That does not mean that you cannot say anything about it. Typically, a written warning will be given to you in person. The supervisor will often be accompanied by someone from human resources. You may be told verbally why you are getting a written warning. You may simply be told to read it or it may be read to you. In any event, try to keep calm and be nonargumentative.

Stay focused on what you are hearing. You cannot stay focused if you become too agitated. Try to center yourself and breathe while you are listening. That way when you are asked if you understood what was just told or read to you, you will be in a position to gather information.

If necessary, seek clarification without being argumentative. Not all managers and people in human resources are clear in their communications. The written warning may not be clear in its identification of the incident on which it is based or in setting forth the expectations for your future performance. You may need to seek clarification about what it is that you may have done to merit the warning. This may be necessary, particularly if no one spoke with you about your perspective on the incident before concluding that you were guilty of the offense.

If you have information about the merits of the charge, you can ask permission to say something in your defense. Rarely, though, will whatever you say make any difference. Basically, you simply want to have the employer explain what it thinks you did wrong and what you need to do to correct the problem.

Performance Improvement Plan

The written warning may take the form of what is sometimes called a *plan of assistance* or *performance improvement plan*. Most often such plans are instituted after a poor annual performance appraisal, but they can follow or become a part of a written warning. Under such plans, you are told that your performance must improve to a certain level within a specified period of time or else you will be terminated. Human resource managers are taught that in developing such plans they are to interject as much objectivity as possible, so that the supervisor and employer will be able to identify aspects of and recognize what the employer deems to be successful performance. Performance goals are then set for the employee to meet within a given time frame. They are taught that those goals are to be realistic and attainable.

If the expectation of you in the written warning or plan of assistance is so subjective that you cannot be sure what performance is expected or how it will be measured, try to negotiate clearer standards. There may be particular obstacles to meet stated goals that should be considered as provisions or exceptions. It could be that you are being asked to adhere to a particular production requirement on a printing press, but that with some jobs you can get that production and others you cannot. It may be that you have firm orders that are about to come in or it is the time of year that a big slow job is about to start. That should be mentioned in your effort to negotiate a fair set of goals. On the other hand, if you contentiously argue that their plan is too vague and demand they make clear exactly what it is you are expected to do—do not worry; they will. It is then likely you will regret having made the point.

Once you commence your performance during the plan, you may be required to meet with your supervisor periodically to update your performance under the plan. Let your supervisor take the lead on that. If your supervisor misses a meeting, do not insist on having one. That may be a sign that he or she is losing interest. Allow the issues your supervisor has with you to take lower priority on his or her list. Likewise, do not remind the supervisor that you are a problem by continually asking, "How am I doing?" Just take care of your performance.

If issues come up during the performance period that call for clarification from your employer, freely seek it and memorialize the instructions you are given in a respectful confirming memo or email.

At the end of the performance period, you are going to be wondering what comes next. You will have a natural urge to seek reassurance that your employer is not planning on firing you. You must resist that urge. If you go to your employer and ask, "Are you going to fire me?" that only reminds your supervisor that they can. Believe it or not, your employer will typically have more pressing issues than you to think of. Your goal is to allow those other pressing issues to be the focus of attention.

SUSPENSION OR INVOLUNTARY LEAVE

The most serious discipline, short of termination, is a *suspension*. Most employers do not suspend for performance deficiencies after a written warning; they just terminate. However, some employers feel that for some offenses, such as excessive absenteeism, it does not hurt to give an otherwise productive employee one more chance to change his or her behavior. Being placed on suspension is like a *last chance agreement*. Once you return, you are bound to strictly comply or else you will be fired.

The most frequent question that arises in the case of suspensions is what happens when you return and your performance is perfect for the rest of that year and the better part of the next year. At what point does the suspension become so old or stale that it is unreasonable for the employer to just terminate you for another offense without going through the disciplinary steps again? If you are an employee at will, no noncontractual obligation will require the employer to start over, unless you can prove that its failure to do so would be discriminatory because of protected class states or protected activity, as compared with other persons in the workforce.

Involuntary leave, with or without pay, is used by employers when employees are charged with serious misconduct in order to get them out of the workplace pending investigation. Employees can be placed on leave with or without previous discipline. Employers who are charged with sexual harassment, who are first-line supervisors charged with abusive conduct of their peers, or are suspected of employee theft are often sent home, typically with pay, while the investigation proceeds. The leave may be converted to an unpaid leave and often is at the point where the employee who is sent home either fails to cooperate with the investigation, abandons employment, or is believed by the employee to be guilty of the offense.

One problem that sometimes occurs in such cases is the employer who uses the occasion of the placement of an employee on leave to discriminate or retaliate against him or her by allowing the leave to go on interminably. Each day a manager is out of the workplace, his or her authority erodes. Sometimes a lawyer's help is required in such cases to gently motivate the employer to expeditiously conclude the investigation, and, if no grounds exist for termination, to restore the employee to his or her rightful position.

UNION EMPLOYEES

Of course, union workers can *grieve* some forms of disciplinary action, depending upon their union contact and its definitions of what constitutes a grievable offense. Since union workers have so much more protection from termination than at-will employees in that they require cause for termination (in many cases, it has been collectively bargained that some form of prior discipline precede a termination for cause), the stakes are higher if a union worker receives a formal written warning. On the one hand, the employee does not want to be perceived as a disgruntled worker who files a grievance with little provocation.

On the other, unless a written warning is challenged, he or she will be one step closer to termination. Therefore, if you are a union worker, consult with your business agent or shop steward on the advisability of filing a grievance. The most important thing to note is that the time for filing such grievances is often very short. Some allow just a matter of days. So know your contract and talk to your union representative immediately.

THE AFTERMATH

Once you survive the formal warning period, there will be the aftermath to deal with. The discipline will remain a part of your personnel file. If there is a recurrence of the offense, more serious discipline could follow. It may influence your next performance review, raise, and whether you get a promotion. But first you have a relationship you need to deal with—the one with your boss. There needs to be a whole lot of mending, as soon as possible. You need to help put closure on this episode and show the supervisor that there are no hard feelings.

One way to start mending the relationship is to employ what is called the *three contact rule*. Pick out three reasons to ask your supervisor's advice about something once each week, over the next three-week period. Select subjects that are safe so that you will be prepared to follow whatever advice they give. Approach your supervisor and ask his or her opinion about that subject. Appear interested in his or her opinion and receptive to your supervisor's advice. Let him or her know later that you have acted on the advice and you appreciate the help.

On the other hand, there are some supervisors who rule by fear and intimidation. That kind of supervisor would never be happy about anyone questioning him or her about anything. If that is your supervisor, you should show respect by simply staying away.

Finally, remember that the best strategy for keeping your job and winning the lawsuit is the same—to be the best employee you can be.

TIPS TO SURVIVE EMPLOYER DISCIPLINE

- Do not make it about a struggle over who is boss.
- Demonstrate your willingness to comply.
- Consider using a *coach* to ensure that you are not acting disrespectfully.
- If your supervisor gives you further discipline, do not react in anger.
- Respectfully try to clarify what is expected.
- Do not keep asking, "How am I doing?"
- Do not insist that your boss keep the scheduled one-on-ones with you.
- Clarify any vague instructions and document your performance and any problems or requests for support.
- Never ask, "Am I going to be fired?"
- Once you survive, consider using the three contact rule to put closure on the crisis period.

–17–
HANDLING A TERMINATION

You have been terminated. You have to explain what happened to your spouse, children, and friends. Worse yet, you have to explain it to yourself. Even when you know you were wrongfully dealt with, you cannot help but wonder why it happened. You will ask yourself whether you could have done something to make a difference or whether you should have handled things in a different way. To feel self-doubt is normal.

You may experience psychological symptoms associated with stress—sleeplessness, loss of appetite, extreme fatigue, etc. You may need the assistance of a psychological counselor. You will certainly need the support of your family. A termination is often unexpected and always traumatic. But do not panic.

If you seek the advice of a lawyer about your termination, here are some things your lawyer may ask you to do during that trying time if you feel you have been wrongly terminated.

- Write a narrative of what occurred in the termination meeting and of the events leading up to the termination.
- Request a copy of your personnel file.
- If you were not given a reason for your termination, ask your boss why you were terminated. If your boss does not know, ask your boss' supervisor. Under the laws of most states, they are not required by law to give you an answer either orally or in writing. If they refuse to give you an answer, however, they would look foolish, if not hostile, in the eyes of a judge and jury.
- Tell your attorney why you believe you were terminated and provide all information that supports your belief. Give your

attorney a copy of your narrative, personnel file, and any other documents you may have that relate to your termination.

- Give your attorney the names, addresses, and telephone numbers of any persons you believe know something helpful about your case.
- Cooperate with your attorney in scheduling interviews of some of your witnesses before proceeding.
- Ensure you receive all the pay and benefits to which you are entitled. Apart from your final wages, this will often include accrued and unused vacation pay or promised severance. You may also stand to receive future commissions or a *pro rata* share of a bonus, depending upon your agreement with your employer.
- **DO NOT SIGN** a *release of liability* in favor of your employer without consulting with your attorney.
- File timely grievances with your union or your civil service commission. Sometimes you can do either. You may wish to consult with your attorney about which avenue to pursue.
- Do not prejudice your case by telling the boss off or by writing long letters of protest to company or political officials. Many cases have been turned away when prejudicial remarks of that sort clouded otherwise good prospects for recovery.
- Do not prejudice your case by improperly removing documents. The Supreme Court has held that damages may be cut off by such acts. If in doubt as to the propriety of a course of action, talk to your lawyer.
- If you are in need of emotional counseling, seek professional help. Your health comes first. Do not be ashamed to admit that you need professional help if you are having trouble coping with the trauma of a termination. On the other hand, in most states, and in most types of cases, you do not have to seek such help to prove a case. A jury can listen to you and assess your damages based on your testimony or the testimony of a family member. Ask your attorney whether you are in a state that requires expert testimony to establish a recoverable loss for the type of claim you will be asserting.

- As soon as you are able, look for other work. A plaintiff in an employee rights case always has the obligation to show that reasonable efforts were made to mitigate (or lessen) damages by seeking other employment. Consult with your attorney about what exactly will be expected of you in terms of the geographical area of your search, the type of work you should be pursuing, and the pay range you would be expected to find acceptable.
- In looking for other work, remember the cardinal rule—work is your best asset and a lawsuit is your least asset. Every lawsuit, even one that looks air tight, is risky. To the extent that you have been able to recover from the damage caused by your employer, so much the better. No responsible attorney would ever advise you to malinger or do anything but exercise your best efforts to get back on your feet and become satisfactorily reemployed as soon as you possibly can. Forget about the effect that reemployment would have on reducing your damages in a lawsuit. An attorney would much rather go into court with a client who found suitable employment within a reasonable period of time, than with a client who failed to secure such employment over an extremely long period of time.
- If you are a member of a protected class and believe that you have been unfairly treated because of that protected class status, consider filing a timely complaint of discrimination with the administrative agencies that investigate those complaints—the Equal Employment Opportunity Commission and your state civil rights enforcement agency. However, your attorney may advise you that a direct action in court on your state law claims would be preferable in your case, so first consult with your attorney.
- If you are a public employee, comply with any applicable tort claims act notice requirements. The law in many states requires that you notify the public body within a given time frame that it will be sued. That is the *quid pro quo* for a waiver by the government of its sovereign immunity. Ask your lawyer whether filing a complaint with the administrative enforcement agencies is

sufficient for tort claims notice purposes or whether a separate filing is required in your jurisdiction.

- If you have filed a complaint of discrimination, cooperate with the investigative agency. After your administrative complaint filing, the agency investigator will contact you. Always be courteous to the investigator.
- The odds are against your case prevailing at the agency level. Only a small percentage of all administrative filings are determined by the agencies to be supported by *substantial evidence* of discrimination. Ask your lawyer whether they will become involved at the agency level. Investigators are typically overworked. You will be counseled to be as helpful as possible to the investigator. You may be asked to provide lists with addresses and telephone numbers of potential witnesses.
- If your complaint is that you were subjected to different treatment from that given to other workers, you will be asked to objectify your performance and treatment as much as possible. That is, to describe your work and the treatment you received in objective terms so that your investigator can compare your performance and treatment with that of other workers.
- Amend your civil rights claim if necessary. Often a person who files a discrimination case is the target of some kind of retaliation. That, too, is illegal. A person who claims such retaliation must file a complaint about that as well within the statute of limitations period or else they lose their right to sue. You may need to amend your civil rights complaint to preserve the retaliation issue for future litigation.
- Communicate and deliberate with your attorney about the results of the agency investigation. At some point, the administrative agency will render its determination. That determination will contain its position on who wins and who loses. However, even if you win at the agency level, the employer can still refuse to accept that determination. If it refuses to accept the judgment of the agency, you will be given a right to sue letter.

Psychologically, a complaint decided in your favor benefits you because the decision will stimulate settlement and make it easier for you to convince a lawyer to take or proceed with your case if the case is not settled by the administrative agency. Occasionally, the enforcement agency will offer to prosecute the case against the employer using government lawyers as your attorney. Should this option arise, consult with a private attorney as to whether this would be your best option.

- Consult about the prospect of withdrawing the complaint. If the agency investigator believes the agency will not find in your favor, the investigator may give you an opportunity to withdraw your complaint so that your case will not be prejudiced by an adverse determination. In most cases, it is wise to take that offer and withdraw the complaint to avoid that prejudice, but check with your attorney before making that decision.
- Consult with your attorney before making any settlement offers. If the agency determination is in your favor, the agency will seek to conciliate or settle the matter. It is extremely important that before responding to any request by the agency representative for you to make an offer, you first consult with your attorney. Whatever you tell the agency may create a ceiling above which your lawyer cannot negotiate a settlement later on if your efforts to settle through the agency are not successful. Alternatively, you may wish to have your lawyer negotiate on your behalf. If you do, be sure you are clear about your fee arrangements with your lawyer to avoid any later controversy.

–18–
EVALUATING YOUR LEGAL CASE

One of the biggest decisions you will ever make is whether to file a lawsuit. One aspect of making that decision relates to your chance of success. Most people have absolutely no idea how to evaluate a case. This chapter is intended to inform you as to how that is done, so that you can better understand your lawyer's advice and make a more informed decision.

POTENTIAL SUCCESS IN COURT

The most frequently asked question of any plaintiff's attorney is, "Do I have a case?" Two things must work in your favor in order to give you a chance of success in the courtroom—the facts and the law. First, you must have a case that falls within the class of cases for which the law affords a remedy. We have reviewed a number of those remedies. Second, the facts must be on your side. This requires an evaluation of the evidence that supports your legal contentions. If the reasons stated by the employer for your firing are proved false, this suggests to the jury that you were terminated for some other reason that the employer is not willing to admit. The only credible evidence the jury will be left with is your evidence that the actual reason was an unlawful one.

Working with an Attorney

Any experienced lawyer in the employment law field rejects many more cases than are accepted. Some cases are accepted during the attorney's first interview with the client. Others are accepted after more extensive contact with the client and perhaps after obtaining independent corroboration of the plaintiff's perspective. Still, other cases are accepted only after an independent fact-finding body has conducted its own investigation into the plaintiff's allegations. In some cases, the attorney may require the person to submit to a lie detector test before deciding whether to accept the case. The attorney's best judgment is the only gauge to measure which cases to accept and after what stage of investigation. Although years of experience may sharpen the attorney's powers of judgment, this method of case selection is an art, not a science.

Some types of cases are more readily accepted than others. Clues lead the attorney to think that the client's report is sincerely believed, was accurately perceived, and is accurately reported. Some of the factors an attorney will look for include:

- the timing of significant events;
- whether the linkage between significant events is probable;
- the absence of other factors to account for adverse personnel decisions;
- whether the employer or the employer's agent has done or would do the act complained of; and,
- the client's believability.

The most important factor is the last. Ultimately, the attorney must believe in the client. That belief must carry an investment of trust and confidence. Every attorney hopes for a client who is direct, candid, perceptive, not defensive, nor vengeful. Lawsuits are not resolved by computers. Rather, they are presented to people. In every lawsuit, the people who decide the case are given two sides to that story. They, too, must inevitably choose whom to believe.

The second most important factor in the lawyer's selection process is the nature of the purported *linkage* between significant events. People believe that employers tend to terminate workers who have had an on-the-job injury. It is as simple as that. Some other linkage factors are not as readily believed. Sometimes the jury must be sensitized to that linkage through expert or anecdotal testimony. Thus, the linkage factor also has to be believable.

Third, the linkage factor is more powerful if the timing of significant events suggests the connection. A worker who is terminated two days after an on-the-job injury is more likely thought to be terminated for that reason than a worker who is terminated years after an injury.

Finally, the absence of other factors for the termination must be established. There is always some plausible explanation why the employee was lawfully discharged. The employer's reason need not be patently absurd. If the employer points to job performance problems as the decisive factor, that explanation can be weakened by proof of disparate treatment, over-scrutinization of work, inadequate warnings, or disproportionate weight given to the problem by the employer.

Fired for filing a workers' compensation claim. For example, suppose that Bob, the client, has reported that he was doing well at work. He received no complaints about his work. Three days after, he fell at work and injured his back and only two days after he filed a workers' compensation claim, he was terminated. The timing of that sequence of events, if accurately reported, tends to support the view that the client was terminated for filing a workers' compensation claim, or for sustaining a back injury at work, or both.

Employers and supervisors who are evaluated for salary purposes in part on safety performance often are hostile to workers who file such claims. Therefore, the relationship between filing the claim and the termination is probable. Because the worker had no other complaints about his work, no other factors account for that linkage of significant events. If, from the client's report or from the attorney's own experience, this has happened to other injured workers in the past, this further strengthens the case. Reports from the client that the supervisor had threatened persons on that shift not to file such claims would likewise aid the plaintiff's case.

If you believe you have been fired for filing a workers' compensation claim, the following considerations would come into play in assessing the strength of your factual case.

- What was your employment history before you filed the claim?
- How soon were you fired after you filed the claim?

- How has your employer treated other workers who had filed such claims? Had anyone else filed such a claim?
- How did your employer treat you after filing such a claim?
- Did your employer freely provide you with the appropriate forms to file such a claim?
- Did your employer make any negative comments when you said you were going to file the claim or when you actually filed your claim?
- Did your performance appraisals change after the claim was filed? If so, how?
- Were you disciplined for any reason after the claim was filed?
- Had you or anyone else been disciplined for the same thing before you filed the claim?
- Did your supervisor's attitude toward you change after the claim was filed? If so, how?
- Were any job duties taken away from you that you could perform after you filed the claim?
- Were any expected promotions or pay increases taken away after you filed the claim?
- How many claims have you filed against this employer?
- Were you reinjured after returning to your old job?
- Did your employer return you to your old job when your doctor released you back to work?
- Were you given light-duty work that was available when your doctor released you back to light-duty work?
- How much time did you lose from work?
- What amount of medical bills did you incur before returning to work?
- Is your employer insured or self-insured for such claims?
- What is its claim history? Is your employer paying an insurance premium that is higher than normal because of its claims history?
- Is management under pressure to reduce the number and cost of such claims?
- Has your boss been singled out by management as having had too many of such claims?

- Is your boss compensated or evaluated in part on his or her safety record?
- How enlightened is your boss? Is he or she tolerant and understanding or unnecessarily rigid and apparently resentful when a worker's civil rights issue comes up?
- What is your employer's attitude toward nondiscrimination for other protected-class workers?
- What kind of witness do you make?
- What kind of witness does your boss make?
- What reasons were given for your termination? Are those reasons valid?

It could be that your employer has a bad reputation for treatment of injured workers. It could be that it has issued memoranda in which your injured status had been taken into account. That status may have been mentioned in management or safety committee meetings. It could be that the reasons stated by the employer for your termination just does not make sense.

Evaluating the believability of the client. Most cases are not as clear as the one described above. This brings us back to the most important factor—the client. While he or she is in the lawyer's office and is being questioned by the lawyer the lawyer is doing two things—examining the facts of the case and evaluating the kind of person the client is. There is much more to a client than how he or she will perform on the stand.

It is true that the lawyer depends on the client to relate facts, describe characters, and remember events. Equally important is that the client be candid, and not vengeful or defensive. Employment cases are naturally sympathetic from a jury's standpoint. The client must not be one who would rob the case of its natural sympathy. The jury should not feel that the employee is merely grasping at straws in attributing a termination to an illegal event or would be one who fails to recognize his or her own faults. In essence, what is required is the truth, and a client who can tell it and not stand in its way.

In meeting with you, the attorney will be looking to select a client who will add to, not detract from, the cause. Do not misunderstand. You need not be physically attractive, highly educated, or even articulate. You just need to be viewed as a good person who intends to tell the truth no matter what.

NO CASE IS PERFECT

Must your case be perfect? No. There is no such thing. Do not be afraid to see a lawyer because of your perception that your case is not perfect. A lawyer may be able to win your case even though:

- you may have done something to prejudice the case;
- your work may not have been perfect;
- the employer may have engaged in smokescreen tactics; or,
- the employer may have made tactical admissions.

You may have Done Something to Prejudice the Case

You may have done something before the initial interview with the attorney to prejudice your own case, such as:

- making prior inconsistent statements about your knowledge or lack of knowledge about the reason for the termination;
- making prior admissions about your own poor quality of work; or,
- engaging in self-help, such as telling the boss off or reporting the company to OSHA.

You need not know the reason why you were terminated. The lawyer, after careful questioning, is the one to try to figure that out. If you have told others that you do not know why the termination occurred, that is okay. Others can establish that, or the facts can speak for themselves. Juries are instructed by the court to rely on direct or circumstantial evidence. When a client must admit that he or she does not know for certain why a termination occurred, a jury may nonetheless conclude based on other evidence that the termination occurred for the reason alleged in your court complaint.

Furthermore, a jury knows that no one is perfect. It knows that an employer can criticize something about any worker if the employer looks hard enough. A plaintiff who admits that he or she was not the best worker or made mistakes has not destroyed the case.

Whenever a worker has told the boss what he or she thinks of the termination, cussed the boss out, or made threats against the boss, this hurts the employee's case because it tends to rob his or her case of its sympathy. If a jury believes that through this self-help the employee has already extracted payment for the termination, the identity between the jury and the worker is weakened.

Your Work may not have been Perfect

The employer's complaints about the employee's work are not fatal to the case if over half the time the employee was given good performance reviews and never heard any complaints about his or her work. This is true because:

- occasional complaints are expected;
- what are characterized as complaints today, were considered suggestions or training during employment;
- others receive the same complaints, but were not terminated; and,
- the plaintiff received complaints while others did not for the same problems.

The Employer may have Engaged in Smokescreen Tactics

Employers, having become more wary of employment lawsuits, will often try to hide a discriminatory or retaliatory discharge in a layoff due to a reorganization, reduction in force, or job elimination. In a lawsuit, however, the jury is allowed to look beneath the surface of a personnel action and scrutinize:

- the process that determined who would be laid off and on what basis;
- whether the decision was subjective and, if so, whether the person who made the decision affecting you did so fairly and in accordance with the criteria the employer purported it was to follow;
- the circumstances that prompted the decision to combine or eliminate your position in the first place; and,

- whether the reorganization achieved the employer's stated goal, so as to appear legitimate, rather than a cover for unlawful discrimination.

The Employer may have Made Tactical Admissions

When a manager has treated a number of employees disrespectfully, defense counsel may argue that the plaintiff has no case because the manager treated everyone poorly. However, an unfair person rarely doles out unfair treatment fairly. Usually there is something distinctive about the mistreatment you and other members of your protected class have received.

Of course, if the employer denies the obvious and embraces the unfair manager as a good manager, that strategy can backfire as well. If the management protects that manager and downplay the horrors that the manager has committed, this could set up a disparity between the testimony of the management witnesses and the testimony of the nonmanagement witnesses, so that the jury smells a cover-up.

Your Case may Improve as it Develops

Your lawyer will also try to exploit opportunities that the employer presents.

The employer's tactics may anger the jury. During the case it frequently develops that:

- a conspiracy existed to get rid of you;
- the employer's witnesses have been coached to modify the truth about your work performance;
- the employer's witnesses give inconsistent deposition testimony;
- important documents have been withheld or destroyed by the employer after the suit is filed;
- the employer has made threats to employees not to give favorable testimony about you; or,
- the employer's witnesses lie on the stand.

Any of these factors will make a jury angry. These factors call the employer's credibility into question on other matters and subvert the employer's position.

The employer may give you an advantage. The employer often gives the employee the advantage in a case by making one of several mistakes that includes:

- depreciating the plaintiff;
- underestimating the plaintiff's attorney;
- failing to acknowledge a natural reaction (for example, the jury's reaction to a statement such as, "No it didn't bother me when he told the president he thought I was doing something illegal"); or,
- blindly supporting subordinate, errant managers without having a reasonable basis for that support.

These mistakes result from the employer's arrogance. They may pervade the lawsuit and serve as the source of the employer's failure in the case.

Human Nature may Work in Your Favor

Human nature and the nature of organizations have not changed much over the years. People tend to act to protect themselves, both financially and emotionally. They act out of anger, fear, hatred, and vengeance. Companies tend to act to protect the continuity and vitality of the organization. These tendencies are powerful and consistent. As a result, plaintiffs' attorneys have an advantage because:

- the wrongdoer seldom admits wrongdoing;
- other people allow a wrongdoer to continue the wrongful acts;
- management tends to support its managers and therefore discounts the legitimate complaints of workers as coming from disgruntled workers;
- defense attorneys and personnel officers tend to perpetuate their own relationship with the organization because the organization often *shoots the messenger*; and,

- attorneys for employers often do a they say type of investigation, where they take self-serving denials at face value, such as, "Sorry, they say they did not do it."

The employee's attorney is further aided because the wrongdoer is not forthcoming about the facts and provides outright denials or shades the truth. The human resource director's job is made more difficult whenever he or she cannot get the truth from his or her own people.

Other related principles are at work here. One is that persons in the workplace tend by inertia to allow wrongdoing to continue. For example, a general manager may sexually harass many women, and all the managers know it and do nothing about it, even though they knew it was part of their job to maintain a nonhostile work atmosphere. It is far easier to ignore wrongdoing. As a result, the human resource director does not get the truth from witnesses who say, "I did not see anything" because they would make themselves out to be bad people if they did see an ongoing wrong and let it continue. So they did not see anything.

Human resource directors have a blind spot, too. Their job is to protect the employer. Some of them are more aggressive than others in recognizing potential liability, reporting it to their supervisors, and fixing a situation. Too often, however, their performance is measured by how well they protect the corporation. In addition, the personnel manager is given responsibilities that involve inherent conflicts of interest. On one hand, they are to clean up the system. On the other hand, they must report to upper management on existing problems that may reflect poorly on their past performance in having cleaned up the system. As a result, everyone wants to put a good face on a problem. This does not happen in every case, everywhere, but it is a natural tendency.

Those same natural tendencies extend to the investigation conducted by the employer's lawyer. The defense lawyer's priority is all too often to keep the client—not necessarily to win the case. The defense lawyer is not always in the best position to severely question or criticize his or her client's employees, particularly if the target of the employee's case is the president who hired the lawyer. The result is a *they say* type of investigation. This response is not useful in resolving the case or in effectively presenting the employer's case at trial.

So, despite what you perceive to be a disparity of power, you may have a real chance to win in court.

–19–
HIRING AN ATTORNEY

The most important decision you make in the quest to vindicate your legal rights is your selection of a lawyer. There are widely varying skill and experience levels of persons who practice employment law. This chapter offers a few tips on how to go about finding an attorney.

DETERMINING IF YOU NEED AN ATTORNEY

If something has caused your antennae to go up that is out of the ordinary and out of your experience, it probably means it would not do any harm to run your problem by a lawyer. Sometimes you are too close to the situation to be able to assess it objectively. Most lawyers do not charge for initial telephone interviews. It would be a simple matter to find several who would not charge you for a call. Call a couple and bounce the facts off of them until you find advice that makes sense.

The dangers of not calling and at least speaking to a lawyer is that you may otherwise prejudice your case by either doing or failing to do something that is contrary to your legal interests. For example, time limits apply to the assertion of legal rights. Similarly, your rights to proceed could be injured if you sent out a letter or an email that was ill advised. The attorney can review your communications and edit out any prejudice.

SELECTING AN ATTORNEY

An attorney who practices employment law may be secured through the *lawyer referral service* of your state bar association. That list is made up of attorneys who choose to participate in the service. Each attorney may designate the types of cases he or she chooses to have referred. Typically, though, there is no screening process to make sure the attorneys are experienced in the particular area they have indicated they wish to receive referrals.

Private referral services are also available, but there is no assurance that those attorneys who sign up for such referrals are the best in the field. There are also Yellow Page advertisements, but there is absolutely no screening process that controls the claims made in those ads.

By far the best way to get a good lawyer in such matters is by *personal referral*. Family, friends, or coworkers may have had a good experience with an employment lawyer. Another good way to obtain a referral is to call a lawyer—either an employment lawyer who is on the defense side, or a lawyer outside the area of specialty who has been around for awhile—and ask that lawyer for a referral to a plaintiff's employment specialist. The lawyer will take care to give you a referral to a good lawyer. Otherwise, he or she could be responsible for a negligent referral. That is great motivation to a lawyer.

The lawyer may refer you to more than one employment law attorney. Ask the lawyer who he or she would go to first with your problem if it were that lawyer or a member of his or her family who needed help.

Next, call and meet with the lawyer or lawyers who were recommended. Do not be afraid to see more than one. Usually only a small fee or no fee at all is charged for a first visit. You will be looking for a lawyer with whom you feel comfortable investing your trust and confidence.

During the interview, discuss the fees and costs with the lawyer. Any responsible lawyer will provide you with detailed information concerning his or her charges and your estimated costs of litigation.

Reference Publications

Two good references that are available are the Martindale-Hubbell legal directory, and the publication, *The Best Lawyers in America*.

Martindale-Hubbell relies on the opinions of lawyers in the community generally, and rates lawyers by quality ("a" or "b") and integrity ("v" is for very high). Look for an "av" attorney or firm. The directory is also available online at **www.martindale.com**.

The *Best Lawyers in America* is also based on local peer ratings, but from specialists in the field. One field of specialty that is rated is *Labor and Employment Law*. Lawyers who represent employees are listed for each of the fifty states. The Best Lawyers listings are available online at **www.bestlawyers.com**. Hardbound volumes may be available at your local library.

In both cases, lawyers cannot purchase their rating or inclusion.

TYPES OF ATTORNEYS

Each lawyer has a different style, but there are many different styles that are effective. There are some lawyers who are quite effective even though they do not take a *barracuda* approach. A lawyer can be assertive in pursuing your interests and still be reasonable.

In fact, a lawyer who is overly aggressive can work against you. If the tone of his or her letters angers your employer while you are employed, your employer could take its resentment out on you and fire you for it. If he or she angers your employer's lawyer during litigation by engaging in sharp or underhanded tactics, settlement could be impeded. You do not want a lawyer who so angers your opponent as to get them personally invested in defeating you so that they expend even more energy and resources trying to do that.

You also do not want your opponents to be able to relate to a jury how they tried to work with you to save your employment, but your lawyer's unreasonable demands or behavior made that impossible. Juries do not like lawyers. They also do not like employees who would sic a rabid lawyer on an employer. You want an effective, competent lawyer who may be aggressive, but not unreasonably so.

FEES

There are two basic ways to hire lawyers—pay an *hourly rate* or hire them on a *contingent basis*. The contingency fee will equal a percentage of what the lawyer recovers for you.

Whether to pay hourly or on a contingent basis usually depends on the services you would like the lawyer to perform. If you want the lawyer to simply write a letter with no prospect for litigation, an hourly fee is probably more appropriate. It would be a good idea to impose a *not to exceed cap* on the hourly fee without your further authority.

In most cases, though, the services you want the lawyer to provide will be to recover substantial dollars for you because of a wrongful termination or some other act of discrimination. Many hours will need to be invested by the lawyer in building and creating value in your case. It is not unusual for several hundred hours to be expended doing that. That is why, in most cases, you will be looking to find someone who is willing to do that on a contingent basis.

If nothing is recovered, you will owe the lawyer nothing, except the out-of-pocket costs your lawyer has expended for filing fees, depositions, and other direct litigation expenses. Typically, those expenses range in the $2,000–$4,000 area for individual cases, depending on the size of the employer, the number of depositions that need to be taken and subpoenas issued, and whether an expert witness must be retained. That may sound like a lot of money, but for every dollar in cost you incur, keep in mind that your lawyer will be expending ten, twenty, or sometimes even fifty times that amount of value in his or her time fighting to advance your interests.

RETAINER AGREEMENTS

Most lawyers will have you sign a *retainer agreement*. That agreement will contain the terms of your lawyer's hiring. It will state the basis for compensation for the lawyer and your payment obligations for court filing fees and litigation expenses. It may contain some conditions that would justify withdrawal of representation. It may also contain provisions making you liable for payment in the event that you change attorneys.

There is not a lot of regulation restricting the content of such agreements, so there is no such thing as a standard agreement. Typically, the content is driven by personal experiences of the lawyer drafting them. So read it carefully. Take it home before signing it if you have any questions about it. Attempt to negotiate out or clarify any objectionable or troublesome clauses. If you have a good case, you have some leverage.

CHANGING ATTORNEYS

Part of the reason you need to be careful in choosing a lawyer is that it is not easy to change lawyers after you get one. First, lawyers do not like stepping on each other's toes. They are reluctant to do anything that would interfere with a current attorney-client relationship. Ethical rules prohibit it. It may be difficult for you to persuade a second lawyer to even see you for a second opinion while you are currently represented. Further, the fact that you are shopping around for a new lawyer may cause people to think that any trouble you are having with your current lawyer is of your own making. Most lawyers will simply encourage you to go back and straighten out any communication problems you are having with your current lawyer.

Second, it does not impress your opponent if you change lawyers. The employer is just as apt to think that your lawyer lost faith in the case. Still, confidence is everything in the attorney-client relationship, so if you have lost confidence in your lawyer, it is appropriate to discover whether your interests could not be better served elsewhere. Take care to read the fine print in your retainer agreement, though, as to whether you will owe your former lawyer a fee if you change lawyers.

Other complications may arise. Your former attorney may not release your file to you or your attorney if you have an outstanding bill for fees or costs. Your former attorney may claim an interest in the fee eventually generated in the litigation based on past work performed. That may need to be worked out by the attorneys. However, the system is designed to accommodate a change of lawyers, and if that is indicated in your case do not worry, the judge will not punish you for it. From the court's standpoint, all it receives is a simple one-page *Notice of Substitution of Attorneys*. Unless a change would jeopardize the court's trial schedule, you will not be called upon to explain to a judge why you did it.

Also, most retainers, if unused, are refundable. So, if you change lawyers, do not be shy about asking if you have some money coming back from your retainer.

–20–
FILING A LAWSUIT

Part of the angst associated with whether to file a lawsuit, or from actually going through the experience after it is filed, arises from not knowing what the process involves. There is no real mystery to it. The system is highly formalized, and there are distinct stages of litigation. In Chapter 1, the basics of each stage were addressed. This chapter is intended to acquaint you with more details of each step.

THE PREFILING STAGE

When you contact a lawyer, you may be asked to assemble documents, provide a narrative, or arrange to have witnesses interviewed. The lawyer is under an obligation to perform due diligence to the extent that is practicable to avoid filing a frivolous lawsuit.

If you have a case, your lawyer may recommend first writing a *demand letter* to the employer to give the employer an opportunity to settle before suit is filed. This is recommended particularly when the case is clearly documented or when it is thought the employer attaches value to avoiding the adverse publicity attendant to a court filing. However, employees generally overestimate the desire of employers to avoid such filings.

Prefiling demand letters have a small success rate, perhaps ten to twenty percent. One reason for that is that employers find that many more lawsuits are threatened than are filed. Until a filing is made, the employer really does not know if a threat is real. As a result, employers and their lawyers are conditioned to say, "No" in the first instance. They save money that way, weeding out the weak cases. That is why it takes exceptional circumstances for a case to stand out and merit early settlement. That is also why it is so important to attach yourself to a lawyer whose reputation is not to make idle threats.

Your lawyer may feel that it is necessary to have you first exhaust administrative remedies by filing with a civil rights enforcement agency at the federal or state level. This may be required because of the nature of your case. It may also be desirable in that it can offer a free investigation into the matter. When your employer contends your performance was the reason for your termination, your lawyer may need the comfort level that such an investigation brings before committing to litigation. If the stated reason was attendance, for example, and you do not have complete records or a complete memory of your absenteeism, the administrative investigation will be the vehicle to learn those facts and how your attendance measured up to that of others. Those investigations can take months. In the meantime, you have to go about the business of living your life and let the legal process run on a separate track.

While your lawyer is waiting for a response to a demand letter, and you both are waiting for the administrative agency to complete its business, there will be events that transpire in your own life that dictate your future involvement with the legal system. If, in the meantime, you get work at, near, or above the pay you were formerly enjoying, the need for litigation can suddenly expire. There is nothing fun about litigation. There is worry when something is about to happen, and worry because nothing at all is happening during long periods of seemingly endless delay. For some, the stress of litigation can sometimes be as onerous as the stress the employer imposed directly.

Once you have substitute employment, you may change the value you place on the pursuit of the case. This is particularly true if your new work takes you to a different locale. Long distance litigation is particularly difficult to maintain an appetite for. Calls from a lawyer about the loss of a job in a distant city readily becomes an intrusion.

However, if your case checks out and your need for litigation and interest remains, you may get to the next step.

THE POSTFILING STAGE

A lawsuit is initiated through the filing of a formal court pleading known as the *complaint*. The complaint contains the various legal theories or *claims* you are asserting. Those claims are stated through allegations of fact that tell why you are suing.

Once the complaint is filed, it must be *served* on the defendant. A sheriff or process server will effect service either by personal or other form of service permitted by law. Once the complaint has been served, the defendant will have a certain amount of time (typically twenty or thirty days) to file a court *appearance*. During this time, the defendant will be turning the matter over to a lawyer, who will contact yours and give your lawyer notice of representation. The opposing lawyer may ask for an extension of time to investigate the matter before an appearance is filed. Extensions are routinely granted out of professional courtesy. Do not worry. Such extensions will not typically cause undue delay. Besides, your lawyer may, and probably will, need an extension at some point in your case. Trust your lawyer's instinct for when it is time to press the other side for an appearance. (Remember that a lawyer who is employed on a contingent fee basis is just as eager as you are to get paid.)

Discovery Requests

During this time, the lawyers will each exchange what are known as *discovery requests*. These require each party to produce documents that may lead to relevant information, or, where permitted, to answer questions called *interrogatories* which are under oath concerning relevant issues in the case. Once the initial document requests have been responded to, the parties are ready to take *depositions*.

Depositions. A *deposition* is testimony taken under oath in a question and answer format. When your deposition is taken, your lawyer will be there with you and be ready to object to any improper questions if need be. The opposing lawyer will be asking you questions, and a court reporter will be typing your verbatim responses. Your lawyer will prepare you for the deposition beforehand, so you will know what to expect. The opposing lawyer will ask all about your background, education, and work history. You will be asked about your work for your former employer, your lawsuit allegations, and the facts you have to support those allegations.

The deposition stage is the most demanding of your time in the process, next to the trial itself. While your deposition may only last a day or a part of a day, you will be strongly encouraged to attend the depositions that your lawyer will be taking of the employer's witnesses. If you have a case, you will enjoy seeing your former manager finally having to account for his or her actions. Those depositions will vary in number and length depending on the type of case and the number of actors involved. Currently, the Federal Rules of Civil Procedure forbid each side from taking more than ten depositions without leave of court.

Motion for Summary Judgment

After the depositions are concluded and all documents have been exchanged, discovery is complete. At this juncture the defendant may try to kick your case out of court by filing what is called a *Motion for Summary Judgment*. That motion contends the employee's case is so weak that, viewing all facts in favor of the employee, there is no genuine issue in dispute of a factual nature for a jury to resolve. Therefore, the court can dismiss the case, as a matter of law, so that a jury trial is not in order.

On *summary judgment*, a judge is not to resolve disputed issues of fact. To withstand such a motion, your lawyer's job is to show that there is a genuine issue of material fact for a jury to resolve. About a quarter of all cases are disposed of on summary judgment. It is a nice hurdle to get over. Once you do, your case will be destined to be tried unless it is settled earlier.

THE TRIAL STAGE

If yours is one of the few which are not settled or disposed of on summary judgment, your case will be tried. Generally, juries find the truth, whatever it is, and declare it in their verdict. To go through a jury trial as a litigant is difficult, but it is not nearly as hard as people might imagine. In truth, going through a deposition can be more hostile because there is no judge present to supervise, nor is the deposing attorney tempered in demeanor by the presence of a jury at trial.

In contrast, lawyers are on their best behavior at trial so as not to raise a jury's ire or the wrath of a judge, whose role in large part is to maintain proper decorum. Nor are there many surprises at trial. With modern rules of discovery, by the time of trial, both attorneys know what witnesses exist and what they will say. At trial, their interest is in constructing a cogent, persuasive, and interesting presentation for the jurors who are strangers to the case.

Most of the stress a litigant experiences during trial is not externally imposed. There will be worry and anxiety, but your lawyer will prepare for your testimony in advance and communicate with you to let you know what is coming next.

Most jury trials of employment cases can be tried in a week in individual cases. Almost all can be tried in two weeks. Your attendance is essential. For most people, that can be arranged without adverse repercussions to their work or family life. Except for your daily attendance and preparation of your testimony, your role will be fairly inactive. Your attorney, though, will be frantically working twelve to fourteen hours a day analyzing the day's developments and anticipating the ones to follow. Be prepared to be on standby. Be ready to assist in providing information or whatever other service your attorney requires. The trial experience will bring you and your lawyer very close as you work together to win your case.

THE APPEAL STAGE

One of the reasons people decide to settle is to avoid the inevitable appeal that follows a successful trial. In most court systems, a party is entitled to one appeal, so long as there is a legal basis for it.

The grounds for appeal vary, from errors of law the judge made in rulings on evidence or instructions to the jury, to other errors that may have allowed unlawful bias to unduly influence the outcome.

An appeal can take a year or two, or sometimes more, to work through the appellate system. Appellate judges have no deadlines. In our system, which is based on legal precedent, a judge decides a point of law that influences, if not determines, the outcome of similar cases that follow. Therefore, appellate judges want to get it right.

Posttrial Motions

The reason an appeal takes so long is that first *posttrial motions* are filed with the trial judge to allow the judge who supposedly erred to correct it. That alone requires weeks, if not months, of briefing and argument. Once the trial judge decides whether to take away the jury verdict (they can do that) or order a new trial, the parties are then given a period of time—typically thirty days—to appeal.

Notice of appeal. They appeal by filing a simple document known as a *notice of appeal*. That begins the appellate process. The notice of appeal goes to a court reporter who must then transcribe the entire court proceedings. Once the lawyer who appealed obtains the court transcript, a briefing schedule is set. Then an opening brief is written by the lawyer who appealed, which takes a couple of months. Then the opposing lawyer is given time to file a responsive brief, typically thirty days. The lawyer who appealed is given another thirty days to file a reply brief. That concludes the briefing activity.

Then the appellate judges (typically there is a panel), having received all of the briefs, will read and analyze them with the assistance of their law clerks. That may take months. At some point, oral argument before the appellate court may be scheduled. After oral argument, the appellate court issues its opinion approving, modifying, or reversing the lower court's judgment. Sometimes that decision is rendered in weeks. In other cases, the opinion may not be issued for a year or more. Sometimes the case is remanded for a new trial. As you can imagine, it is not a process over which you or your lawyer have control. However, at any point along the road, settlement remains an option.

• • • • •

While the intent of this chapter is to enlighten you about what may be required as you proceed through litigation, no amount of information can eliminate the stress you will feel throughout that process. Whether you are a plaintiff or defendant, there is nothing fun about it. Hopefully, this information will help lessen your burden as you move through it. While the material in this chapter is a general description of the process, each case presents its own level and array of stresses. Your attorney will want to help you through the rough patches. Do not be afraid to consult with your attorney to soothe your anxiety as your case proceeds.

–21–
SETTLING YOUR CASE

Most cases that are brought are eventually settled. There is risk to litigation for both sides and, in most cases, the parties will be able to come to terms to avoid the risk of loss. In the federal courts, lawyers are required to discuss settlement after a case is filed. Some state systems have a similar requirement. Even before those requirements were instituted, judges would typically ask lawyers if they had discussed settlement and would encourage them to do so.

The days when it was a sign of weakness to mention the *S word* first are now gone. In fact, the skillful lawyer can punctuate a favorable development by behaving as if, in light of that development, the other side would surely want to discuss it. This chapter will discuss a few of the questions that arise about settlement.

Q: If I get a lawyer and file a case, does that mean the case will not settle?

A: No. Over 80% of civil cases are generally settled after they are filed. During the course of litigation settlement, *windows* will appear. These windows typically relate to stages in the case. During each window of opportunity, which may last but a few days, the parties are temporarily on hold, having just finished one stage and about to commence another. Because cases cannot remain long in a static position, the settlement window closes when one of the attorneys chooses to put the case back in gear. Lawyers only know two speeds—go and stop. If your attorney is skillful, he or she will be sensitive to the opportunities that present themselves.

Settlement windows typically open at the following times:

- on receipt of a prefiling demand letter;
- just after the case is filed;
- after depositions are taken;
- after surviving pretrial motions to dismiss your case;
- just before preparation for trial; and,
- at or after trial.

Rarely do both parties believe it is in their interest to settle at the same time. At the outset, you may be too angry to even consider it. One of your attorney's jobs is to protect you from your own anger. Likewise, the employer may stubbornly believe it did nothing wrong. It may take some unfavorable depositions before it receives counsel from its attorneys that it has some liability exposure.

Even after you recover from your own anger, other obstacles to settlement may exist. You may have an unrealistic notion of the value of the case. Hopefully, before you selected your lawyer, he or she was wise enough to communicate what he or she believed to be a fair range of value for the case and made sure they explored your expectations before taking you on as a client. Further, as the litigation process is dynamic, unfavorable developments may make the case less valuable than originally thought. Good communication with your attorney throughout the process will help to minimize any surprises down the road.

The employer has a completely different set of challenges. The attorney that is handling the case may be the same one who initially advised the employer that it was legal to terminate you. It is difficult for the attorney who gave that advice to think otherwise, or to tell the employer it did something wrong, particularly after billing the client $10,000 or $20,000 defending the case. In that situation, the defense lawyer may need to be shown that they were basing their initial advice on incomplete or inaccurate information from one of the managers for the employer. That realization may not come until that manager is questioned under oath by your attorney.

Likewise, the employer's human resources manager may have previously told the CEO that they had taken care of a problem, and it is embarrassing for them to admit that perhaps the matter had not been taken care of at all. They may feel that to concede is an admission that they did not perform their job, placing them at risk of termination. Or the case may involve a charge of wrongdoing against the person employed by the defendant who will be making the decision whether to settle, and until the case develops, will be too apt to confuse settlement with a confession of guilt.

Eventually, however, emotions will take a back seat to the economic aspects of the case—the value it represents to you and the risk it represents to the employer. Before a settlement can be reached, however, both sides must be persuaded that a settlement is to their benefit.

Q: Can I save money by first trying to settle the case myself?

A: Typically, no. This holds true for three reasons. First, without sound legal advice, you are too apt to set your original demand too low. You may think you are only trying to simplify matters by getting right to your bottom line and giving it to your employer. The problem is that even if you characterize it as your bottom line, the tendency is for people not to believe that. It is highly unusual for an employer to accept an initial offer. Once you speak and put a value on your case, you restrict your lawyer who will find it difficult to negotiate for more than a figure your employer has already been advised to reject.

Second, you may not appreciate the full value of your case. It would be well worth an initial consultation fee, or two or three, before you start throwing figures out.

Third, if your case is substantial, no one will pay you substantial dollars without an attorney. Having an attorney who believes in your case is a demonstration to your employer that you have convinced at least one person that your case has substance. If one person can be convinced of that, perhaps a jury would also be convinced. Having an attorney also tells the employer that if they do not settle with you, they will be in it for the long haul. That represents not only significant cost, but also potentially damaging disruption to the business. It is rare that an attorney cannot bring more value to your case than the fee the attorney will generate.

Q: What is my case worth in settlement?

A: There is no book you can use to value employment cases. That is why it is important to seek out an experienced practitioner in the field who will have a sense for the value of your case in that market. Each case will have its own value, depending on a number of different factors that include:

- the type of damages recoverable for that type of case in your jurisdiction;
- the amount of money you have lost, or stand to lose;
- the emotional distress or injury to reputation you have suffered;
- the egregiousness of the employer's conduct;
- your personal jury appeal;
- the jury appeal of your antagonist;
- the probability your case will survive a pretrial motion to dismiss;
- the probability of a favorable jury verdict; and,
- the likely verdict range at trial in the event of a plaintiff's verdict.

The verdict range will be influenced by the strength of your case and the evidence in favor and against it. It will also be greatly influenced by the size of the employer.

After factoring in all of those elements, your attorney can come to an opinion of a likely verdict range at trial. The settlement value of the case can then also be estimated. One method of doing that is to take the average favorable jury verdict, if the case were hypothetically tried ten times, and multiply that number by the probability of success. If, for example, the average favorable jury verdict was $100,000 and the probability of winning was 60%, then the settlement value of the case would be $60,000.

Q: If we try to settle now and are unsuccessful, can we ask for more at trial?

A: Yes. Settlement discussions are confidential and will not be admissible at trial. The judge and jury will not hear any numbers that were discussed during the settlement discussions.

Q: What can I get in settlement besides money?

A: If you do not settle, all the jury can do is give you money. In addition, in statutory discrimination cases, the judge has injunctive power to order reinstatement. There may be other things that are just as important to you that only a settlement can provide. Typically, noneconomic factors, such as recommendations, an agreed upon procedure for responding to employer inquiries, and an agreement not to disparage you, are all factors to consider. Your employer may be willing to remove a disparaging memo or evaluation from your file. It may be willing to let you resign retroactively to the last active date of employment to remove the stain of an involuntary termination from your record. It may agree not to contest your application for certain benefits such as unemployment benefits. It may agree to finance continued health benefits or outplacement services. Nearly anything both sides will agree to can be placed into a settlement agreement.

Q: My lawyer has mentioned something about mediation. What is mediation?

A: *Mediation* is a process whereby a third party attempts to work with both parties to try to facilitate settlement. Mediation is not *arbitration*. A mediator does not decide the case. Typically, the parties jointly select a third party to serve as mediator and a date is set for mediation. At mediation, both sides are represented and the mediator will do shuttle diplomacy—taking offers and counter offers back and forth until the case is either settled or settlement fails.

From the employee's perspective, mediation is a no-lose proposition. If the amount offered in settlement at the mediation is insufficient, you should just proceed with the case.

SECTION THREE:

Frequently Asked Questions About Your Rights in the Workplace

Q: ***When I am pursuing employment, what can I do to protect myself?***

A: The best way to protect yourself is to get information. In some states you can hold your employer to whatever promises have been made to you, whether oral or written, so long as the *promises* have not been effectively disclaimed. Ask to see a copy of the employee handbook. Ask to see copies of the personnel rules and procedures.

In the hiring interview, ask questions about matters that are important to you. The answers that you get about such things as job title, salary, line of authority, fringe benefits, and longevity in the job are material to your decision to take the job. They are representations your employer makes to induce you to accept the job. In many states, they are promises you can hold your employer to in a court of law.

If you are an out-of-state recruit, before agreeing to move you could memorialize the promises by writing a letter to the employer that recite the promises. Then, request the employer to signify its agreement by returning a copy of the letter signed by an authorized representative in a space indicated beneath the statement "IT IS SO AGREED," inserted at the bottom of your letter. Be sure to show the letter to your attorney before you send it to make sure it says what you mean to say and covers all the points.

If you are an out-of-state recruit, you can ask pointed questions about the stability of your position. It would be helpful to ask the employer about the financial condition of the company and whether the employer foresees any problem that would prevent that position from being continued indefinitely into the future.

Problems besides economic woes can surprise the employee. Sometimes an employee is recruited to a company only to find that the company is soon sold to outsiders who have their own staff they wish to bring with them. Holdovers from previous administrations are viewed with distrust. You can inquire whether the company is presently engaged in, or is likely to engage in, sale or merger discussions.

As a prospective employee, you may think that you are pushing it to expect such cooperation or to expect the employer to put its promises down in black and white. Some employers are willing to put their promises in writing. If the issues are critical to your personal decision to pull up stakes and move, however, you may decide the risk you take is necessary.

Q: ***I know I am an employee at will. Does that mean I have no right to sue under any circumstances?***

A: No. All that means is that you can be terminated at any time without cause, except for an unlawful reason. Unlawful reasons include reasons that violate federal or state discrimination laws (see Chapter 2), whistleblowing laws (see Chapter 10), or state tort laws for wrongful discharge. (see Chapter 3.) You may also be able to sue under federal or state laws for discrimination in hiring, pay, promotion, or demotion. In addition, the manner in which you have been treated or terminated may give rise to liability for other torts for such things as invasion of privacy, defamation of character, or intentional inflection of emotional distress. (see Chapter 4.)

Q: *The document I signed says I am an independent contractor. Does that mean I have no protection?*

A: No. Whether you are an employee or not is not completely dependent upon labels. In one case, for example, the Supreme Court held professional golfer Casey Martin could challenge the PGA even though he was classified as an independent contractor.[239] An *economics realities* test is sometimes applied in cases brought under Title VII, the ADEA, and ERISA. Under that and similar tests the courts will look principally to whether the employer has the right to control the person in the performance of the work.[240]

In one case, the Supreme Court said it would look to such factors such as:

- the skill required;
- the source of the instrumentalities and tools;
- the location of the work;
- the duration of the relationship between the parties;
- whether the hiring party has the right to assign additional projects to the third party;
- the extent of the hired party's discretion over when and how long to work;
- the method of payment;
- the hired party's role in hiring and paying assistants;
- whether the work is part of the regular business of the hiring party;
- whether the hiring party is in business;
- the provision of employee benefits; and,
- the tax treatment of the hired party.[241]

This test is very similar to the traditional common law *right to control* test that is applied today in many states in which the issue principally turns on the employer's right to control the manner and means by which the work is accomplished.

Q: *Can they reduce my pay or fringe benefits?*

A: The employer is allowed to make prospective changes in the wages of most fringe benefits offered to employees. The employer cannot say at the end of your work day, "Oh, by the way, for the last four hours on your shift, I cut your pay by $2 an hour." The reason is that you have already performed your part of the bargain. However, in the absence of any other understanding and apart from other considerations, the employer can say at the end of your shift, "I can no longer afford to pay you the same wages. Starting tomorrow you will be paid $2 an hour less." If you show up and work, you have accepted that new offer.

Some benefits that are provided in the future or over a period of time may follow a different rule. Vacation benefits, for example, are usually made available on an annual basis. The understanding may be that the employee is entitled to one week of vacation at the end of the first six months on the job. Different states have different rules, but after you start working, the employer may not be able to change the rules and defer your entitlement to the vacation until after one year of service. Likewise, if the understanding is that during the current year you are entitled to two weeks' vacation, the employer may not be able to reduce that benefit or change the benefit in midstream during that year. However, the employer will likely be able to reduce future vacation benefits subject to any contrary express or implied understanding between the parties.

For pension and health plan benefits for employees that are subject to *Employee Retirement Income Security Act* (ERISA), vested pension rights cannot be taken away, while other benefit plans typically can be reduced prospectively or abolished if the employer satisfies certain criteria.

Q: *My performance review was not as high as it should have been. What should I do?*

A: More employment relationships are wrecked by inappropriate responses by employees to their performance reviews than any other cause. No one likes to think he or she is less than perfect, especially when he or she devotes great effort to a job. Nor does anyone like to think that his or her performance has slipped. But sometimes that happens. And even when you have been unfairly criticized by your boss, it usually does you no good to:

- tell the boss that he or she is being unfair;
- write a lengthy rebuttal;
- go over your boss' head to complain about this treatment;
- call your boss a liar; or,
- ask your boss to step outside.

In most cases, if you strongly disagree with a negative appraisal, you should apply the *overnight, cool-off rule*. Do not react immediately. If you are angry, whatever you do will be wrong. When you go to work the next day, arrange to speak with the boss at the best time of the day for that boss to hear what you have to say (some bosses are better in the morning, some just after lunch). Tell the boss your concern. Relay your message in a way that does not convey to the boss that you reject his or her judgment. Otherwise, the boss will think you lack perception. Instead, begin by telling the boss how the evaluation makes you feel. You can be disappointed by an appraisal without rejecting its message. Then tell the boss why your expectations were higher. Relate your accomplishments, the special project, and the company award in an organized, articulate manner. This approach is more apt to get the boss to revise the appraisal.

Do not be surprised, however, if the appraisal is not revised. Realize that the boss may have graded you down to assert authority over you. To revise the appraisal would be tantamount to losing the struggle for control. Or your reasons just may not be sufficient to merit a revised appraisal. Remember that if your appraisal is upgraded from your employer's perspective, everyone else will want theirs upgraded too.

Appraisals are typically so subjective that substantially identical performance by two individuals in the office can be perceived by the manager to be quite different in quality. Many managers do not begin to downgrade performance in performance appraisals unless some other problem occurs that arouses their hostility. Usually, it is that other issue that you need to address rather than anything that is said in the appraisal itself.

Q: *I have just received a written warning. What should I do?*

A: The considerations expressed for the previous question apply equally when you have received a written warning, except that you may be one step closer to termination because you received formal *corrective action*.

Theoretically, corrective action gives the employee notice of a perceived deficiency and an opportunity to correct it. Corrective action policies most often incorporate a ladder of *progressive discipline*—from oral to written warnings, followed by probation or suspension, followed by termination. There is nothing wrong with legitimate corrective action, but a problem arises when the employer uses it for some other purpose.

You may feel that you are in jeopardy because you have had your *one warning* and you need to contest it to protect yourself. On the other hand, contesting it may be futile and may only hasten the final blow. It is best to get legal advice before reacting. Your reaction itself could precipitate a termination. (For more on surviving discipline, see Chapter 16.)

Q: *What about probation? When does that come into play?*

A: *Probation* is a term that today is largely restricted to apply to public employers or union work forces where an employee must serve an initial period of satisfactory performance before being entitled to civil service or union contract cause for termination protection.

While it is often said that during your probationary period you can be fired for any reason, it is more accurate to say you can be fired for any lawful reason. During that period, you still cannot be fired because of race, sex, age, national origin, religion, disability, or other protected class status or activity.

Some private employers still use the term probation to refer to either an initial period of employment before which you have no benefits or to a stage of discipline during which it reserves the right to fire you if you repeat an offense.

Q: *When should I speak up and object to the discriminatory treatment?*

A: When you have a good relationship with your employer, communication is always healthy. On the other hand, if your relationship is rocky, the tendency is to speak up—when you have nothing left to lose; when it does not matter that speaking up may cost you your job; when you cannot take it any longer without relief anyway; or when your need to speak out outweighs any fear that your employer may tell a prospective employer that you are a troublemaker. You also speak up when you cannot afford to leave; when you have been with the same company for an extended period doing the same thing and do not know anything else; when your skill is so specialized that if you are forced out there is no place left in town to go; or when you are unemployable elsewhere because of your physical condition.

If the situation has not become severe, you have to make a personal decision that no one can later second guess as to when to put yourself and your job on the line. Objecting may cost you your job. Not objecting could cause you to give up and abandon your job. Not objecting could also prejudice any legal case you would later wish to bring. It could cause doubt that the condition you expressed strong disapproval of existed. It could also deprive you of the protection afforded to those who engage in whistleblowing activities.

In sexual harassment and other discrimination cases, current employees who are victims of on-the-job harassment that does not involve a *tangible employment action*, such as a termination or demotion, are required to speak up in order to claim the legal protection of the law that prohibits such harassment. (see Chapter 15.) Unless you speak up, your legal protection may be lost if it is later determined that you unreasonably failed to do so.

Q: *Is there any way I can relieve some pressure at work?*

A: If you want or need to hold onto your job after a blowup with the boss, one helpful strategy is the *three contact rule*. Use this to create three positive contacts once a week, over the next three weeks with the boss.

The object is to allow issues besides you to preoccupy your boss. So think of something about which you can solicit your boss' input, something that is safe so that you can positively receive and act upon the input regardless of its substance. Here, you want to convey the impression that you are not so distracted by your boss' wrath and frozen by fear into inaction.

Structure the contact in a nonadversarial and nonthreatening way. Just a casual conversation in a hallway will do. You want the boss to be thinking of you as you are walking away after each contact, "I can work with this person."

Q: *Should I be keeping a log or diary?*

A: Lawyers are divided on whether a plaintiff should keep a log or diary of events pertaining to the case. In particular, *pain diaries* are controversial. If you merely forget to record how you are feeling on a particular day, the mistaken impression can be made that you had no pain that day.

However, words used by your boss in conversations are important, as are specific incidents of harassment and the exact sequence of events. Your lawyer may wish that you keep a log rather than forget important details. If you do start keeping a log, be sure to make your entries at home rather than at work. You do not want the people who you work with to start thinking that you are writing about them.

Q: *Should I involve my human resources department?*

A: Again, unless you communicate observable discrimination in the workplace, you may prejudice any later claims that it existed. (see Chapter 2.) Further, you may be required to report it under the terms of your employee handbook.

You should not be naive about the situation. Most human resources departments operate to assist and support management.

Companies have set up internal grievance procedures, ombudsmen, counselors, and the like to encourage disputes to remain *all in the family*. Such devices are sometimes effective as a means of correcting discrimination. Still, they are misused as vehicles to promote the company line and discourage further pursuit of claims. More often, however, depending on the competence of the people at your company and your level of trust, you may wish to first go through the internal process to relieve a conflict. Be careful, though, because anything you say may be used against you later on.

This is not to say that all human resources employees are ill willed or conspire together to vanquish the innocent employee. By nature, however, we act to protect ourselves. Human resources staff learn early that they best protect themselves by supporting line management. They learn they do not get very far in the organization by bucking the managers they serve.

Also, if you consider pursuing an *internal grievance*, be careful that in doing so you do not subject yourself to a final and binding internal decision that the employer will argue precludes you from pursuing any court remedy. On the other hand, yours may provide that such pursuit is mandatory. Your employer may contend later on that you cannot pursue certain legal claims if you failed to pursue the mandatory grievance machinery. If there is any doubt about what yours provides or what course to take, seek legal advice.

Q: ***If I have a problem, do I have to go through my union?***

A: If you are a union member or are given protection under a union contract and your collective bargaining agreement has a grievance mechanism that allows your particular dispute a hearing, the law is structured so that you are strongly urged to use that grievance mechanism. If you do not, you may be precluded from bringing a court suit because you failed to exhaust your internal remedies.

There are exceptions to this rule, most notably in discrimination cases. Some other exceptions put a heavy burden of proof on the employee. You should ordinarily speak with a lawyer about what to do in your case. However, be aware of the sometimes short deadlines for filing a grievance under your collective bargaining agreement.

Read the agreement yourself and speak with your union steward or business agent about those time lines and about whether your issue is grievable.

Q: *I lost my union grievance. Can I still pursue other legal remedies?*

A: Even if your grievance went to arbitration and you lost, you may pursue your discrimination remedies even if discrimination was one of the issues you raised at the arbitration hearing. Judges understand that your ability to gather favorable evidence during union grievance proceedings is more limited than under liberal court discovery rules.

Also, in some cases, you are entitled to sue the union, the employer, or both in what is known as *unfair representation* cases, where the union failed to fulfill its duty of fair representation to you. (see Chapter 11.)

Other claims you may have, such as those created by an assault, battery, or defamation, may not relate at all to the arbitration. You may be able to pursue those other claims in court.

Q: *I got hurt on the job on a machine my employer did not properly maintain. Can I sue my employer for negligence?*

A: Probably not. Workers' compensation is said to be the *exclusive remedy* for employer negligence leading to injury. Statutory exceptions are typically provided for injuries intentionally caused by the employer. Litigation in each state have fleshed out the exact requirements to fall within the exception. There may be a way in your state to sue if a *third party* contributed to the injury by supplying defective equipment, for example, or if the injury did not *arise out of* the work itself. (see Chapter 11.) However, workers' compensation laws were passed to avoid these very types of lawsuits.

Q: *My employer is not accommodating my disability. What should I do?*

A: Sometimes the solution is simple. Sometimes you may have been talking to the wrong person at work. A first-line supervisor may not have had sufficient training to understand the need to accommodate your request or at least to pass on your request to higher ups or human resources. Sometimes if your supervisor is unwilling to give you accommodation, you may have to go directly to human resources yourself. If there is no human resources department, go to that person's supervisor to obtain relief.

On other occasions, the problem can be solved by providing the proper medical documentation to support your need for accommodation. You cannot doctor yourself. Nor are you an expert in worksite modification. You know your job and the demands of your position. You also know the physical limitations you have. It may seem obvious to you that a particular accommodation is required. However, your own medical opinion about your limitations is not authoritative to your employer. But that same opinion coming from your doctor about a weight lifting limitation, for example, will be taken seriously.

It is often the case that one's physical condition changes over time, for better or worse. Your need for accommodation may have extended over a considerable period. You may have become used to working out minor adjustments to your workplace informally with your supervisor. But if your condition has deteriorated over time and you can do less and less of your job, at some point your request for accommodation will be viewed as moving to such a level that the informal relationship you have relied on is insufficient to obtain relief without outside medical support. Do not panic if you find you have reached the apparent limit of your employer's willingness to work with you. It just may be time to go back to your doctor for more support.

Finally, it could be that what you are requesting is unsupportable. The employer is not obligated to fulfill every desire of yours. It must only reasonably accommodate your disability. You may be asking for something beyond what is required. You may be focused on the deluxe lift truck you saw on television, when a simple hoist will do. The employer must reasonably accommodate you. While it should listen to your ideas, it does not necessarily have to select the form of accommodation you are requesting. (For more information about the *Americans with Disabilities Act*, see Chapter 2.)

Q: *If I am being sexually harassed, what should I do?*

A: The laws are skewed in favor of the person who reports the harassment. (see Chapters 7 and 15.) If you and your attorney decide the thing to do is report it, report it to the human resources manager of the company. If there is no human resources manager, you can report it to the general manager or owner. If the person who is doing the harassing is the owner, you can tell him or her to stop the harassment. If that person does not stop, you can write a memo to that person restating your request. If you do, keep a copy of the memo. Also, you can speak to another company manager about it and ask that person to intercede. The memo and this witness will provide evidence later on of the harassment and the protest. They will also impress upon the the boss that your protests are serious and help dispel the fantasy that you are just playing *hard to get*.

Power is intoxicating. Sadly, some people at the top of business organizations believe that they are irresistible and that all subordinates desire them as sexual partners. Fortunately, resistance and disclosure often provide a quick cure. The problem is that the worker usually is too afraid of retaliation to disclose the harassment, believes erroneously that he or she can handle it personally, or has been discouraged in the past from believing that disclosure is the best way to remedy the situation.

If the preceding steps do not take care of the problem, a courteous letter from your attorney to upper management can sometimes be quite sobering to the offender, so long as upper management reacts responsibly, rather than defensively to protect the harasser.

Q: *I am being harassed at work by my boss. Can I quit without losing my rights?*

A: You may jeopardize some rights if you quit because of boss harassment. Boss harassment is a favorite tool of management to get rid of certain workers. Sometimes this method is used because of a worker's race, sex, or age; because he or she has engaged in a protected activity; or when cause is required to discharge a worker.

Many courts have recognized the principle of *wrongful constructive discharge*. This means that if a person quits under certain circumstances, the resignation will be treated as a discharge by the employer.

Under federal discrimination law, if you quit because the employer maintained objectively intolerable working conditions because of your protected class status or protected activity and you resign because of those conditions, the resignation will be treated as a wrongful constructive discharge. The discharge is supplied as a legal construct or fiction. Similarly, many states recognize wrongful constructive discharge in public policy tort cases if the circumstances fall within one of the accepted categories of wrongful discharge and the plaintiff can meet the requisite proof of intent in that jurisdiction. (see Chapter 3.)

The test is an objective one, however. If you quit, you are taking the chance that a juror, a year or two later, will second guess you and vote against you because the juror believed you should have held on a little longer.

Furthermore, you may place your unemployment compensation benefits in jeopardy by quitting. In some states, you forfeit those benefits if you voluntarily resign without good cause.

Consult an attorney before any planned resignation. Therefore, you can learn the law of constructive discharge in your state and obtain a professional assessment as to how close your situation comes in that jurisdiction to the body of case law on what amounts to *intolerable working conditions*.

Q: *My employer is offering me a demotion with a reduction in pay or a severance package. What should I do?*

A: What you choose to do is a highly personal choice. Certainly your feelings will be hurt by an offer of a lesser position. It may be embarrassing. Usually, however, any fear you may have about others holding you in scorn if you accept the lesser position is unfounded or exaggerated. Regardless, your decision should be based not on what others may think of you, but on what will be best for you.

Typically, it is easier to look for employment from a position of employment. It is also better to have a job that is paying you during your job search, even though it pays a few dollars less than you were formerly making. An offered severance may seem like a good deal until the money runs out and you are still without a job.

Q: *I have been told to resign or I will be terminated. What should I do?*

A: Sometimes workers are asked for their resignation or are told that, unless they resign, they will be fired. If this happens to you, obtain legal advice. Your lawyer may ask you to consider which—resignation or termination—would do you the most harm. I say *harm* rather than *good* because either result will have the potential for some damage and the object is to contain the damage.

If you are terminated, then in any later job application that asks whether you have been terminated you must respond, "yes." To give false information on an application form is grounds for termination. Résumé fraud may also cut off damages in your wrongful discharge case as of the date of discovery by the employer.

A termination can have a chilling effect on obtaining employment elsewhere. Employers like to hire persons who are currently employed and who are doing well with their current employer. They do not like to hire problem employees.

Consider your prospects for obtaining other employment. If the prospects are good and you believe that a termination would reverse the prospects, and you are not willing to sue your employer, then you and your lawyer may feel you should resign. If you are unsure of those prospects, however, and other factors make it difficult to get other employment anyway—such as a bad economic climate in the industry, your own limited specialty, or poor past employment history—then the two of you may balk at resigning. There is always the chance your employer will change its mind. Then, too, perhaps the termination warning was an idle threat.

While a resignation may, in some other cases, prejudice any legal rights you wish to assert against your employer, in most states, if your employer tells you to resign or be fired, those rights will not be lost. How can you prove you were given that ultimatum? Consider memorializing the conversation and your decision in writing as part of your resignation letter.

Philosophically, you should conduct yourself in life so as to maximize your chances of getting work and not live to further a lawsuit. Sometimes, however, a lawsuit will be all you have left to advance. Consult a lawyer about how a resignation would affect your legal rights before you decide whether to resign.

Q: *The hammer is about to fall. What should I be doing?*

A: Do not assume that just because things are rocky at work you will be fired. This will only cause further strain in what may be a salvageable employer-employee relationship. The first thing to do is to take steps to clear the air. Communication with your boss will relieve any unwarranted fear for both parties. Paranoia breeds in silence. If you believe that you are being set up for termination and that your meeting would only cause a blow up, consider taking the problem to your human resources manager for advice. Some companies are not opposed to using third-party mediators to facilitate the resolution of a dispute. If the problems with your supervisor are simply beyond repair, consider requesting a transfer to another department.

If you have decided to leave the company, you may want to negotiate time to look for another position, a severance pay package, or both. Be aware, though, that as soon as you express a desire to leave, they will want you to go immediately. Also, if you express that desire, you may have deflated your negotiating leverage. Consult with a lawyer on the pros and cons of announcing your desire to leave or broaching the subject of a negotiated severance. By all means, however, continue to do your job to the best of your ability while you are being paid to do it.

Q: *My boss lied to me about why I was terminated. Is that illegal?*

A: Except, arguably, in the few states where by state statute the employer is required to tell you in writing the reason for your termination, to be lied to is not itself illegal.

On the other hand, if you claim you were terminated because of unlawful discrimination on the basis of protected class status and are able to prove the employer's stated reason is false, that will greatly assist your case. The Supreme Court has held that if you disprove the employer's stated reason for termination, it will ordinarily raise an inference of unlawful discrimination.[242]

Q: *When I was first hired I signed an agreement to arbitrate any employment dispute. Is that agreement valid?*

A: Maybe. In 2001, the Supreme Court held that employment agreements are subject to the *Federal Arbitration Act* that is designed to compel the resolution of legal disputes outside the courts.[243]

Even so, courts have since tested the enforceability of arbitration agreements against the *common law* contract law of the state in which the agreements were made. Some arbitration agreements have been found to be unenforceable on grounds of *unconscionability*. The Supreme Court has held that generally applicable state law contract defenses, such as fraud, duress, or unconscionability, may be applied to invalidate arbitration agreements. The Supreme Court has also held that arbitration is enforceable only if substantive state rights are preserved, such as the right to recover punitive damages, where those are available.

Q: *What protection do I have if I file a complaint?*

A: Civil rights laws make discrimination illegal, as well as retaliation for opposing unlawful discrimination. It is also illegal to discriminate or retaliate against a person because the person has used the system set up by the antidiscrimination laws by filing a complaint of discrimination.

Does this mean the employer will not retaliate against you? No. In fact, retaliation under those circumstances is common. That is why legislators have passed laws prohibiting it. But if the employer retaliates against you, you have one more ground for complaint. Usually, proving retaliation is easier than proving the underlying discrimination that led to the initial complaint. (For more on whistleblowing and retaliation, see Chapter 10.)

Q: *I am an employee at will. I believe I have been terminated because* I know too much. *Is that wrongful discharge?*

A: Unfortunately, while it may be just as reprehensible for an employer to terminate someone whom it thinks may report unlawful conduct to the authorities as someone who actually has made such a report, the law of wrongful discharge has been developed to protect persons who have actually engaged in protected activity—even if that activity is a mere threat to report illegal activity. (see Chapter 3.)

Even if you cannot sue for wrongful discharge, alternative tort theories might be applicable. If, in the process of terminating you, the employer attacks your competence to effect your termination because of your knowledge of illegal activity, that could be the basis for a *defamation* claim. Similarly, if the firing manager is the person who is personally motivated to get you out of the way because of that knowledge, that could be the basis for a suit against that individual for *intentional interference with economic relations*. In the few states that permit it, it would be against the employer as well. (see Chapter 4.)

Q: *I am not a union employee. I work for a private employer. I have been terminated because my competence threatens my boss. Can I do anything about it?*

A: An employee at will can be terminated for any or no reason, except for one that violates a statute or public policy. No wrongful discharge claim for an at-will employee may be predicated upon a firing *without cause*, because none is needed. However, the employer may generate liability for defamation of character if it makes false and derogatory statements about your performance. Sometimes when a manager is called upon to justify a termination of a highly regarded employer, he or she succumbs to the temptation to *gold plate* the employee's alleged sins in order to save face with the boss or the workforce that remains. Ironically, it is often the case that the better the employee, the greater the sin that the firing manager feels pressure to assert to justify the discharge. If the manager succumbs to that pressure, liability for defamation may be generated. (see Chapter 4.)

GLOSSARY

A

Americans with Disabilities Act (ADA). A federal statute concerning discrimination against persons with disabilities.

administrative remedy. An available proceeding before an agency charged to enforce a law.

appeal. The stage of a lawsuit after a case is tried.

arbitrator. A person who decides the issues in dispute in an arbitration proceeding.

arbitration. A proceeding that is used to decide cases as an alternative to trial, typically under more streamlined rules and procedures.

at-will employment. Employment that is terminable without cause at the pleasure of the employer.

B

back pay. Lost wages from the date of termination to the date of trial.

C

civil law. The law that regulates the affairs of people and entities other than criminal law.

claim for relief. A legal theory advanced by a party in a court pleading.

COBRA (Consolidated Omnibus Budget Reconciliation Act). A federal statute that allows for the continuation of health insurance coverage after employment is terminated.

common law. Judge made law based upon prior case precedent.

complainant. The charging party in an administrative proceeding.
complaint. The legal document that starts a lawsuit.
contract. A legally enforceable agreement.

D

damages. The monetary relief a person in a lawsuit is requesting to be awarded.
defamation. A verbal or written statement that injures a person's reputation.
defendant. The person or entity that is being sued in a lawsuit.
deposition. An interrogation under oath by an attorney after a lawsuit is filed.
discharge. An involuntary termination of employment.
disclaimer. A statement that purports to negate a promise.
discrimination. To treat someone differently than others (which is usually unlawful only if the different treatment is because of protected class status or activity such as race, sex, age, etc.).
disparate impact. A test or other seemingly neutral selection tool that adversely affects a particular protected class.
disparate treatment. To treat members of a particular protected class differently.
due process. Procedural fairness, found typically in public or union employment, that usually includes notice of the charges and a fair opportunity to be heard.

E

economic damages. Typically, lost income.
EEOC (Equal Employment Opportunity Commission). A federal agency charged with investigating discrimination claims.
ERISA (Employee Retirement Income Security Act). A federal statute regarding the regulation of retirement accounts and certain other employment benefits.
exemplary damages. *See punitive damages.*

F

Family and Medical Leave Act (FMLA). A federal statute concerning unpaid leave for certain family and medical situations.

fraud. A misrepresentation by commission or omission.

front pay. Future lost income, measured from the date of trial forward.

G

grievance. An internal remedy, typically given to union workers, to contest an adverse personnel action.

H

HIPAA (Health Insurance Portability and Accountability Act). A federal statute allowing for immediate and continued health care coverage for employees switching employers.

hostile work environment. A charge in a discrimination case, typically that the number of acts of unlawful discrimination is so frequent, or that the acts of unlawful discrimination are so severe, so that discrimination pervades the working environment.

I

independent contractor. Typically, one who works for another, but is so free from the control of the other in doing the work so that an employment relationship is not formed.

intent. A state of mind that most often in tort law means acting to cause injury, or with knowledge that if an act occurs injury will likely result.

interrogatory. A written question that must be answered under oath after a lawsuit is filed.

J

just cause. Having a good reason to act.

L

layoff. A termination of employment, typically because of a reduction in force.

liquidated damages. A statutory penalty under the ADEA equal to two times the backpay award.

M

mediation. A dispute resolution process whereby a third party is used to facilitate a voluntary settlement between the parties.

mediator. A person who, unlike an arbitrator, does not decide who prevails, but serves as a facilitator to help the parties voluntarily settle a lawsuit.

N

noneconomic damages. Damages other than for lost income and expenses, such as for emotional distress or injury to reputation.

O

OSHA (Occupational Safety and Health Act). A federal statute concerning workplace safety.

P

plaintiff. The person or entity in a lawsuit that initiates it.

private sector employment. Employment other than with a government body.

probationary period. Typically found in public sector or union employment, the period that must be served before an employee acquires full rights, including just cause protection.

progressive discipline. A disciplinary system that involves ascending levels of discipline if performance does not improve after notice, typically including a verbal warning and at least one written warning before termination.

protected class. A classification of persons to which Congress or a state legislature has afforded legal protection against discrimination or retaliation.

public sector employment. Employment with any government body.

punitive damages. Damages awarded not to compensate a victim for damages suffered, but to punish the defendant and set an example for others.

Q

qualified privilege. In the law of defamation, a conditional right to speak ill of another, which is lost if abused in certain ways.

R

reasonable accommodation. An adjustment or allowance that employers are required to give to disabled workers to enable them to perform their work, such as a job modification, a work aid, or a leave of absence.

recklessness. A state of mind in which a person acts without regard to the consequences that will likely result from their acts or with an *I do not care* attitude.

reinstatement. As a remedy in a discrimination case, a court order that the employee be rehired.

respondent. The party against which an administrative complaint is filed.

retainer agreement. A document that formalizes an attorney-client relationship and expresses its terms.

reverse discrimination. A claim that a member of a majority racial group, for example, is being or has been discriminated against.

right to sue letter. A letter issued by a federal or state administrative agency that grants the right to initiate a lawsuit within a stated period of time.

S

settlement. An agreed upon resolution of a lawsuit by the parties.

sexual harassment. Any verbal or physical conduct of a sexual nature that is unwelcome, and would be offensive to a reasonable victim.

statute. A bill passed by Congress or a state legislature that is signed into law by the president or a governor.

summary judgment. A pretrial motion in which a party contends its opponent is not entitled to a jury trial because there are no factual issues in dispute to be resolved by a jury, and that the judge can decide the case as a matter of law.

T

termination. A cessation of employment, including a layoff, other than a voluntary resignation.

Title VII. That part of the Civil Rights Act of 1964 that prohibits employment discrimination.

tort. A civil wrong of a noncontractual nature, such as assault, battery, or defamation.

trial. A formal court proceeding in which a factfinder, be it judge or jury, is called upon to decide who prevails after a full presentation of the evidence.

U

undue hardship. That level of hardship that makes a proposed accommodation unreasonable for an employer to bear.

V

verdict. A jury's decision.

W

WARN Act (Worker Adjustment and Retraining Act). A federal statute requiring notice to workers of plant closings and mass layoffs.

whistleblower laws. Laws that protect those who oppose illegal activity.

wrongful constructive discharge. A resignation induced by an employer under circumstances in which had the person been terminated, the termination would have been unlawful.

wrongful discharge. A termination of employment under circumstances that makes it unlawful, such as for opposing illegal activity.

–Appendix A–
EEOC OFFICE DIRECTORY

The Equal Employment Opportunity Commission (EEOC) is the federal agency charged with receiving most federally-based administrative complaints of discrimination including those for race, color, national origin, religion, sex, age, and disability. You may be able to make a joint federal and state filing through your state civil rights enforcement agency if your state has one.

This appendix provides information on how to reach your regional EEOC office directly.

HEADQUARTERS

U.S. Equal Employment Opportunity Commission
1801 L Street, N.W.
Washington, DC 20507
202-663-4900

FIELD OFFICES

To be automatically connected with the nearest EEOC field office, call: 800-669-4000.

Albuquerque District Office
505 Marquette Street, N.W.
Suite 900
9th Floor
Albuquerque, NM 87102
505-248-5201

Atlanta District Office
Sam Nunn Atlanta Federal Center
100 Alabama Street, S.W.
Suite 4R30
Atlanta, GA 30303
404-562-6800

Baltimore District Office
City Crescent Building
10 South Howard Street
3rd Floor
Baltimore, MD 21201
410-962-3932

Birmingham District Office
Ridge Park Place
1130 22nd Street South
Suite 2000
Birmingham, AL 35205
205-212-2100

Boston Area Office
John F. Kennedy Federal Building
475 Government Center
Boston, MA 02203
617-565-3200

Buffalo Local Office
6 Fountain Plaza
Suite 350
Buffalo, NY 14202
716-551-4441

Charlotte District Office
129 West Trade Street
Suite 400
Charlotte, NC 28202
704-344-6682

Chicago District Office
500 West Madison Street
Suite 2800
Chicago, IL 60661
312-353-2713

Cincinnati Area Office
John W. Peck Federal Office Building
550 Main Street
10th Floor
Cincinnati, OH 45202
513-684-2851

Cleveland District Office
Tower City Skylight Office Tower
1660 West Second Street
Suite 850
Cleveland, OH 44113-1412
216-522-2003

Dallas District Office
207 South Houston Street
3rd Floor
Dallas, TX 75202
214-253-2700

Denver District Office
303 East 17th Avenue
Suite 510
Denver, CO 80203
303-866-1300

Detroit District Office
Patrick V. McNamara Building
477 Michigan Avenue
Room 865
Detroit, MI 48226
313-226-4600

El Paso Area Office
300 East Main Street
Suite 500
El Paso, TX 79901
915-534-6700

Fresno Local Office
1265 West Shaw Avenue
Suite 103
Fresno, CA 93711
559-487-5793

Greensboro Local Office
2303 West Meadow View Road
Suite 201
Greensboro, NC 27407
336-547-4188

Greenville Local Office
301 North Main Street
Suite 1402
Greenville, SC 29601-9916
864-241-4400

Honolulu Local Office
300 Ala Moana Boulevard
Room 7-127
P.O. Box 50082
Honolulu, HI 96850-0051
808-541-3120

Houston District Office
Mickey Leland Federal Building
1919 Smith Street
Suites 600 and 700
Houston, TX 77002-8049
713-209-3320

Indianapolis District Office
101 West Ohio Street
Suite 1900
Indianapolis, IN 46204
317-226-7212

Jackson Area Office
Dr. A.H. McCoy Federal Building
100 West Capitol Street
Suite 207
Jackson, MS 39269
601-965-4537

Kansas City Area Office
Gateway Tower II
4th and State Avenues
9th Floor
Kansas City, KS 66101
913-551-5655

Little Rock Area Office
820 Louisiana Street
Suite 200
Little Rock, AR 72201
501-324-5060

Los Angeles District Office
Roybal Federal Building
255 East Temple Street
4th Floor
Los Angeles, CA 90012
213-894-1000

Louisville Area Office
600 Dr. Martin Luther King, Jr. Place
Suite 268
Louisville, KY 40202
502-582-6082

Memphis District Office
1407 Union Avenue
Suite 621
Memphis, TN 38104
901-544-0115

Miami District Office
One Biscayne Tower
2 South Biscayne Boulevard
Suite 2700
Miami, FL 33131
305-536-4491

Milwaukee District Office
Reuss Federal Plaza
310 West Wisconsin Avenue
Suite 800
Milwaukee, WI 53203-2292
414-297-1111

Minneapolis Area Office
Towle Building
330 South Second Avenue
Suite 430
Minneapolis, MN 55401-2224
612-335-4040

Nashville Area Office
50 Vantage Way
Suite 202
Nashville, TN 37228-9940
615-736-5820

Newark Area Office
1 Newark Center
21st Floor
Newark, NJ 07102-5233
973-645-6383

New Orleans District Office
701 Loyola Avenue
Suite 600
New Orleans, LA 70113-9936
504-589-2329

New York District Office
33 Whitehall Street
11th Floor
New York, NY 10004
212-336-3620

Norfolk Area Office
Federal Building
200 Granby Street
Suite 739
Norfolk, VA 23510
757-441-3470

Oakland Local Office
1301 Clay Street
Suite 1170-N
Oakland, CA 94612-5217
510-637-3230

Oklahoma Area Office
210 Park Avenue
Suite 1350
Oklahoma City, OK 73102
405-231-4911

Philadelphia District Office
The Bourse Building
21 South 5th Street
Suite 400
Philadephia, PA 19106
215-440-2600

Phoenix District Office
3300 North Central Avenue
Suite 690
Phoenix, AZ 85012-2504
602-640-5000

Pittsburgh Area Office
Liberty Center
1001 Liberty Avenue
Suite 300
Pittsburgh, PA 15222-4187
412-644-3444

Raleigh Area Office
1309 Annapolis Drive
Raleigh, NC 27608-2129
919-856-4064

Richmond Area Office
830 East Main Street
6th Floor
Richmond, VA 23219
804-771-2200

San Antonio District Office
Mockingbird Plaza II
5410 Fredericksburg Road
Suite 200
San Antonio, TX 78229
210-281-7600

San Diego Area Office
Wells Fargo Bank Building
401 B Street
Suite 510
San Diego, CA 92101
619-557-7235

San Francisco District Office
350 The Embarcadero
Suite 500
San Francisco, CA 94103-1260
415-625-5600

San Jose Local Office
96 North 3rd Street
Suite 200
San Jose, CA 95112
408-291-7352

San Juan Area Office
525 F.D. Roosevelt Avenue
Plaza Las Americas
Suite 1202
San Juan, Puerto Rico 00918-8001
787-771-1464

Savannah Local Office
410 Mall Boulevard
Suite G
Savannah, GA 31406-4821
912-652-4234

Seattle District Office
Federal Office Building
909 First Avenue
Suite 400
Seattle, WA 98104-1061
206-220-6883

St. Louis District Office
Robert A. Young Federal Building
1222 Spruce Street
Room 8.100
St. Louis, MO 63103
314-539-7800

Tampa Area Office
501 East Polk Street
Suite 1000
Tampa, FL 33602
813-228-2310

Washington Field Office
1801 L Street, N.W.
Suite 100
Washington, DC 20507
202-419-0700

–Appendix B–

STATE DISCRIMINATION LAWS AND AGENCIES

There are many differences from state to state in the content of state discrimination laws. Listed here in alphabetical order is a description of the discrimination laws of each state and the District of Columbia so that you may find what yours provides. Also listed is information on how to reach your state discrimination enforcement agency, if you have one, for questions or claim filings.

ALABAMA

Law

Prohibits discrimination against employees 40 years and over on the basis of age. (Ala. Code Secs. 25-01-20 and following.) There is no statutory provision regarding discrimination on the basis of race, color, religion, sex, national origin, or disability, except in state employment.

Agency

There is no state civil rights agency.

ALASKA

Law

Prohibits discrimination because of race, religion, color, national origin, age, sex, physical or mental disability, marital status, pregnancy, or parenthood where reasonable demands of position do not require distinction.
(Alaska Stat. Secs. 18.80.010 and following.)

Agency

Alaska State Commission for Human Rights
800 A Street
Suite 204
Anchorage, Alaska 99501-3669
907-274-4692

ARIZONA

Law

Prohibits discrimination on basis of race, color, religion, sex, results of a genetic test, handicap, national origin, or age. (Ariz. Rev. Stat. Secs. 41-1461 and following.)

Agency

Arizona Civil Rights Division
Office of Arizona Attorney General
1275 West Washington Street
Phoenix, Arizona 85007
602-542-5263

ARKANSAS

Law

Prohibits discrimination on basis of race, religion, ancestry, national origin, gender, or sensory, mental, or physical disability. (Ark. Code Ann. Secs. 16-123- 102 and following.)

Agency

Equal Employment Opportunity Commission
Little Rock Area Office
820 Louisiana Street
Suite 200
Little Rock, Arkansas 72201
501-324-5060

CALIFORNIA

Law

Prohibits discrimination on basis of race, religious creed, color, national origin, ancestry, physical or mental disability, medical condition related to a history or diagnosis of cancer or to genetic characteristics, marital status, sex, age, or sexual orientation. (Cal. Govt C. Sec. 12940.)

Agency

California Department of Fair Employment and Housing
Sacramento District Office
2000 O Street
Suite 120
Sacramento, California 95814-5212
916-445-5523

COLORADO

Law

Prohibits discrimination on basis of disability, race, creed, color, sex, age, national origin, or ancestry. (Colo. Rev. Stat. Sec. 24-34-402.) Makes unlawful termination for engaging in lawful activity off employer's premises, unless restriction relates to a bona fide occupational requirement, is reasonably and rationally related to employment activities and responsibilities of a particular employee or employee group, or is necessary to avoid conflict of interest or appearance thereof.
(Colo. Rev. Stat. Sec. 24-34-402.5.)

Agency

Colorado Civil Rights Division Commission
1560 Broadway
Suite 1050
Denver, Colorado 80202
303-894-2997

CONNECTICUT

Law

Prohibits discrimination on basis of race, color, religious creed, age, sex, marital status, national origin, ancestry, present or past history of mental disability, mental retardation, learning disability or physical disability, and genetic information or sexual orientation. (Conn. Gen. Stat. Secs. 46a–60 and following.)

Agency

Connecticut Commission on Human Rights and Opportunities
21 Grand Street
Hartford, Connecticut 06106
860-541-3400

DELAWARE

Law

Prohibits discrimination on basis of race, marital status, genetic information, color, age, religion, sex, or national origin
(Del. Code Ann Tit. 19, Sec. 711.)

Agency

Delaware Department of Labor
4425 North Market Street
Wilmington, Delaware 19802

DISTRICT OF COLUMBIA

Law

Prohibits discrimination on basis of actual or perceived race, color, religion, national origin, sex, age, marital status, personal appearance, sexual orientation, familial status, family responsibilities, disability, matriculation, or political affiliation.
(D.C. Code Sec. 2-1402.11.)

Agency

Office of Human Rights
441 4th Street, N.W.
Suite 570 North
Washington, DC 20001
202-727-4559

FLORIDA

Law

Prohibits discrimination on basis of race, color, religion, sex, national origin, age, handicap, or marital status.
(Fla. Stat. Sec. 760.01.)

Agency

Florida Commission on Human Relations
2009 Apalachee Parkway
Suite 100
Tallahassee, Florida 32301
850-488-7082

GEORGIA

Law

Prohibits discrimination on basis of sex (Ga. Code Ann. Sec. 34-5-1), age (40–70) (Ga. Code Ann. Sec. 34-1-2), handicap (Ga. Code Ann. Secs. 34-6A-1 and following), and attendance at a judicial proceeding except where employee is charged with a crime. (Ga. Code Ann. Sec. 34-1-3.)

Also prohibits discrimination in public employment on basis of race, color, religion, national origin, sex, handicap, or age (40–70). (Ga. Code Ann. Sec. 45-19-29.)

Agency

Georgia Commission on Equal Opportunity
Suite 710—International Tower
229 Peachtree Street, N.E.
Atlanta, Georgia 30303-1605
404-656-1736

HAWAII

Law

Prohibits discrimination on basis of race, sex, sexual orientation, age, religion, color, ancestry, disability, marital status, or arrest and court record not rationally related to job. Also prohibits discrimination against lactating employee who breast-feeds or expresses milk during meal or break period. (Haw. Rev. Stat. Sec. 378-10-2.) Prohibits discrimination solely on ground employer is summoned as garnishee for employee's debt, or because of work injury compensable under workers' compensation law. (Haw. Rev. Stat. Sec. 378-32.)

Agency

Hawaii Civil Rights Commission
Princess Keelikolani Building
830 Punchbowl Street #441
Honolulu, Hawaii 96813
808-586-8636

IDAHO

Law

Prohibits discrimination on the basis of race, color, religion, sex, national origin, age (40 and over), or disability.
(Idaho Code Sec. 67-5909.)

Agency

Idaho Human Rights Commission
P.O. Box 83720
650 West State Street
Room 100
Boise, Idaho 83720-0306
208-332-1820

ILLINOIS

Law

Prohibits discrimination on basis of race, color, religion, national origin, ancestry, age (40 to 70), sex, marital status, physical or mental handicap, military status, or unfavorable discharge except for dishonorable discharge.
(775 ILCS 5/1-102 and following.)

Agency

Illinois Human Rights Commission
James R. Thompson Center
100 West Randolph Street
Suite 5-100
Chicago, Illinois 60601
312-814-6269

William G. Stratton Office Building
Room 404
Springfield, Illinois 62706
217-785-4350

INDIANA

Law

Prohibits discrimination on basis of race, religion, color, sex, disability, national origin, ancestry, and age (40–70). (Ind. Code Sec. 22-9-1-1 and following.)

Agency

Indiana Civil Rights Commission
100 North Senate Avenue
Indiana Government Center North
Room N103
Indianapolis, Indiana 46204
317-232-2600

IOWA

Law

Prohibits discrimination on basis of age, race, creed, color, sex, national origin, religion, or disability. (Iowa Code Sec. 216.6.)

Agency

Iowa Civil Rights Commission
Grimes State Office Building
400 East 14th Street
Des Moines, Iowa 50319-1004
515-281-4121

KANSAS

Law

Prohibits discrimination on basis of race, religion, color, sex, disability, national origin, or ancestry, without business necessity. (Kan. Stat. Ann. Sec. 44-1009.) Age discrimination for reasons of age 18 or more is prohibited unless a valid business motive exists, except that executives may be forced to retire at age 65 if they will receive at least $44,000 per year in retirement benefits. (Kan. Stat. Ann. Secs. 44-1113 and -1118.)

Agency

Kansas Human Rights Commission
Landon State Office Building
900 S.W. Jackson
Suite 568-S
Topeka, Kansas 66612-1258
785-296-3206

KENTUCKY

Law

Prohibits discrimination on basis of race, color, religion, national origin, sex, disability, age (40 and over), or because the person is a smoker or nonsmoker so long as the person complies with any workplace policy concerning smoking. (Ky. Rev. Stat. Ann. Secs. 344.030 and following.)

Agency

Kentucky Commission on Human Rights
332 West Broadway
Suite 700
Louisville, Kentucky 40202
502-595-4024

LOUISIANA

Law

Prohibits discrimination on basis of age (40 and over), race, color, religion, pregnancy, childbirth and related medical conditions, disability, protected genetic information, sex, and national origin. (La. Rev. Stat. Ann. 23:301 and following.)

Agency

Louisiana Commission on Human Rights
1001 North 23rd Street
Suite 262
Baton Rouge, Louisiana 70802
225-342-6969

MAINE

Law

Prohibits discrimination on basis of race, color, sex, physical or mental disability, religion, age, ancestry, national origin, for previous assertion of claim or right under workers' compensation laws, or for previous activity under state Whistleblower's Protection Act. Also prohibits discrimination on the basis of sexual preference. (Me. Rev. Stat. Ann. Tit 5, Sec. 4553 (10-g).)

Agency

Maine Human Rights Commission
51 State House Station
Augusta, Maine 04333-0051
207-624-6050

MARYLAND

Law

Prohibits discrimination on basis of race, color, religion, sex, age, national origin, marital status, genetic information, sexual orientation, physical or mental disability unrelated in nature and extent so as to reasonably preclude performance of employment for refusing to submit to a genetic test or make available the results of a genetic test, or for opposing any unlawful practice or participation in proceeding. (Md. Ann. Code Art. 49B, Sec. 16.)

Agency

Maryland Commission on Human Relations
William Donald Schaefer Towers
6 St. Paul Street
Suite 900
Baltimore, Maryland 21202
410-767-8600

MASSACHUSETTS

Law

Prohibits discrimination on basis of race, color, religious creed, national origin, sex, sexual orientation, which shall not include persons whose sexual orientation involves minor children as the sex object, genetic information, ancestry, age (40 and over), handicap, or membership in labor unions. (Mass. Gen. Laws Ch. 151 B, Sec. 4 and following.) Also prohibits discrimination against persons refusing to provide information regarding arrests not leading to conviction, and first convictions for certain violations and misdemeanors. (Sec. 4 [9].) Also prohibits discrimination against persons who failed to inform of commitment to mental institution, provided person has been discharged and has psychiatric certification of mental competence. (Sec. 4 [9A].) Also prohibits discrimination against person who opposed practices forbidden by civil rights laws (Sec. 4 [4]) or who aid or encourage any other person to exercise civil rights. (Sec. 4 [4A].) Also prohibits discrimination on basis of political activity.
(Mass. Gen. Laws Ch. 56, Sec. 33.)

Agency

Massachusetts Commission Against Discrimination
One Ashburton Place
6th Floor
Room 601
Boston, Massachusetts 02108
617-994-6000

MICHIGAN

Law

Prohibits discrimination on basis of religion, race, color, national origin, sex, age, height, weight, or marital status. (Mich. Comp. Laws Secs. 37.2101 and following.) Also prohibits discrimination because of disability or genetic condition unrelated to ability to perform work.
(Mich. Comp. Laws Secs. 37.1101 and following.)

Agency

Michigan Department of Civil Rights
Capitol Tower Building
Suite 800
Lansing, Michigan 48933
517-335-3165

MINNESOTA

Law

Prohibits discrimination on basis of race, color, religious creed, national origin, sex, marital status, status with regard to public assistance, membership or activity in any antidiscrimination agency, disability, sexual orientation, and age (over 25). (Minn. Stat. Secs. 363.01 and following.) Also prohibits discrimination for not contributing to charity or community organization. (Minn. Stat. Sec. 181.937.) Also prohibits discrimination for lawful use of consumable products off employer's premises during

working hours. (Minn. Stat. Sec. 181.938.) Also prohibits discrimination for certain whistle blowing activities.
(Minn. Stat. Secs. 181.932 and 181.935.)

Agency

Minnesota Department of Human Rights
190 East 5th Street
Suite 700
St. Paul, Minnesota 55101
651-296-5663

MISSISSIPPI

Law

Does not regulate private employers. Prohibits discrimination in state employment on basis of race, color, religion, sex, national origin, age, or handicap. (Miss. Code Ann. Sec. 25-9-149.)

Agency

There is no state civil rights agency.

MISSOURI

Law

Prohibits employers of more than six persons from discriminating on basis of race, color, religion, national origin, sex, ancestry, age (40–70), or disability.
(Mo. Rev. Stat Secs. 213.010 and following.)

Agency

Missouri Commission on Human Rights
P.O. Box 1129
3315 West Truman Boulevard
Jefferson City, Missouri 65012-1129
573-751-4091

MONTANA

Law

Prohibits discrimination on the basis of race, creed, religion, color, national origin, age, physical or mental disability, marital status, or sex, when the reasonable demands of the position do not require an age, physical or mental disability, marital status, or sex distinction. (Mont. Code Ann. Sec. 49-2-303.)

Agency

Montana Human Rights Commission
P.O. Box 1728
1625 11th Avenue
Helena, Montana 59624-1728
406-444-2884

NEBRASKA

Law

Prohibits discrimination on basis of race, color, religion, sex, age (40–70), disability, marital status, or national origin.
(Neb. Rev. Stat. Secs. 48-1101 and following.)

Agency

Nebraska Equal Opportunity Commission
Nebraska State Office Building
301 Centennial Mall South
5th Floor
P.O. Box 94934
Lincoln, Nebraska 68509-4934
402-471-2024

NEVADA

Law

Prohibits discrimination because of race, color, religion, sex, sexual orientation, age, disability, or national origin.
(Nev. Rev. Stat. Sec. 613.330.)

Agency

Nevada Equal Rights Commission
1515 East Tropicana Avenue
Suite 590
Las Vegas, Nevada 89119-6522
702-486-7161

NEW HAMPSHIRE

Law

Prohibits discrimination on basis of age, sex, race, color, marital status, physical or mental disability, religious creed, national origin, or sexual orientation. (N.H. Rev. Stat. Ann. Sec. 354-A:7.)

Agency

New Hampshire Commission For Human Rights
2 Chenelle Drive
Concord, New Hampshire 03301-8501
603-271-2767

NEW JERSEY

Law

Prohibits discrimination on basis of race, creed, color, national origin, ancestry, age, marital status, affectional or sexual orientation, genetic information, sex, or atypical cellular or blood trait, disability for military service, nationality, refusal to submit to genetic tests or to make results available to employer, and age (to 70). (N.J. Stat. Ann. Sec. 10:5-12.) Also under Conscientious Employee Protection Act, prohibits discrimination against employee who discloses or threatens to disclose to supervisor or public body activity, policy or practice or employer co-employee or another employee with whom employer has a business relationship, that employee objectively reasonably believes violated law, testifies about any such violation, or objects to or refuses to participate in such activity, or one that is fraudulent or criminal, or incompatible with clear mandate of public policy concerning health, safety, welfare, or protection of the environment. (N.J. Stat. Ann. Sec. 34:19-3.)

Requires employee to first bring notice of such activity, policy or practice to attention of supervisor in writing, except in certain circumstances, including reasonable fear of personal safety. (N.J. Stat. Ann. Sec. 34:19-3.)

Agency

New Jersey Department of Laws and Safety
Divisions of Civil Rights
P.O. Box 089
Trenton, New Jersey 08625-0089
609-292-4605

NEW MEXICO

Law

Prohibits discrimination by reason of race, age, religion, color, national origin, ancestry, sex, spousal affiliation, physical or mental handicap, or serious medical condition.
(N.M. Stat. Ann. Secs. 28-1-7 and following.)

Agency

New Mexico Human Rights Commission
New Mexico Department of Labor Education Bureau
1596 Pacheco Street
Santa Fe, New Mexico 87505
800-566-9471

NEW YORK

Law

Prohibits discrimination because of age, race, creed, color, national origin, sexual orientation, sex, disability, genetic predispositions or carrier status, or marital status.
(N.Y. Exec. Law Sec. 296.)

Agency

New York State Division of Human Rights
One Fordham Plaza
Bronx, New York 10458
719-741-8400

NORTH CAROLINA

Law

Prohibits discrimination on account of race, religion, color, national origin, age, sex, handicap, or disability. (N.C. Gen. Stat. Sec. 143-422.2.) Also prohibits retaliation for filing complaint under Workers' Compensation Act, Wage and Hour Act, Office Safety and Health Act, or Occupational Safety and Health Act. (N.C. Gen. Stat. Sec. 95-196.) Also prohibits discrimination based on genetic testing or genetic information. (N.C. Gen. Stat. Sec. 95-196.) Also prohibits discrimination against persons who have complied with court ordered parental duties under juvenile code. (N.C. Gen. Stat. Sec. 95-241.) Also prohibits discrimination against persons using lawful products during nonworking hours, except that employer can restrict use if related to bona fide occupational requirements, fundamental objectives of organization, or violates substance abuse prevention programs. (N.C. Gen. Stat. Sec. 95-28.2.) Also prohibits discrimination against military personnel. (N.C. Gen. Stat. Sec. 127B-10-12.) Also prohibits discrimination for taking leave up to four hours annually to participate in or attend activities at child's school. (N.C. Gen. Stat. Sec. 95-28.3 [b].) Also prohibits discrimination against persons having AIDS or HIV infection in determining suitability for continued employment, but not prohibited to deny employment to job applicant based on confirmed positive test for AIDS virus infection.
(N.C. Gen. Stat. Sec. 130A-148[i].)

Agency

North Carolina Human Relations Commission
217 West Jones Street
4th Floor
Raleigh, North Carolina 27603
919-733-7996

or

North Carolina Human Relations Commission
1318 Mail Service Center
Raleigh, North Carolina 27603-1318

NORTH DAKOTA

Law

Prohibits discrimination because of race, color, religion, sex, national origin, age, physical or mental disability, marital status, receipt of public assistance, or participation in lawful activity off employer's premises during nonworking hours which is not in direct conflict with essential business-related interest of employer. (N.D. Cent. Code Sec. 14-02.4-03.)

Agency

North Dakota Department of Labor
600 East Boulevard Avenue
Department 406
Bismarck, North Dakota 58505-0340
701-328-2660

OHIO

Law

Prohibits discrimination on basis of race, color, religion, sex, nationl origin, disability, age, or ancestry. (Ohio Rev. Code Ann. Sec. 4112.02.) Also prohibits discrimination against those who file or pursue workers' compensation claims.
(Ohio Rev. Code Ann. Sec. 4123.90.)

Agency

Ohio Civil Rights Commission
1111 East Broad Street
Suite 301
Columbus, Ohio 43205
888-278-7101

OKLAHOMA

Law

Prohibits discrimination on basis of race, color, religion, sex, national origin, age, or handicap, unless action is related to a bona fide occupational qualification reasonably necessary to the normal operation of the employer's business or enterprise. (Okla. Stat. Tit 25, Sec. 1302.) Act specifically does not require preferential treatment of individual or group on account of imbalance with respect to total number or percentage of persons of any group. (Okla. Stat. Tit 25, Sec. 1310.)

Agency

Oklahoma Human Rights Commission
2101 North Lincoln Boulevard
Room 480
Oklahoma City, Oklahoma 73105-4904
405-521-2360

OREGON

Law

Prohibits discrimination on basis of race, religion, color, sex, national origin, marital status, age (18 or older) or the race, religion, color, sex, national origin, marital status, or age of any other person with whom the person associates, or because of an expunged juvenile record, or disability. (Or. Rev. Stat. Sec. 659A.030.) Also prohibits retaliation against persons for making safety complaints (Or. Rev. Stat. Sec. 654.062), making complaints about health care facilities, testifying in good faith in unemployment compensation hearings (Or. Rev. Stat. Sec. 659A.233), giving legislative testimony (Sec. 659A.270), for whistleblowing (Or. Rev. Stat. Secs. 659A.200 and .230), for performing jury service (Or. Rev. Stat. Sec. 10.090), solely because certain persons related by blood or marriage works or has worked for the company (Or. Rev. Stat. Sec. 659A.309), because the person filed a workers' compensation claim (Or. Rev. Stat. Sec. 659A.109), or has made a wage claim. (Or. Rev. Stat. Sec. 652.355.)

Agency

Oregon Bureau of Labor and Industries Civil Rights Division
Portland State Office Building
800 NE Oregon
Suite 32
Portland, Oregon 97232
503-731-4075

PENNSYLVANIA

Law

Prohibits discrimination because of race, color, religious creed, ancestry, age, sex, national origin, non-job related handicap or disability, or use of a guide dog or support animal.
(Pa. Stat. Ann. Tit 43, Sec. 955.)

Agency

Pennsylvania Human Relations Commission
301 Chestnut Street
Suite 300
Harrisburg, Pennsylvania 17101
717-787-4410

RHODE ISLAND

Law

Prohibits discrimination on basis of race, color, religion, disability, age (40–70), sexual orientation, gender identity or expression, or country of ancestral origin.
(R.I. Gen. Laws Sec. 28-5-7.)

Agency

Rhode Island Commission For Human Rights
180 Westminster Street
3rd Floor
Providence, Rhode Island 02903
401-222-2661

SOUTH CAROLINA

Law

Prohibits discrimination on basis of race, religion, color, sex, age, national origin, or disability. (S.C. Code Ann. Sec. 1-13-80.)

Also prohibits discrimination against employee who complies with valid subpoena to testify in court or administrative proceeding, or for institution or participating in workers' compensation actions. (S.C. Code Ann. Sec. 41-1-80.)

Agency

South Carolina Human Rights Commission
2611 Forest Drive
Suite 200
P.O. Box 4490
Columbia, South Carolina 29204
803-737-7800

SOUTH DAKOTA

Law

Prohibits discrimination on basis of race, color, creed, religion, sex, ancestry, disability, or national origin.
(S.D. Codified Laws Secs. 20-13-1 and following.)

Agency

South Dakota Division of Human Rights
700 Governors Drive
Pierre, South Dakota 57501
605-773-4493

TENNESSEE

Law

Prohibits discrimination on basis of race, creed, color, religion, sex, age, or national origin. (Tenn. Code Ann. Sec. 4-21-401.)

Also prohibits discrimination solely on basis of a physical, mental or visual handicap and makes violation a Class C misdemeanor. (Tenn. Code Ann. Sec. 8-50-103.)

Agency

Tennessee Human Rights Commission
530 Church Street
Suite 305
Cornerstone Square Building
Nashville, Tennessee 37243-0745
615-741-5825

TEXAS

Law

Prohibits discrimination on basis of race, color, disability, religion, sex, national origin, or age. (Tex. Lab. Code Ann. Sec. 21.051.) Also prohibits discrimination for participating in public evacuation (Sec. 22.002), for participating in a strike (Tex. Lab. Code Ann. Sec. 52.031), or against persons who in good faith filed a workers' compensation claim, hired a lawyer for representation in such a claim, or instituted or testified in a workers' compensation proceeding.
(Tex. Lab. Code Ann. Secs. 451.001 to .003.)

Agency

Texas Commission on Human Rights
6330 Highway 290 East
Suite 250
Austin, Texas 78723
512-437-3450
or
P.O. Box 13006
Austin, Texas 78711-3006

UTAH

Law

Prohibits discrimination because of race, color, sex, pregnancy, childbirth, pregnancy related conditions, age (40 or over), religion, national origin, or disability.
(Utah Code Ann. Sec. 34A-5-106.)

Agency

Utah Anti-Discrimination Division
160 East 300 South
3rd Floor
Salt Lake City, Utah 84114
801-530-6801
or
P.O. Box 146630
Salt Lake City, Utah 84114-6630

VERMONT

Law

Prohibits discrimination on basis of race, color, religion, ancestry, national origin, sex, sexual orientation, place of birth, age, or disability. (Vt. Stat. Ann. Tit 21, Sec. 495.)

Agency

Vermont Human Rights Commission
135 State Stree
Drawer 33
Montpelier, Vermont 05633-6301
802-828-2480

VIRGINIA

Law

Prohibits discrimination on basis of race, color, religion, national origin, sex, pregnancy, childbirth or related medical conditions, age (40 and over), marital status, or disability.
(Va. Code Ann. Sec. 2.2-3900.)

Agency

Virginia Council on Human Rights
900 East Main Street
Pocahontas Building
4th Floor
Richmond, Virginia 23219
804-225-2292

WASHINGTON

Law

Prohibits discrimination on basis of age (40 and over), sex, marital status, race, creed, color, national origin, presence of sensory, mental or physical disability, or the use of a dog guide or service animal by a disabled person. (Wash. Rev. Code Sec. 49.60.180.) Also prohibits discrimination on basis of HIV test results, unless absence of HIV is bona fide occupational qualification.
(Wash. Rev. Code Secs. 49.60.172-.210.)

Agency

Washington State Human Rights Commission
711 South Capitol Way, #402
Olympia, Washington 98504-2490
360-753-6770

WEST VIRGINIA

Law

Prohibits discrimination on basis of race, religion, color, national origin, ancestry, sex, age (40 or over), blindness, or disability. (W. Va. Code Sec. 5-11-9.) Also prohibits discrimination for employee receiving or attempting to receive workers' compensation benefits. (W. Va. Code Sec. 23-5A-1.) Also prohibits discharge of worker off work due to compensable injury, except where employee committed separate dischargeable offense. (W. Va. Code Sec. 23-5A-3.)

Agency

West Virginia Human Rights Commission
1321 Plaza East
Room 108A
Charleston, West Virginia 25301-1400
304-558-2616

WISCONSIN

Law

Prohibits discrimination by reason of age (40 and over), race, creed, color, disability, marital status, sex, national origin, ancestry, arrest or conviction record, membership in national guard or military, or use or non-use of lawful products off employer's premises during nonworking hours. (Wis. Stat. Sec. 111.321.) Also prohibits discrimination because of sexual orientation. (Wis. Stat. Sec. 111.36.) Also prohibits discrimination against person for attempting to enforce statutory right, opposing discriminating practice, making complaint, or aiding or testifying in proceeding. (Wis. Stat. Sec. 111.322.) Exception to age discrimination provided to allow age distinction where knowledge or experience to be gained is required for future advancement to arrangement or executive positions, or where employee is exposed to physical danger or hazards, such as certain employment in law enforcement or fire fighting. (Wis. Stat. Sec. 111.33.)

Agency

Wisconsin Equal Rights Division, Civil Rights Bureau
201 East Washington Avenue
Room A300
P.O. Box 8928
Madison, Wisconsin 53708-8928
608-266-6860

WYOMING

Law

Prohibits discrimination because of age (40–70), sex, race, creed, color, national origin, ancestry, or disability.
(Wyo. Stat. Ann Sec. 27-9-105.)

Agency

Wyoming Department of Employment
1510 East Pershing Boulevard
Cheyenne, Wyoming 82002
307-777-5488

–Appendix C–
NOTABLE WRONGFUL DISCHARGE CASES

The public policy tort of wrongful discharge (discussed in Chapter 3), has been widely recognized in the United States over the past twenty-five years. The following is a listing of some of the cases from around the country that have fostered its development. A review of these cases will give you a good idea of the type of situations in which it has been held to apply.

ALABAMA

Overton v. Amerex Corp., 642 So.2d 450
(Ala. 1994) (for seeking workers' compensation).
Refusal to expand tort to other cases expressed in *Wright v. Dothan, Chrysler, Plymouth, Dodge, Inc.*, 658 So.2d 428 (Ala. 1995).

ARIZONA

Wagenseller v. Scottsdale Memorial Hospital, 710 P.2d 1025
(Ariz. 1985) (for refusal to engage in *mooning*).
Vermillion v. AAA Pro Moving & Storage, 704 P.2d 1360
(Ariz. 1985) (for reporting theft by his employer).
Murcott v. Best Western, Int'l, 9 P.3d 1088
(Ariz. 2000) (for complaining internally about possible antitrust violations).

ARKANSAS

Webb v. HCA Health Servs, 780 S.W.2d 571
(Ark. 1989) (for a hospital employee's refusal to falsify patient records).
Sterling Drug, Inc. v. Oxford, 743 S.W.2d 380
(Ark. 1998) (for reporting employer submitted false information to government—but contract damages only).

CALIFORNIA

Tameny v. Atlantic Richfield Co., 610 P.2d 1330
(Cal. 1980) (for refusing to participate in illegal price fixing).
Petermann v. Int'l Brotherhood of Teamsters, Local 396, 344 P.2d25
(Cal. 1959) (for refusing to commit perjury).
Stevenson v. Superior Court, 16 Cal.4th 880
(1997) (for discharge contrary to public policy expressed in state age-discrimination statute).
Grant-Burton v. Covenant Care, Inc., 99 Cal.App.4th 1361
(2002) (for discussing wages, where such discussions were protected by statute).

COLORADO

Martin Marietta Corp v. Lorenz, 823 P.2d 100
(Colo. 1992) (for refusal to misrepresent quality control deficiencies and unrealistic cost assessments to government).
Rocky Mountain Hosp. v. Mariani, 916 P.2d 519
(Colo. 1996) (for refusing to falsify accounting information).

CONNECTICUT

Sheets v. Teddy's Frosted Foods, Inc., 427 A.2d 385
(Conn. 1980) (for reporting food labeling irregularities).
Lewis v. Nationwide Mut. Ins. Co., 19 IER 1470
(D. Conn. 2003) (for demonstrating loyalty to company insureds as required by Rules of Professional Conduct).

DELAWARE

Heller v. Dover Warehouse Market, Inc., 515 A.2d 178
(Del. 1986) (on basis of reports of unlawful polygraph).
Schuster v. Derocili, 775 A.2d 1029
(Del. 2001) (discharge contrary to public policy against sexual harassment expressed in state's discrimination statute).

DISTRICT OF COLUMBIA

Adams v. George W. Cochran & Co., Inc., 597 A.2d 28
(DC Ct App. 1991) (for refusal to drive a truck without a required inspection sticker).

HAWAII

Parnar v. Americana Hotels, 652 P.2d 625
(Haw. 1982) (for reporting potential anti-trust violations to a company attorney).
Smith v. Chaney Brooks Realty, 865 P.2d 170
(Haw. 1994) (for inquiring about the propriety of certain paycheck deductions).

IDAHO

Jackson v. Minidoka Irr. Dist., 563 P.2d 54
(Id. 1977) (must violate public policy).
Ray v. Nampa School Dist. No. 131, 814 P.2d 17
(Id. 1991) (for reporting electrical and building codes violations).
Hummer v. Evans, 923 P.2d 981
(Id. 1996) (for complying with court issued subpoena).
Crea v. FMC Corp., 16 P.3d 272
(Id. 2000) (for disclosing employer's responsibility for arsenic contamination of groundwater).

ILLINOIS

Palmateer v. International Harvester Co., 421 N.E.2d 876 (Ill. 1981) (for reporting the crime of a coworker).

Hinthorn v. Roland's of Bloomington, Inc., 519 N.E.2d 909 (Ill. 1988) (for seeking medical attention associated with work-related injury).

Pietruszynski v. The McClier Corp., 788 N.E.2d 82 (Ill. 2003) (for testifying or expressing intent to testify in workers' compensation proceedings).

INDIANA

Frampton v. Central Indiana Gas Co., 297 N.E.2d 425 (Ind. 1973) (for filing workers' compensation claim).

McClanahan v. Remington Freight Lines, Inc., 517 N.E.2d 390 (Ind. 1988) (for refusing to drive an overweight truck in violation of law).

IOWA

Springer v. Weeks & Leo Co., Inc., 429 N.W.2d 558 (Iowa 1988) (for filing workers' compensation claim).

Woodruff v. Associated Grocers of Iowa, Inc., 364 N.W.2d 215 (Iowa 1985) (for reporting that employer was keeping two sets of accounting books).

Fitzgerald v. Salsbury Chemical, Inc., 613 N.W.2d 275 (Iowa 2000) (for providing truthful testimony in coworkers' discrimination case).

KANSAS

Palmer v. Brown, 752 P.2d 685 (Kan. 1988) (for reporting medicaid fraud).

KENTUCKY

Firestone Textile Co. Div. Firestone Tire & Rubber Co. v. Meadows, 666 S.W.2d 730 (Ky. 1983) (for pursuing workers' compensation claim).

Brown v. Physician's Mut. Ins. Co., 679 S.W.2d 836
(Ky. App. 1984) (for attempting to report procedural irregularities to outside agency).
Northeast Health Management Inc. v. Cotton, 56 S.W.3d 440
(Ky.Ct.App. 2001) (constructively discharged for refusal to commit perjury on behalf of supervisor).

LOUISIANA

Cahill v. Frank's Door & Building Supply Co., Inc., 590 So.2d 53
(La. 1991) (for filing workers' compensation claim).
Bartlett v. Reese, 569 So.2d 195
(La. Ct. App. 1990) (for reporting possible environmental violations by third party to state agency).

MARYLAND

Kessler v. Equity Management, Inc., 572 A.2d 1144
(Md. 1990) (refusal to conduct unlawful search).

MICHIGAN

Watassek v. Michigan Dept. of Mental Health, 372 N.W.2d 617
(Mich. 1985) (for reporting patient abuse).
Trombetta v. Detroit, Toledo & Fronton R. Co., 265 N.W.2d 385
(Mich. 1978) (for refusing to alter pollution reports).
Sventko v. Kroger Co., 245 N.W.2d 151
(Mich. 1976) (for filing workers' compensation claim).
Garavaglia v. Centro, Inc., 536 N.W.2d 805
(Mich. Ct.App. 1995) (discharged as employer's bargaining representative due to union pressure).

MINNESOTA

Phipps v. Clark Oil & Refining Corp, 408 N.W.2d 569
(Minn. 1987) (for refusal to pump leaded gasoline into vehicle designed for unleaded gasoline).

MISSISSIPPI

McArn v. Allied Bruce - Terminex Co., 626 So.2d 603 (Miss. 1993) (for refusing to defraud a customer).

Drake v. Advance Constr. Serv., 117 F.3d 203 (5th Cir. 1997) (interpreting Mississippi law) (for refusing to conceal deficiencies in employer's government contract performance).

MISSOURI

Kirk v. Mercy Hospital Tri-County, 851 S.W.2d 617 (Mo. App. 1993) (for refusal by nurse to *stay out of it* in case of questionable patient care).

Saffels v. Rice, 40 F.3d 1546 (8th Cir. 1994) (interpreting Missouri law) (discharge due to employer's mistaken belief employee had reported FLSA violations to authorities).

NEBRASKA

Ambroz v. Cornhuskers Square Ltd., 416 N.W.2d 510 (Neb. 1987) (for refusing to take unlawful polygraph examination).

Jackson v. Morris Communications Corp., 657 N.W.2d 634 (Neb. 2003) (for exercising workers' compensation rights).

NEVADA

Hansen v. Harrah's, 675 P.2d 394 (Nev. 1984) (for filing workers' compensation claim).

D'Angelo v. Gardner, 819 P.2d 206 (Nev. 1991) (for refusal to work in an unsafe and unhealthful work environment).

NEW HAMPSHIRE

Cloutier v. Great Atlantic & Pacific Tea Co., Inc., 436 A.2d 1140 (N.H. 1981) (for attempting to comply with OSHA statute in maintaining safe workplace).

NEW JERSEY

Lally v. Copygraphics, 428 A.2d 1317
(N.J. 1981) (for filing workers' compensation claim).
Pierce v. Ortho Pharmaceutical Corp., 417 A.2d 505
(N.J. 1980) (by doctor refusing to violate Hippocratic Oath).
MacDougall v. Weichert, 677 A.2d 162
(N.J. 1996) (for casting vote on town council opposed by employer's client).

NEW MEXICO

Chavez v. Manville Products Corp., 777 P.2d 371
(N.M. 1989) (for opposing unauthorized use of employees' name in employer's lobbying efforts).

NEW YORK

Wieder v. Skala, 609 N.E.2d 105
(N.Y. 1992) (refusal to violate professional ethics code).

NORTH CAROLINA

Coman v. Thomas Mfg. Co. Inc., 381 S.E.2d 445
(N.C. 1989) (for refusing to falsify records and drive truck in violation of federal law).
Deerman v. Beverly Cal. Corp., 518 S.E.2d 804
(N.C. 1999) (for fulfilling statutory duties as nurse in providing advice to family of patient to change physicians).

NORTH DAKOTA

Krein v. Marian Manor Nursing Home, 415 N.W.2d 793
(N.D. 1987) (for seeking workers' compensation benefits).
Resler v. Humane Soc'y, 480 N.W.2d 429
(N.D. 1992) (for giving truthful testimony pursuant to subpoena).

OHIO

Greeley v. Miami Valley Maintenance Contractors, Inc., 551 N.E.2d 981 (Ohio 1990) (for having wages assigned to satisfy support obligations).

Celeste v. Wiseco Piston, 784 N.E.2d 1198 (Ohio 2003) (for expressing concerns to management about safety of company's products).

OKLAHOMA

Burk v. K-Mart Corp., 770 P.2d 24 (Okla. 1989) (must be contrary to clear mandate of public policy in constitutional, statutory or decisional law).

McGehee v. Florafax Int'l, Inc., 776 P.2d 852 (Okla. 1989) (for refusing to commit perjury).

Sargent v. Central Nat'l Bank & Trust Co., 809 P.2d 1298 (Okla. 1991) (for refusing to alter report to audit committee).

OREGON

Delaney v. Taco Time Int'l, Inc., 681 P.2d 114 (Or. 1984) (for refusing to defame a coworker).

Nees v. Hocks, 536 P.2d 512 (Or. 1975) (for reporting to jury duty).

PENNSYLVANIA

Shick v. Shirey, 716 A.2d 1231 (Penn. 1998) (for filing workers' compensation benefits).

Raykovitz v. K-Mart Corp., 665 A.2d 833 (Pa.Super.Ct. 1995) (where part-time employee who had lost full-time position was discharged for seeking to collect unemployment compensation for loss of full-time work).

Rothrock v. Rothrock Motor Sales, Inc., 810 A.2d 114 (Pa.Super. 2002) (for refusing to dissuade subordinate from filing workers' compensation claim).

SOUTH CAROLINA

Ludwick v. This Minute of Carolina, Inc., 337 S.E.2d 213 (S.C. 1985) (for honoring subpoena).

Garner v. Morrison Knuden Corp., 456 S.E.2d 907 (S.C. 1995) (for reporting and testifying about radioactive contamination and unsafe working conditions at nuclear facility).

SOUTH DAKOTA

Johnson v. Kreiser's, Inc., 433 N.W.2d 225 (S.D. 1988) (for refusing to commit unlawful act).

Dahl v. Combined Ins. Co., 621 N.W.2d 163 (S.D. 2001) (for reporting missing insurance premiums to regulators).

TENNESSEE

Clanton v. Cain-Sloan Co., 677 S.W.2d 441 (Tenn. 1984) (for exercise of workers' compensation rights).

Hodges v. S.C. Toof & Co., 833 S.W.2d 896 (Tenn. 1992) (for performing jury service).

Crews v. Buckman Labs Int'l, Inc., 78 S.W.3d 852 (Tenn. 2002) (for reporting the employer's general counsel did not possess a Tennessee license to practice law).

TEXAS

Sabine Pitot Service, Inc. v. Hauck, 687 S.W.2d 733 (Tex. 1985) (for refusal to illegally pump ships bilges into coastal waters prohibited by federal law).

Ed Rachal Foundation v. D'Unger, 117 S.W.3d 348 (Tex.Ct.App. 2003) (for disobeying instructions to ignore mistreatment of transient trespassers).

UTAH

Peterson v. Browning, 832 P.2d 1280 (Utah 1992) (for refusing to falsify documents in violation of law).

Heslop v. Bank of Utah, 839 P.2d 828
(Utah 1992) (for objecting to false reporting of bank's income and assets contrary to law).
Spratley v. State Farm Mut. Auto Ins. Co., 78 P.3d 603
(Utah 2003) (lawyer constructively discharged by requirement to violate ethical rules).

VERMONT

Payne v. Rozendaal, 520 A.2d 586
(Vt. 1986) (discriminatory discharge on basis of age stated cause of action under public policy exception).

VIRGINIA

Bowman v. State Bank of Keysville, 331 S.E.2d 797
(Va. 1985) (for refusing to succumb to duress to vote shares of stock in way favorable to employer).
Lockhart v. Commonwealth Educ. Sys. Corp., 439 S.E.2d 328
(Va. 1994) (tort claim of alleged discriminatory discharge based on race and gender).

WASHINGTON

Thompson v. St. Regis Paper Co., 685 P.2d 1081
(Wash. 1984) (for attempting to bring company in compliance with Foreign Corrupt Practice Act).
Gardner v. Loomis Armored, 913 P.2d 377
(Wash. 1996) (for leaving truck unattended to help rescue hostages who were being threatened by a man with a knife).
Hubbard v. Spokane Co., 50 P.3d 602
(Wash. 2002) (over difference of opinion concerning the legality of issuing a hotel building permit).

WEST VIRGINIA

Harless v. First Nat'l Bank in Fairmont, 246 S.E.2d 270
(W. Va. 1978) (for telling superiors at a bank customers were being mischarged on installment loans).

Kanagy v. Fiesta Salons, Inc., 541 S.E.2d 616 (W. Va. 2000) (providing information to regulatory board).

Lilly v. Overnight Transp. Co., 425 S.E.2d 214 (W.Va. 1992) (for refusing to operate a vehicle with brakes so unsafe as to create a danger to the public).

WISCONSIN

Strozinsky v. School District of Brown Deer, 614 N.W.2d 443 (Wis. 2000) (for complying with federal income tax withholding laws).

Strozinsky v. School District of Brown Deer, 614 N.W.2d 443 (Wis. 2000) (for complying with federal income tax withholding laws).

WYOMING

Griess v. Consolidated Freightways Corp. of Delaware, 776 P.2d 752 (Wyo. 1989) (filing a workers' compensation claim).

NOTES

[1]McDonnell Douglas Corp. v. Green, 411 U.S. 792 (1973); Texas Dept. of Community Affairs v. Burdine, 450 U.S. 248 (1981).
[2]Reeves v. Sanderson Plumbing Products, Inc., 530 U.S. 133 (2000).
[3]Hazlewood School District v. United States, 433 U.S. 299 (1977).
[4]Loiseau v. Department of Human Services, 567 F. Supp. 1211 (D. Or. 1983).
[5]Watson v. Fort Worth Bank & Trust, 487 U.S. 977 (1988).
[6]Hazlewood School District v. United States, 433 U.S. 299 (1977).
[7]EEOC v. Steamship Clerks Union, 48 F.3d 594 (1st Cir. 1995).
[8]Monge v. Beebe Rubber Co., 316 A.2d 549 (N.H. 1974).
[9]Nees v. Hocks, 536 P.2d 512 (Or. 1975).
[10]Fortune v. National Cash Register Co., 364 N.E.2d 1251 (Mass. 1977).
[11]Toussaint v. Blue Cross & Blue Shield of Michigan, 292 N.W.2d 880 (Mich. 1980).
[12]Cleary v. American Airlines, Inc., 168 Cal. Rptr. 722 (1980).
[13]Gantt v. Sentry Ins., 824 P.2d 680 (Cal. 1992).
[14]Birthisel v. Tri-Cities Health Service Corp., 424 S.E.2d 606 (W. Va. 1992); Hennessey v. Coastal Eagle Point Oil Co. 609 A.2d 11 (N.J. 1992); Painter v. Graley 639 N.E.2d 51 (Ohio 1994).
[15]Rackley v. Fairview Care Centers, Inc., 23 P.3d 1022 (Utah 2001).
[16]Weider v. Skala, 609 N.E.2d 105 (N.Y. 1992).
[17]Palmateer v. International Harvester Co., 421 N.E.2d 876 (Ill. 1981).
[18]Banaitis v. Mitsubishi Bank, Ltd., 879 P.2d 1288 (Or. App. 1994).

[19]Troy v. Inter-Financial Inc., 320 S.E.2d 872 (Ga. 1984) (No claim for refusal to commit perjury); Evans v. Bibb Co., 342 S.E.2d 484 (Ga. 1986).
[20]Smith v. Piezo Technology & Professional Administrators, 427 So.2d 182 (Fla. 1983); but see, Hartley v. Ocean Reef Club, Inc., 476 So.2d 1327 (Fla. App. 1985) (refusing to recognize the tort).
[21]Austin v. Healthtrust, Inc., 967 S.W.2d 400 (Tex. App. 1998).
[22]Ran Ken, Inc. v. Schlapper, 963 S.W.2d 102 (Tex. App. 1998).
[23]Adams v. George W. Cochran & Co., 597 A.2d 28 (D.C. App. 1991).
[24]Gray v. Citizens Bank of Washington, 609 A.2d 1143 (D.C. App. 1992).
[25]Murray v. Commercial Union Ins. Co., 782 F.2d 432 (3rd Cir. 1986).
[26]Petermann v. Int'l Broth. of Teamsters, Local 396, 344 P.2d 25 (Cal. 1959).
[27]Vermillian v. AAA Pro Moving & Storage, 704 P.2d 1360 (Ariz. 1985).
[28]Nees v. Hocks, 536 P.2d 512 (Or. 1975).
[29]Griess v. Consolidated Freightways Corp. of Delaware, 776 P.2d 752 (Wyo. 1989).
[30]See, e.g., Fox v. MCI Comm Corp., 931 P.2d 857 (Utah 1997).
[31]See, e.g., Belline v. K-Mart Corp., 940 F.2d 184 (7th Cir. 1991) (applying Illinois law).
[32]McQuary v. Bel Air Convalescent Home, Inc., 684 P.2d 21 (Or. 1984).
[33]Clark v. Modern Group, Ltd., 9 F.3d 321 (3rd Cir. 1993) (applying Pennsylvania law).
[34]Retherford v AT&T Comm. of the Mountain States, 844 P.2d 949 (Utah 1992).
[35]See, e.g., Dominguez v. Stone, 638 P.2d 423 (N.M. App. 1981).
[36]Manfield v. AT&T Corp., 747 F. Supp. 1329 (WD Ark 1990).
[37]Milton v. Illinois Bell Tel. Co., 427 N.E.2d 829 (Ill.1981).
[38]Armano v. Federal Reserve Bank of Boston, 468 F. Supp. 674 (D. Mass. 1979).
[39]Restatement Torts, Second, Section 46.

[40]Beasley v. Affiliated Hospital Products, 712 S.W.2d 557 (Mo. App. 1986).
[41]Miniodis v. Cook, 494 A.3d 212 (M.D. 1985).
[42]Kidder v. AmSouth Bank, NA, 639 So.2d 1361 (Ala. 1994).
[43]Hoff v. Bower, 492 N.W.2d 912 (S.D. 1992).
[44]Hunter v. Up-Right, Inc., 12 Cal. Rptr. 193 (1993).
[45]DuSesoi v. United Refining Co., 540 F. Supp. 1260 (W.D. Pa. 1982).
[46]Lenk v. Total-Western, Inc., 108 Cal. Rptr. 2d 34 (2001).
[47]Lord v. Souder, 748 A.2d 393 (Del. 2000).
[48]Telesphere Intern, Inc. v. Scollin, 489 So.2d 1152 (Fla. App. 1986).
[49]Wildes v. Pens Unlimited, Inc., 389 A.2d 837 (Me. 1978).
[50]Yaindl v. Ingersoll - Rand Co., 422 A.2d 611 (Pa. 1981).
[51]Powers v. Delnor Hosp., 481 N.E.2d 968 (Ill. App. 1985).
[52]Ettenson v. Burke, 17 P.3d 440 (N.M. App. 2000).
[53]Chapman v. Crown Glass Co., 557 N.E.2d 256 (Ill. App. 1990).
[54]Jones v. Lake Park Care Center, Inc., 569 N.W.2d 369 (Iowa 1997).
[55]Marczak v. Drexel Nat. Bank, 542 N.E.2d 787 (Ill. App. 1989).
[56]Pratt v. Prodata, Inc., 885 P.2d 786 (Utah 1994).
[57]Restatement Torts, Second, Section 652B.
[58]Norman-Bloodsaw v. Lawrence Berkeley Laboratory, 135 F.3d 1260 (9th Cir. 1998) (applying California law).
[59]K-Mart Corp. Store No. 7441 v. Trotti, 677 S.W.2d 632 (Tex. App. 1984).
[60]Cramer v. Consolidated Freightways, Inc., 255 F.3d 683 (9th Cir. 2001) (applying California law).
[61]Vernars v. Young, 539 F.2d 966 (3rd Cir. 1976) (applying Pennsylvania law).
[62]Levias v. United Airlines, 500 N.E.2d 370 (Ohio App. 1985).
[63]Schmidt v. Ameritech Corp., 115 F.3d 501 (7th Cir. 1997) (applying Illinois law).
[64]Phillips v. Smalley Maintenance Services, Inc., 711 F.2d 1524 (11th Cir. 1983).

[65]O'Brien v. Papa Gino's of America, Inc., 780 F.2d 1067 (1st Cir. 1986) (applying New Hampshire law).
[66]Bratt v. IBM Corp., 785 F.2d 352 (1st Cir. 1986) (applying Massachusetts law).
[67]Lyons v. National Car Rental Systems, Inc., 30 F.3d 240 (1st Cir. 1994) (applying Massachusetts law).
[68]Miles v. Perry, 529 A.2d 199 (Com App. 1987).
[69]Tedeschi v. Smith, Barney, Harris Upham & Co, Inc., 548 F. Supp. 1172 (S.D.N.Y. 1982) (applying New York law).
[70]Staples v. Bangor Hydro-Electric Co., 561 A.2d 499 (Me. 1989).
[71]Carney v. Memorial Hospital and Nursing Home, 475 N.E.2d 451 (N.Y. 1985).
[72]Mendez v. M.S. Walker, Inc., 528 N.E.2d 891 (Mass. App. 1988).
[73]Steinberg v. Thomas, 659 F. Supp. 789 (D. Colo. 1987).
[74]Gaudio v. Griffin Health Services Corp., 733 A.2d 197 (Conn. 1999).
[75]Ezekiel v. Jones Motor Co., 372 N.E.2d 1281 (Mass. 1978).
[76]Agriss v. Roadway Express Co., 483 A.2d 456 (Pa. Super. 1984).
[77]Oberbroeckling v. Lyle, 362 S.E.2d 682 (Va. 1987).
[78]Griswold v. Fresenius USA, Inc., 978 F. Supp. 718 (N.D. Ohio 1997) (in failing to provide work environment safe from sexual harassment).
[79]Chea v. Men's Warehouse, 932 P.2d 1261 (Wash. App. 1997) (race); Byrd v. Richardson-Greenshields, Inc. 552 So.2d 1099 (Fla. 1989) (sex).
[80]Cox v. Brazo, 303 S.E.2d 71 (Ga. App. 1983), affirmed 307 S.E.2d 474 (Ga. 1983).
[81]See discussion, Consolidated Rail Corp. v. Gottshall, 512 U.S. 532 (1994).
[82]See, e.g., Coffee v. McDonnell Douglas Corp., 503 P.2d 1366 (Cal. 1972).
[83]See, e.g., Toussaint Blue Cross & Blue Shield of Michigan, 292 N.W.2d 880 (Mich. 1980).
[84]See, e.g., Wagenseller v. Scottsdale Mem. Hosp., 710 P.2d 1025 (Ariz. 1985).
[85]Zaccardi v. Zale Corp., 856 F.2d 1473 (10th Cir. 1988).

[86]Forrester v. Parker, 606 P.2d 191 (N.M. 1980); Foley v. Interactive Data Corporation, 765 P.2d 373 (Cal. 1988).

[87]Lukosi v Sandia Indian Mgmt. Co., 748 P.2d 507 (N.M. 1988).

[88]See e.g., McDonald v. Mobil Coal Producing, Inc., 820 P.2d 986 (Wyo. 1991) (conspicuous); Johnson v. Nasca, 802 P.2d 1294 (Okla. App. 1990) (clear).

[89]See e.g., Feges v. Perkins Restaurants, Inc., 483 N.W.2d 701 (Minn. 1992).

[90]Stahl v. Sun Microsystems, Inc.,19 F.3d 533 (10th Cir. 1994).

[91]Mers v. Dispatch Printing Co., 483 N.E.2d 150 (Ohio 1985).

[92]Kern v. Levolor Lorenteen, Inc.. 899 F.2d 772 (9th Cir. 1990) (applying California law).

[93]Pickell v. Arizona Components Co., 931 P.2d 1184 (Colo. 1997).

[94]Seibel v. Liberty Homes, Inc., 752 P.2d 291 (Or. 1988).

[95]Boothby v. Texon, Inc., 608 N.E.2d 1028 (Mass. 1993).

[96]Sanderson v. First Sec. Hearing Co., 844 P.2d 303 (Utah 1992).

[97]Lopez v. Kline, 953 P.2d 304 (N.M. Ct. App. 1997).

[98]Weiner v. McGraw-Hill, 443 N.E.2d 441 (N.Y. 1982).

[99]Allegri v. Providence - St. Margaret Health Center, 684 P.2d 1031 (Kan. 1984).

[100]Foley v. Interactive Data Corporation, 765 P.2d 373 (Cal. 1988).

[101]Guz v. Bechtel Nat. Inc., 8 P.3d 1089 (Cal. 2000).

[102]Romack v. Public Service Co. of Indiana, 511 N.E.2d 1024 (Ind. 1987).

[103]Torosyn v. Boehringer Ingelheim Pharmaceuticals, Inc., 662 A.2d 89 (Conn. 1995).

[104]Amoco Fabrics & Fibers Co. v. Hilson, 669 So.2d 832 (Ark. 1995).

[105]Restatement 2d, Contracts, Section 205 (1981).

[106]See, e.g., Hall v. Farmer's Insurance Exchange, 713 P.2d 1027 (Okla. 1985) (commissions on renewal premiums).

[107]Cross v. CCL Custom Mfg., Inc., 951 F. Supp. 124 (WD Tenn. 1997).

[108]Handler v. Fast Lane, Inc., 868 F. Supp. 1138 (E.D. Ark. 1994).

[109]Ross v. Douglas County, 234 F.3d 391 (8th Cir. 2000).

[110]Rowlett v. Anheuser - Busch, 832 F.2d 194 (1st Cir. 1987).

[111]Davenport v. Riverview Garden School Dist., 30 F.3d 940 (8th Cir. 1994).

[112]Kline v. Tennessee Valley Authority, 128 F.3d 337 (6th Cir. 1997).

[113]Saint Francis College v. Al-Khazraji, 481 U.S. 604 (1987).

[114]McDonald v. Santa Fe Trail Transp. Co., 427 U.S. 273 (1976).

[115]Calcote v. Texas Educational Foundation, Inc., 578 F.2d 95 (5th Cir. 1978).

[116]Crowley v. Prince George's County, 890 F.2d 683 (4th Cir. 1989).

[117]Reynolds v. School Dist. No. 1, 69 F.3d 1523 (10th Cir. 1995).

[118]Shehadeh v. Chesapeake R. Potomac Tel. Co. of Maryland, 595 F.2d 711 (D.C. Cir. 1978).

[119]Hossaini v. Western Missouri Medical Center, 97 F.3d 1085 (8th Cir. 1996).

[120] Chaiffetz v. Robertson Research Holding, Ltd., 798 F.2d 731 (5th Cir. 1986).

[121]Sumitomo Shoji America, Inc. v. Avagliano, 457 U.S. 176 (1982).

[122]Diaz v. Pan Am World Airways, Inc., 442 F.2d 385 (5th Cir. 1971).

[123]Hayes v. Shelby Memorial Hospital, 726 F.2d 1543 (11th Cir. 1984).

[124]Pacourek v. Inland Steel Co., 65 FEP 758 (W.D. Ill. 1994).

[125]Ponton v. Newport News School Bd, 632 F. Supp. 1056 (E.D. Va. 1986).

[126]United Auto Workers v. Johnson Controls Inc., 499 U.S. 187 (1991).

[127]EEOC v. Wooster Brush Co. Employees Relief Association, 727 F.2d 566 (6th Cir. 1984).

[128]Oncale v. Sundowner Offshore Services, Inc., 523 U.S. 75 (1998).

[129]Doe v. City of Belleville, 119 F.3d 563 (7th Cir. 1997).

[130]Wrightson v. Pizza Hut of America, Inc., 99 F.2d 138 (4th Cir. 1996).

[131]Garcia v. Elf Atochem - North America, 28 F.3d 446 (5th Cir. 1994).

[132]Higgins v. New Balance Athletic Shoes, 194 F 3d 252 (1st Cir. 1999); Simonton v. Runyon, 232 F.3d 33 (2nd Cir. 2000);

Bibby v. Phila. Coca Cola Bottling Co., 260 F.3d 257 (3rd Cir. 2001); Schmedding Tnemec Co., 187 F.3d 862 (8th Cir. 1999).

[133]Nichols vs. Azteca Restaurant Enterprises, Inc., 256 F.3d 864 (9th Cir. 2001).

[134]Rene v. MGM Grand Hotel, Inc., 305 F.3d 1061 (9th Cir. 2002).

[135]Vetter v. Farmland Indus., Inc., 120 F.3d 749 (8th Cir. 1997).

[136]Turner v. Barr, 811 F. Supp. 1 (D.D.C. 1993).

[137]Meritor Savings Bank v. Vinson, 477 U.S. 57 (1986).

[138]Harris v. Forklift Systems, Inc., 510 U.S. 17 (1983).

[139]Heller v. EBB Auto Co., 8 F.3d 1433 (9th Cir. 1993).

[140]Kelly v. Metro-North Commuter R.R., 51 FEP Cases 1136 (S.D.N.Y. 1989).

[141]Yudovich v. Stone, 839 F. Supp. 382 (E.D. Va. 1993).

[142]EEOC v. Townley Eng., & Mfg., Co., 859 F.2d 610 (9th Cir. 1988), cert. denied 489 U.S. 1077.

[143]See note 139.

[144]See note 139.

[145]Trans World Airlines, Inc. v. Hardison, 432 U.S. 63 (1977).

[146]See note 145.

[147]Ansonia Board of Education v. Philbrook, 479 U.S. 60 (1986).

[148] Newport News Shipbuilding Dry Dock Co. v. EEOC, 462 U.S. 669 (1983).

[149]Oncale v. Sundowner Offshore Services, Inc., 523 U.S. 75, (1998).

[150]Harris v. Forklift Systems, Inc., 510 U.S. 17 (1993).

[151]Meritor Savings Bank, FSC v. Vinson, 477 U.S. 57 (1986).

[152]See note 151.

[153]See note 149.

[154]See note 151.

[155]Burlington Industries, Inc. v. Ellerth, 524 U.S. 742 (1998); Faragher v. City of Boca Raton, 524 U.S. 775 (1998).

[156]See note 155.

[157]Intlekofer v. Turnage, 973 F.2d 773 (9th Cir. 1992).

[158]Sempier v. Johnson & Higgins, 45 F.3d 724 (3rd Cir. 1995).

[159]O'Connor v. Consolidated Coin Caterers Corp., 517 U.S. 308 (1996).

[160]See note 159.

[161]See, e.g., Armbruster v. Unisys Corp., 32 F.3d 768 (3rd Cir. 1994).

[162]Nidds v. Schindler Elevator Corp., 113 F.3d 912 (9th Cir. 1996), cert. denied 522 U.S. 950 (1997).

[163]Norris v. City and County of San Francisco, 900 F.2d 1326 (9th Cir. 1990).

[164]Yartzoff v. Thomas, 809 F.2d 1371 (9th Cir. 1987).

[165]Hazen Paper Co. v. Biggins, 507 U.S. 604 (1993).

[166]Conway v. Electro Switch Corp., 825 F.2d 593 (1st Cir. 1987); Heyne v. Caruso, 69 F.3d 1475 (9th Cir. 1990).

[167]Maldonado-Maldonado v. Pantasia Mfg., Corp., 956 F. Supp. 73 (D. P.R. 1997).

[168]Kells v. Sinclair Buick-GMC Truck, 210 F.3d 827 (8th Cir. 2000).

[169]Siegel v. Alpha Wire Corp. 894 F.2d 50 (3rd Cir. 1990).

[170]Denesha v. Farmers Ins. Exchange, 161 F.3d 491 (8th Cir. 1998), cert. denied 119 S Ct. 1763 (1999).

[171]Giacoletto v. Amax Zinc Co., Inc., 954 F.2d 424 (7th Cir. 1992); Miller v. Fairchild Indus., Inc., 876 F.2d 718 (9th Cir. 1989).

[172]Reeves v. Sanderson Plumbing Products, Inc., 530 U.S. 133 (2000).

[173]Cassino v. Reichold Chemicals, Inc., 817 F.2d 1338, (9th Cir. 1987), cert. denied 484 U.S. 1047 (1988).

[174]Trans World Airlines, Inc. v. Thurston, 469 U.S. 111 (1985); Hazen Paper Co. v. Biggins, 507 U.S. 604 (1993).

[175]See note 165.

[176]Gavalik v. Continental Can Co., 812 F.2d 834 (3d Cir. 1987).

[177]Dister v. Continental Group, Inc., 859 F.2d 1108 (2d Cir. 1988).

[178]Jess v. Pandick, Inc., 699 F. Supp. 698 (N.D. Ill. 1988).

[179]Burditt v. Kerr-McGee Chemical Corp., 982 F. Supp. 404 (ND Miss. 1997).

[180]Arnett v. Tuthill Corp., 849 F. Supp. 654 (N.D. Ill. 1994).

[181]Carlos v. White Consolidated Industries, Inc., 934 F. Supp. 227 (W.D. Tex.as 1996).

[182]Inter-Modal Rail Employers Ass'n v. Atchison, Topeka and Santa Fe Ry., 520 U.S. 510 (1997).

[183]Hirsch for Estate of Hirsch v. National Mail Service Inc., 989 F. Supp. 977 (N.D. Ill. 1997).

[184]Fitzgerald v. Codex Corp., 882 F.2d 586 (1st Cir. 1989).

[185]Bragdon v. Abbott, 524 U.S. 624 (1998).

[186]Gillen v. Fallon Ambulance Service, 283 F.3d 11 (1st Cir. 2002).

[187]McAlindin v. County of San Diego, 192 F.3d 1226 (9th Cir. 1999).

[188]Taylor v. Phoenixville School Dist., 184 F.3d 296 (3d Cir. 1999).

[189]Nunes v. Wal Mart Stores, 164 F.3d 1243 (9th Cir. 1999).

[190]Humphrey v. Memorial Hospitals Association, 239 F.2d 1128 (9th Cir. 2001), cert. denied 535 U.S. 1011 (2002).

[191]Barnett v. U.S. Air, Inc., 228 F.3d 1105 (9th Cir. 2000), vacated on other grounds 535 U.S. 391 (2002).

[192]McAlindin v. County of San Diego, 192 F.3d 1226 (9th Cir. 1999), amended 201 F.3d 1211 (9th Cir. 2000), cert. denied 530 U.S. 1243 (2000).

[193]Sanders v. ABC, 978 P.2d 67 (Cal. 1999).

[194]Deal v. Spears, 980 F.2d 1153 (8th Cir. 1992).

[195]Walker v. Darby, 911 F.2d 1573 (11th Cir. 1990).

[196]Fitzpatrick v. Bitzer, 427 U.S. 445 (1976).

[197]Kimel v. Florida Board of Regents, 528 U.S. 62 (2000).

[198]Board of Trustees of University of Alabama v. Garrett, 531 U.S. 356 (2001).

[199]Johnson v. Railway Express Agency, Inc., 421 U.S. 454 (1975).

[200]McDonald v. Santa Fe Trail Transportation Co., 427 U.S. 273 (1976).

[201]Johnson v. Railway Express Agency, Inc., 421 U.S. 454 (1975); Jones v. Alfred H. Mayer Co., 392 U.S. 409 (1968).

[202]Poolaw v. City of Anadarko, 660 F.2d 459 (10th Cir. 1981); Garner v. Giarrusso, 571 F.2d 1330 (5th Cir. 1978).

[203]City of Canton v. Harris, 489 U.S. 378 (1989).

[204]City of St. Louis v. Prapotnik, 485 U.S. 112 (1988).

[205]Will v. Michigan Department of State Police, 491 U.S. 58 (1989).

[206]Hafer v. Melo, 502 U.S. 21 (1991).

[207]Newport v. Fact Concerts, Inc., 453 U.S. 247 (1981).

[208]Smith v. Wade, 461 U.S. 30 (1983).
[209]Alexander v. Holden, 66 F.3d 62 (4th Cir. 1995).
[210]Lankford v. Hobart, 73 F.3d 283 (10th Cir. 1996).
[211]Burtnick v. McLean, 76 F.3d 611 (4th Cir. 1996).
[212]Suissa v. Fulton County, 74 F.3d 266 (11th Cir. 1996).
[213]Chambers v. Omaha Public School District, 536 F.2d 222 (8th Cir. 1976).
[214]Pickering v. Board of Education, 391 U.S. 563 (1968).
[215]Gillette v. Delmore, 886 F.2d 1194 (9th Cir. 1989).
[216]Roth v. Veteran's Administration of Government of United States, 856 F.2d 1401 (9th Cir. 1988).
[217]Connick v. Myers, 461 U.S. 138 (1983).
[218]Givhan v. Western Line Consol. School Dist., 439 U.S. 410 (1979).
[219]Lee v. Nicholl, 197 F.3d 1291 (10th Cir. 1999).
[220]Moore v. Kilgore, 877 F.2d 364 (5th Cir. 1989).
[221]Sexton v. Marten, 210 F.3d 905 (8th Cir. 2000).
[222]Cliff v. Board of School Commissioners, 42 F.3d 403 (7th Cir. 1994).
[223]Clinger v. New Mexico Highlands University, 17 IER 333 (10th Cir. 2000).
[224]Ayoub v. Texas A&M, 927 F.2d 834 (5th Cir. 1991).
[225]Wachsman v. Dallas, 704 F.2d 160 (5th Cir. 1983), cert. denied, 464 U.S. 1012 (1983).
[226]McCloud v. Testa, 97 F.3d 1536 (6th Cir. 1996).
[227]Arnett v. Kennedy, 416 U.S. 134 (1974).
[228]Ford v. Wainwright, 477 U.S. 399 (1986).
[229]Cleveland Board of Education v. Loudermill, 470 U.S. 532 (1985).
[230]Owen v. Independence, 445 U.S. 622 (1980).
[231]Textile Workers v. Lincoln Mills, 353 U.S. 448 (1957).
[232]Linn v. Plant Guard Workers, 383 U.S. 53 (1966).
[233]Belknap, Inc. v. Hale, 463 U.S. 491 (1983).
[234]Lingle v. Norge Division of Magic Chef, 486 U.S. 399 (1988).
[235]Vaca v. Sipes, 386 U.S. 171 (1967).
[236]Republic Steel v. Maddox, 379 U.S. 650 (1965).

[237]Hines v. Anchor Motor Freight, 424 U.S. 554 (1976).
[238]Dutrisac v. Caterpillar Tractor Co., 749 F.2d 1270 (9th Cir. 1983).
[239]PGA Tour, Inc. v. Martin, 532 U.S. 661 (2001).
[240]Fields v. Hallsville Independent School Dist., 906 F.2d 1017.
[241]Nationwide Mut. Ins. Co. v. Darden, 503 U.S. 318 (1992).
[242]Reeves v. Sanderson Plumbing Products, Inc., 530 U.S. 133 (2000).
[243]Circuit City v. Adams, 532 U.S. 105 (2001).

INDEX

C

E

F

G

H

I

J

K

L

M

N

O

P

T

U

V

W

Z

ABOUT THE AUTHOR

Richard C. Busse was born in Philadelphia, Pennsylvania. He grew up in Southern California and graduated from San Diego State University in 1971 with a B.S. degree in marketing. He obtained his law degree in 1974 from the University of California, Hastings College of the Law.

From 1975 to 1981, Mr. Busse defended employment cases, both with a defense firm and in his capacity as Chief Deputy County Counsel for Multnomah County, Oregon, the state's most populous county, where Portland is situated.

In 1981, he set out on his own to develop a plaintiff's employment litigation practice, and has practiced in that field ever since. He is now senior partner in the Portland law firm Busse & Hunt, which is devoted exclusively to the practice of plaintiff's employment law. Mr. Busse represents victims of race, sex, age, disability, and other forms of unlawful discrimination. He also represents employees who have been the subject of wrongful discharge, defamation, and other workplace torts. His cases have established important legal precedents in the field. He is a frequent speaker and has published articles on employment law since 1981.

Mr. Busse has been listed in the national peer review publication *The Best Lawyers in America* every year since 1989 for labor and employment law in Oregon. His firm has been named as the leading *plaintiff's employment law firm* in Oregon by Chambers US; America's Leading Business Lawyers, 2003–04; and he has been awarded its highest individual rating.

He is a fellow in the International Society of Barristers. He is a former master in the American Inns of Court. The nationally known legal directory, Martindale-Hubbell, gives Mr. Busse and his firm its highest rating for legal ability and ethics.

SPHINX® PUBLISHING'S STATE TITLES

Up-to-Date for Your State

California Titles	
How to File for Divorce in CA (5E)	$26.95
How to Settle & Probate an Estate in CA (2E)	$28.95
How to Start a Business in CA (2E)	$21.95
How to Win in Small Claims Court in CA (2E)	$18.95
Landlords' Legal Guide in CA (2E)	$24.95
Make Your Own CA Will	$18.95
Tenants' Rights in CA	$21.95
Florida Titles	
Child Custody, Visitation and Support in FL	$26.95
How to File for Divorce in FL (8E)	$28.95
How to Form a Corporation in FL (6E)	$24.95
How to Form a Limited Liability Co. in FL (3E)	$24.95
How to Form a Partnership in FL	$22.95
How to Make a FL Will (7E)	$16.95
How to Probate and Settle an Estate in FL (5E)	$26.95
How to Start a Business in FL (7E)	$21.95
How to Win in Small Claims Court in FL (7E)	$18.95
Land Trusts in Florida (7E)	$29.95
Landlords' Rights and Duties in FL (9E)	$22.95
Georgia Titles	
How to File for Divorce in GA (5E)	$21.95
How to Start a Business in GA (4E)	$21.95
Illinois Titles	
Child Custody, Visitation and Support in IL	$24.95
How to File for Divorce in IL (3E)	$24.95
How to Make an IL Will (3E)	$16.95
How to Start a Business in IL (4E)	$21.95
Landlords' Legal Guide in IL	$24.95
Maryland, Virginia and the District of Columbia Titles	
How to File for Divorce in MD, VA, and DC	$28.95
How to Start a Business in MD, VA, or DC	$21.95
Massachusetts Titles	
How to Form a Corporation in MA	$24.95
How to Start a Business in MA (4E)	$21.95
Landlords' Legal Guide in MA (2E)	$24.95
Michigan Titles	
How to File for Divorce in MI (4E)	$24.95
How to Make a MI Will (3E)	$16.95
How to Start a Business in MI (4E)	$24.95

Minnesota Titles	
How to File for Divorce in MN	$21.95
How to Form a Corporation in MN	$24.95
How to Make a MN Will (2E)	$16.95
New Jersey Titles	
How to File for Divorce in NJ	$24.95
How to Start a Business in NJ	$21.95
New York Titles	
Child Custody, Visitation and Support in NY	$26.95
File for Divorce in NY	$26.95
How to Form a Corporation in NY (2E)	$24.95
How to Make a NY Will (3E)	$16.95
How to Start a Business in NY (3E)	$21.95
How to Win in Small Claims Court in NY (2E)	$18.95
Landlords' Legal Guide in NY	$24.95
Tenants' Rights in NY	$21.95
North Carolina and South Carolina Titles	
How to File for Divorce in NC (3E)	$22.95
How to Make a NC Will (3E)	$16.95
How to Start a Business in NC or SC	$24.95
Landlords' Rights & Duties in NC	$21.95
Ohio Titles	
How to File for Divorce in OH (3E)	$24.95
How to Form a Corporation in OH	$24.95
How to Make an OH Will	$16.95
Pennsylvania Titles	
Child Custody, Visitation and Support in PA	$26.95
How to File for Divorce in PA (4E)	$26.95
How to Form a Corporation in PA	$24.95
How to Make a PA Will (2E)	$16.95
How to Start a Business in PA (3E)	$21.95
Landlords' Legal Guide in PA	$24.95
Texas Titles	
Child Custody, Visitation and Support in TX	$22.95
How to File for Divorce in TX (4E)	$24.95
How to Form a Corporation in TX (3E)	$24.95
How to Make a TX Will (3E)	$16.95
How to Probate and Settle an Estate in TX (4E)	$26.95
How to Start a Business in TX (4E)	$21.95
How to Win in Small Claims Court in TX (2E)	$16.95
Landlords' Legal Guide in TX	$24.95

SPHINX® PUBLISHING ORDER FORM

BILL TO:		SHIP TO:	
Phone #	Terms	F.O.B. Chicago, IL	Ship Date

Charge my: ❒ VISA ❒ MasterCard ❒ American Express ❒ **Money Order or Personal Check**

Credit Card Number **Expiration Date**

SPHINX PUBLISHING NATIONAL TITLES

Qty	ISBN	Title	Retail
____	1-57248-363-6	101 Complaint Letters That Get Results	$18.95
____	1-57248-361-X	The 529 College Savings Plan (2E)	$18.95
____	1-57248-483-7	The 529 College Savings Plan Made Simple	$7.95
____	1-57248-460-8	The Alternative Minimum Tax	$14.95
____	1-57248-349-0	The Antique and Art Collector's Legal Guide	$24.95
____	1-57248-347-4	Attorney Responsibilities & Client Rights	$19.95
____	1-57248-382-2	Child Support	$18.95
____	1-57248-487-X	Cómo Comprar su Primera Casa	$8.95
____	1-57248-148-X	Cómo Hacer su Propio Testamento	$16.95
____	1-57248-462-4	Cómo Negociar su Crédito	$8.95
____	1-57248-463-2	Cómo Organizar un Presupuesto	$8.95
____	1-57248-147-1	Cómo Solicitar su Propio Divorcio	$24.95
____	1-57248-373-3	The Complete Adoption and Fertility Legal Guide	$24.95
____	1-57248-166-8	The Complete Book of Corporate Forms	$24.95
____	1-57248-383-0	The Complete Book of Insurance	$18.95
____	1-57248-499-3	The Complete Book of Personal Legal Forms	$24.95
____	1-57248-500-0	The Complete Credit Repair Kit	$19..95
____	1-57248-458-6	The Complete Hiring and Firing Handbook	$19.95
____	1-57248-353-9	The Complete Kit to Selling Your Own Home	$18.95
____	1-57248-229-X	The Complete Legal Guide to Senior Care	$21.95
____	1-57248-498-5	The Complete Limited Liability Company Kit	$21.95
____	1-57248-391-1	The Complete Partnership Book	$24.95
____	1-57248-201-X	The Complete Patent Book	$26.95
____	1-57248-369-5	Credit Smart	$18.95
____	1-57248-163-3	Crime Victim's Guide to Justice (2E)	$21.95
____	1-57248-251-6	The Entrepreneur's Internet Handbook	$21.95
____	1-57248-235-4	The Entrepreneur's Legal Guide	$26.95
____	1-57248-346-6	Essential Guide to Real Estate Contracts (2E)	$18.95
____	1-57248-160-9	Essential Guide to Real Estate Leases	$18.95
____	1-57248-375-X	Fathers' Rights	$19.95
____	1-57248-450-0	Financing Your Small Business	$17.95
____	1-57248-459-4	Fired, Laid-Off or Forced Out	$14.95
____	1-57248-502-7	The Frequent Traveler's Guide	$14.95
____	1-57248-331-8	Gay & Lesbian Rights	$26.95
____	1-57248-139-0	Grandparents' Rights (3E)	$24.95
____	1-57248-475-6	Guía de Inmigración a Estados Unidos (4E)	$24.95
____	1-57248-187-0	Guía de Justicia para Víctimas del Crimen	$21.95
____	1-57248-253-2	Guía Esencial para los Contratos de Arrendamiento de Bienes Raices	$22.95
____	1-57248-334-2	Homeowner's Rights	$19.95
____	1-57248-164-1	How to Buy a Condominium or Townhome (2E)	$19.95
____	1-57248-384-9	How to Buy a Franchise	$19.95
____	1-57248-497-7	How to Buy Your First Home (2E)	$14.95
____	1-57248-472-1	How to File Your Own Bankruptcy (6E)	$21.95
____	1-57248-343-1	How to File Your Own Divorce (5E)	$26.95
____	1-57248-390-3	How to Form a Nonprofit Corporation (3E)	$24.95
____	1-57248-345-8	How to Form Your Own Corporation (4E)	$26.95
____	1-57248-232-X	How to Make Your Own Simple Will (3E)	$18.95
____	1-57248-479-9	How to Parent with Your Ex	$12.95
____	1-57248-379-2	How to Register Your Own Copyright (5E)	$24.95
____	1-57248-394-6	How to Write Your Own Living Will (4E)	$18.95
____	1-57248-156-0	How to Write Your Own Premarital Agreement (3E)	$24.95
____	1-57248-504-3	HR for Small Business	$14.95
____	1-57248-230-3	Incorporate in Delaware from Any State	$26.95
____	1-57248-158-7	Incorporate in Nevada from Any State	$24.95
____	1-57248-474-8	Inmigración a los EE.UU. Paso a Paso (2E)	$24.95
____	1-57248-400-4	Inmigración y Ciudadanía en los EE. UU. Preguntas y Respuestas	$16.95
____	1-57248-377-6	The Law (In Plain English)® for Small Business	$19.95
____	1-57248-476-4	The Law (In Plain English)® for Small Writers	$16.95
____	1-57248-453-5	Law 101	$16.95
____	1-57248-374-1	Law School 101	$16.95
____	1-57248-223-0	Legal Research Made Easy (3E)	$21.95
____	1-57248-449-7	The Living Trust Kit	$21.95
____	1-57248-165-X	Living Trusts and Other Ways to Avoid Probate (3E)	$24.95
____	1-57248-486-1	Making Music Your Business	$18.95
____	1-57248-186-2	Manual de Beneficios para el Seguro Social	$18.95
____	1-57248-220-6	Mastering the MBE	$16.95
____	1-57248-455-1	Minding Her Own Business, 4E	$14.95
____	1-57248-480-2	The Mortgage Answer Book	$14.95
____	1-57248-167-6	Most Val. Business Legal Forms You'll Ever Need (3E)	$21.95
____	1-57248-388-1	The Power of Attorney Handbook (5E)	$22.95
____	1-57248-332-6	Profit from Intellectual Property	$28.95
____	1-57248-329-6	Protect Your Patent	$24.95
____	1-57248-376-8	Nursing Homes and Assisted Living Facilities	$19.95
____	1-57248-385-7	Quick Cash	$14.95
____	1-57248-350-4	El Seguro Social Preguntas y Respuestas	$16.95
____	1-57248-386-5	Seniors' Rights	$19.95
____	1-57248-217-6	Sexual Harassment: Your Guide to Legal Action	$18.95
____	1-57248-378-4	Sisters-in-Law	$16.95
____	1-57248-219-2	The Small Business Owner's Guide to Bankruptcy	$21.95
____	1-57248-395-4	The Social Security Benefits Handbook (4E)	$18.95
____	1-57248-216-8	Social Security Q&A	$12.95
____	1-57248-328-8	Starting Out or Starting Over	$14.95
____	1-57248-525-6	Teen RIghts (and Responsibilities) (2E)	$14.95
____	1-57248-457-8	Tax Power for the Self-Employed	$17.95
____	1-57248-366-0	Tax Smarts for Small Business	$21.95
____	1-57248-236-2	Unmarried Parents' Rights (2E)	$19.95
____	1-57248-362-8	U.S. Immigration and Citizenship Q&A	$18.95

Form Continued on Following Page **SubTotal**______

Qty	ISBN	Title	Retail
_____	1-57248-387-3	U.S. Immigration Step by Step (2E)	$24.95
_____	1-57248-392-X	U.S.A. Immigration Guide (5E)	$26.95
_____	1-57248-478-0	¡Visas! ¡Visas! ¡Visas!	$9.95
_____	1-57248-477-2	The Weekend Landlord	$16.95
_____	1-57248-451-9	What to Do—Before "I DO"	$14.95
_____	1-57248-330-X	The Wills, Estate Planning and Trusts Legal Kit	$26.95
_____	1-57248-473-X	Winning Your Personal Injury Claim (3E)	$24.95
_____	1-57248-225-7	Win Your Unemployment Compensation Claim (2E)	$21.95
_____	1-57248-333-4	Working with Your Homeowners Association	$19.95
_____	1-57248-380-6	Your Right to Child Custody, Visitation and Support (3E)	$24.95
_____	1-57248-505-1	Your Rights at Work	$14.95
		CALIFORNIA TITLES	
_____	1-57248-489-6	How to File for Divorce in CA (5E)	$26.95
_____	1-57248-464-0	How to Settle and Probate an Estate in CA (2E)	$28.95
_____	1-57248-336-9	How to Start a Business in CA (2E)	$21.95
_____	1-57248-194-3	How to Win in Small Claims Court in CA (2E)	$18.95
_____	1-57248-246-X	Make Your Own CA Will	$18.95
_____	1-57248-397-0	Landlords' Legal Guide in CA (2E)	$24.95
_____	1-57248-241-9	Tenants' Rights in CA	$21.95
		FLORIDA TITLES	
_____	1-57248-396-2	How to File for Divorce in FL (8E)	$28.95
_____	1-57248-356-3	How to Form a Corporation in FL (6E)	$24.95
_____	1-57248-490-X	How to Form a Limited Liability Co. in FL (3E)	$24.95
_____	1-57071-401-0	How to Form a Partnership in FL	$22.95
_____	1-57248-456-X	How to Make a FL Will (7E)	$16.95
_____	1-57248-354-7	How to Probate and Settle an Estate in FL (5E)	$26.95
_____	1-57248-339-3	How to Start a Business in FL (7E)	$21.95
_____	1-57248-204-4	How to Win in Small Claims Court in FL (7E)	$18.95
_____	1-57248-381-4	Land Trusts in Florida (7E)	$29.95
_____	1-57248-338-5	Landlords' Rights and Duties in FL (9E)	$22.95
		GEORGIA TITLES	
_____	1-57248-340-7	How to File for Divorce in GA (5E)	$21.95
_____	1-57248-493-4	How to Start a Business in GA (4E)	$21.95
		ILLINOIS TITLES	
_____	1-57248-244-3	Child Custody, Visitation, and Support in IL	$24.95
_____	1-57248-206-0	How to File for Divorce in IL (3E)	$24.95
_____	1-57248-170-6	How to Make an IL Will (3E)	$16.95
_____	1-57248-265-9	How to Start a Business in IL (4E)	$21.95
_____	1-57248-252-4	Landlord's Legal Guide in IL	$24.95
		MARYLAND, VIRGINIA AND THE DISTRICT OF COLUMBIA	
_____	1-57248-240-0	How to File for Divorce in MD, VA, and DC	$28.95
_____	1-57248-359-8	How to Start a Business in MD, VA, or DC	$21.95
		MASSACHUSETTS TITLES	
_____	1-57248-115-3	How to Form a Corporation in MA	$24.95
_____	1-57248-466-7	How to Start a Business in MA (4E)	$21.95
_____	1-57248-398-9	Landlords' Legal Guide in MA (2E)	$24.95

Qty	ISBN	Title	Retail
		MICHIGAN TITLES	
_____	1-57248-467-5	How to File for Divorce in MI (4E)	$24.95
_____	1-57248-182-X	How to Make a MI Will (3E)	$16.95
_____	1-57248-468-3	How to Start a Business in MI (4E)	$21.95
		MINNESOTA TITLES	
_____	1-57248-142-0	How to File for Divorce in MN	$21.95
_____	1-57248-179-X	How to Form a Corporation in MN	$24.95
_____	1-57248-178-1	How to Make a MN Will (2E)	$16.95
		NEW JERSEY TITLES	
_____	1-57248-239-7	How to File for Divorce in NJ	$24.95
_____	1-57248-448-9	How to Start a Business in NJ	$21.95
		NEW YORK TITLES	
_____	1-57248-193-5	Child Custody, Visitation and Support in NY	$26.95
_____	1-57248-351-2	File for Divorce in NY	$26.95
_____	1-57248-249-4	How to Form a Corporation in NY (2E)	$24.95
_____	1-57248-401-2	How to Make a NY Will (3E)	$16.95
_____	1-57248-468-1	How to Start a Business in NY (3E)	$21.95
_____	1-57248-198-6	How to Win in Small Claims Court in NY (2E)	$18.95
_____	1-57248-197-8	Landlords' Legal Guide in NY	$24.95
_____	1-57248-122-6	Tenants' Rights in NY	$21.95
		NORTH CAROLINA AND SOUTH CAROLINA TITLES	
_____	1-57248-185-4	How to File for Divorce in NC (3E)	$22.95
_____	1-57248-129-3	How to Make a NC Will (3E)	$16.95
_____	1-57248-371-7	How to Start a Business in NC or SC	$24.95
_____	1-57248-091-2	Landlords' Rights & Duties in NC	$21.95
		OHIO TITLES	
_____	1-57248-503-5	How to File for Divorce in OH (3E)	$24.95
_____	1-57248-174-9	How to Form a Corporation in OH	$24.95
_____	1-57248-173-0	How to Make an OH Will	$16.95
		PENNSYLVANIA TITLES	
_____	1-57248-242-7	Child Custody, Visitation and Support in PA	$26.95
_____	1-57248-495-0	How to File for Divorce in PA (4E)	$26.95
_____	1-57248-358-X	How to Form a Corporation in PA	$24.95
_____	1-57248-094-7	How to Make a PA Will (2E)	$16.95
_____	1-57248-357-1	How to Start a Business in PA (3E)	$21.95
_____	1-57248-245-1	Landlords' Legal Guide in PA	$24.95
		TEXAS TITLES	
_____	1-57248-171-4	Child Custody, Visitation, and Support in TX	$22.95
_____	1-57248-399-7	How to File for Divorce in TX (4E)	$24.95
_____	1-57248-470-5	How to Form a Corporation in TX (3E)	$24.95
_____	1-57248-255-9	How to Make a TX Will (3E)	$16.95
_____	1-57248-496-9	How to Probate and Settle an Estate in TX (4E)	$26.95
_____	1-57248-471-3	How to Start a Business in TX (4E)	$21.95
_____	1-57248-111-0	How to Win in Small Claims Court in TX (2E)	$16.95
_____	1-57248-355-5	Landlords' Legal Guide in TX	$24.95

SubTotal This page _______

SubTotal previous page _______

Shipping— $5.00 for 1st book, $1.00 each additional _______

Illinois residents add 6.75% sales tax _______

Connecticut residents add 6.00% sales tax _______

Total _______